THE UNCIVIL WAR

Washington During the Reconstruction 1865 - 1878

by James H. Whyte

TWAYNE PUBLISHERS
New York

Library of Congress Catalog Card No.: 57-14776

MANUFACTURED IN THE UNITED STATES OF AMERICA BY
UNITED PRINTING SERVICES, INC.
NEW HAVEN, CONN.

DEDICATION

To those whose prejudices have stimulated me to undertake this study and to those whose sympathetic advice has made its realization possible this book is gratefully dedicated.

J. H. W.

Foreword

Although local historians of the District of Columbia have devoted their attention to earlier and later periods, the Reconstruction era has been a neglected field. The student must turn back to W. B. Bryan's *History of The National Capital* published in 1916 to find out what took place in Washington during the decade which followed the Civil War: indeed, apart from brief mention by such historians of the national scene as James Ford Rhodes and James Schouler and a scattering of papers and monographs no more comprehensive account of the period exists.

The Reconstruction period in the District has become of special interest today because many of the political and social questions of that time are once more uppermost in the public consciousness. In May, 1953, the Supreme Court upheld in the Thompson Restaurant Case laws forbidding racial discrimination in public places passed in 1872 by the Territorial Legislature of the District, laws which had been considered "lost" and ineffective for many years. The same decision, by confirming the authority of Congress to delegate municipal government in the District by elected representatives of the people, also gave fresh impetus to the movement for District Home Rule. Since so few Americans—even so few Washingtonians—are aware that self-government existed in the District for more than seventy years, and since almost none of them fully understand why Congress took away this privilege in 1874, it is important that the facts be re-examined fully and objectively in order to sweep away the cobwebs of hearsay and prejudice.

It has been the object of this study to consider the question of local suffrage—and especially that of Negro suffrage—in the District during Reconstruction in a larger frame than that previously used by local historians. The background of national politics has been sketched so that local suffrage should be seen in relationship to national issues of the period. Readers will also find in this study many facts concerning the life of the colored population of Washington during the Reconstruction period which have hitherto been passed over by historians of the District. Although considerable attention has been devoted to society in its various aspects, the emphasis has not been primarily on its romantic or antiquarian characteristics, but rather to provide additional insight into the spirit of the times.

It is unfortunate that no biography has yet been written of Alexander Shepherd, the key personality of the entire period, through whose untiring efforts Washington was transformed within a period of three years from a sleepy Southern town into a city worthy of the national capital. Though the Shepherd papers in the Library of Congress contain relatively little matter concerning his administration of the Board of Public Works, and while the District Archives remain uncatalogued and difficult of access, it is hoped that sufficient fresh material, gleaned from these sources and from the newspapers of the period, has been uncovered to stimulate a long-overdue re-appraisal of Shepherd as a man and as an administrator.

J. H. W.

WASHINGTON, D. C.

Acknowledgments

I should like to single out among the many friends who have helped with their encouragement and advice to make this study possible Dr. William Neumann of Goucher College, Maryland, Mr. Meredith Colket, Jr. of the National Archives; and Professor John Hope Franklin of Brooklyn College. My thanks are also due to Dr. Laurence Schmeckebier of the Columbia Historical Society and to Miss Jorgenson of the National Archives for their help regarding illustrative material and for other fruitful suggestions. To Mrs. Dorothy Porter, librarian of the Moorland Collection at Howard University, I am indebted for unfailing interest and assistance. The Washingtoniana Division of the Central Public Library, under the able administration of Miss Ethel Lacy and Miss Saul, has proved an invaluable source of material on Washington history. I am also grateful to Col. Thornett, Secretary to the District Commissioners, and to Mr. West, his assistant, for their kindness in permitting me to look through the old District records. To Miss Imogene Wormley, Miss Carrie Gray, Mrs. Ulysses Houston and Mrs. Molly Hundley I owe many interesting details of family history. Mr. Klaus Wust has provided much useful information regarding the German population in Washington during the years following the Civil War.

J. H. W.

Acknowledgments

[illegible]

Contents

Chapter 1

Washington After the War

In the spring of 1865 Washington presented to the visitor an appearance far from glamorous. The overgrown town was unkempt and slovenly as ever; there was the persisting contrast between the "magnificent distances" of L'Enfant's grandiose plan and the sordid reality. Only a few handsome government buildings had been completed: the Treasury, the Post Office and the Patent Office, all in a severely classical style of architecture, while across the Mall the towers of the Smithsonian Institute overgrown with ivy provided a unique touch of the Romantic. The dome of the Capitol was at last finished, but the Washington Monument was only a pile of masonry, the funds for its erection long since exhausted.

The streets and avenues of the city had always been a scandal and disgrace. L'Enfant's plan had provided for thoroughfares far wider than existed in any American city of the time, and quite out of proportion to the population of the District which, even after the War, numbered only 120,000. Pennsylvania Avenue had been paved with cobblestones by the Federal Government, though, as a result of wartime traffic, its gravel surface had become a mass of ruts and potholes. On many of the side streets pigs, goats, cattle and geese roamed unmolested and occasionally strayed into the open vestibules of private homes. Drainage was by means of surface gutters which were overgrown with weeds and filled with green-scummed slime. Crossing the streets in irregular ruts, they obliged the drivers of vehicles to come to a cautious stop before bumping over them. At night the city was so badly illuminated that few ventured to take their carriages outside the center of the city. John Randolph's dictum of three decades before that "a Washington pedestrian should provide himself with an overcoat, a duster, a pair of rubber shoes and a fan" was still valid in 1865.

Pennsylvania Avenue was hardly worthy to be the main thoroughfare of the nation's capital. Most of the three-story brick houses which bordered the Avenue housed saloons, boarding-houses, restaurants, the offices of newspapers, patent attorneys and solicitors, dealers in second-hand clothing, and pawnshops. Fine stores, such as were to be found in Baltimore, Philadelphia and New York, were nonexistent in Washington. The hotels on the Avenue were second-class hostelries which could not compare with those in other large American cities. The St. Charles, the Ebbitt House, the National, the Kirkwood House were patronized by politicians, lobbyists and office-seekers who left the city immediately after the sessions of Congress. The hotel furniture was old-fashioned and well-filled by corpulent guests. At the close of the day the air was heavy with cigar smoke and the floor slippery with tobacco juice. Contractors, clerks, lobbyists and loafers occupied the chairs; in a corner here or there a "card writer" would be working steadily and silently in the glare of a St. Germain lamp.[1] Even the Willard, which catered to the wealthy and the diplomats, was hardly superior in its furnishings and facilities.

The south side of the Avenue from 15th Street to the Capitol was occupied by cheap saloons, gambling houses and pawnshops. At its rear, where Constitution Avenue now runs, was the Canal, which stretched from Georgetown to Southwest Washington. Little used by commerce for many years, it had become by this time a dumping-ground for garbage, dead dogs and cats, and occasionally an illegitimate child. The stench was so strong that people in its vicinity actually held their noses.

The Avenue during the day was bustling and noisy. Street cars had gradually come to replace the old rickety omnibus during the War; their jangling bells and rumblings mingled with the cries of Negro street vendors of oysters, milk and vegetables.

The entertainments of the capital were pitifully few. Since Lincoln's assassination Ford's Theatre had been taken over by the government; and the National, already twice destroyed by fire, and Walls's Opera House provided the sole source of amusement. The Canterburies, low vaudeville houses, which had sprung up during the War, still catered to government clerks and the few remaining soldiers, but they were frequently raided by the police and had begun to disappear.

Gambling houses, which had once numbered more than a hundred, were no longer as plentiful, but still flourishing. They might be recognized by the heavily curtained windows, through which the gas light shone dimly, and by the brightly-lit numbers in gilt letters over the vestibule doors. Some of the houses were magnificently furnished, with fine carpets, frescoed walls and cut-glass chandeliers. Elegantly-dressed and attentive Negro servants were on hand to serve the wealthy patrons, who consisted of congressmen, contractors, high army officers and out-of-town visitors. In the second-class establishments gambling was often associated with other vices, and unsuspecting clerks were frequently decoyed by pimps and robbed of all their possessions.

Besides the potholes of the Avenue the War had left many other scars on the face of the city. Unpainted wooden buildings, which had served as barracks and stables for army mules, still remained many months after Appomattox. The fifty-six forts built in the early days of the conflict to defend the capital were still standing in the suburbs. Plundered of their lumber by nearby farmers, they now served as shelter for the many freedmen who had poured into the District from the nearby plantations of Maryland and Virginia; from the wrecks of battery wagons and sentry boxes, they had improvised the flimsiest constructions. The forts were a grim reminder of the days, as late as July 1864, when Confederate troops had entered the District limits and had all but captured the city.

The condition of Washington before the War had been such that few members of Congress wished to reside there. Apart from Cabinet officers and diplomats and a few of the wealthier Senators, the majority of congressmen were content to remain in boarding-houses. Some of these, such as Cruchet's, were elegant establishments which charged $25 a week with board; others, catering to government clerks, charged as little as $5 without food. Though low by contemporary standards, rents were high for government employees, whose yearly incomes averaged only $1200. Female clerks who had come to Washington during the War to work for the Treasury Department earned only $900 at most, which made a respectable existence still more precarious. Besides the government employees, there were always "sundry women with no visible means of support," with whom, in an effort to be civil, the stranger could be compromised in a manner little dreamed of at the outset.[2] Horace Greeley advised government clerks who complained that they could not live on what they earned to go to Kansas or Nebraska instead of beseeching Congress to give them bigger salaries. "Washington is not a nice place to live in," he wrote. "The rents are high, the food is bad, the dust is disgusting, the mud is deep, and the morals are deplorable."

Yet for the affluent and those with family connections, life in the capital had its charm. Henry Adams, recalling the early days which he had spent there on his return from London in 1867, wrote: "Washington was the easiest society he had ever seen . . . Society went along excellently without houses or carriages or jewels or toilettes or pavements or shops or *grandezza* of any kind, and the market was excellent as well as cheap. One could not stay there a month without loving the shabby town . . . Life ceased to be strenuous, and one thanked God for it. Politics and reform had become the detail and waltzing the profession . . . He could have spared a world of superannuated history, science or politics to have reversed better in waltzing."[3]

The organized society of the capital in 1865 could be divided into four almost watertight sections: the Cabinet officers and members of old families, the Bureau heads, the clerks and merchants, and the lower classes. Little intimacy existed between them, but promotion in the government could break down some of the barriers. Before the War, Washington had been a Southern city, and Southern institutions had been generally accepted. Abolitionists were frowned on, and New England civilization was sneered at as being composed of "strong-minded women and weak-minded men." "It was not a very cultivated society," recalled the former newspaper correspondent Don Piatt. "People did not talk about books and had not pretensions to artistic taste or scientific achievement. We dealt largely in politics and little social chit-chat . . . Mere wealth had little or no influence. To be a member of a good family, to have position officially, was all that was necessary."[4]

However, four years of civil war, during which the capital itself was just behind the front lines, had transformed Washington completely. In 1861, when it had become apparent that Lincoln and the Republicans were to take over the government, there had been wholesale resignations by Southerners from official positions and from the armed forces. The former sleepy Southern town had become filled with men from the North, the Middle and the Far West. Fortunes were to be made in government contracts by men of initiative who could act quickly. "New England civilization had come in," wrote Donn Piatt, "and Southern ways, tastes and enthusiasms are driven into the keeping of a few old families. Wealth is omnipresent, and the humanities drive about in gorgeous carriages and live among stunning upholstery. It freezes and snows like a Northern town. We laugh at the old families and measure our belle by the depth of her pocket."[5] The population of the District had risen in five years from 75,000 to 120,000, and for the first time in the history of Washington the Southerners were in the minority.

In spite of the small size of the District population, in the past there had existed three distinct governments within its tiny area. The City of Washington, which had received its first charter from Congress in 1803, was bounded on the South by the Potomac River, on the North by Florida Avenue (then known as Boundary Street), on the West by Rock Creek, and on the East by the Anacostia, or Eastern Branch. In common with other American municipalities Washington City had its Board of Common Council and Board of Aldermen, and an elected Mayor. The city was divided into seven wards, which elected councillors to serve for a period of one year and elected aldermen for two years. The Mayor, City Register, Surveyor and Collector of Taxes were also elected for two-year terms.

Georgetown had received its charter many years before Washington and had the same system of local government. It was at this time a settlement of some 10,000 persons, with an active shopping center and the remains of an ancient but now moribund harbor. The atmosphere of Georgetown had remained more distinctly Southern than that of Washington, and during the War a number of its most prominent citizens, related by ties of blood and marriage to slave-owning families of Virginia and Maryland, had departed to fight for the Confederacy. Their ladies had taken up residence in Richmond and had remained there until it had become apparent that the cause of the Confederacy was hopeless. After the War the age-old antagonism between the two cities had been aggravated by the influx into Washington of so many government employees from the North and West, many of them with strong Abolitionist sympathies.

The County of Washington, which extended outside of the built-up areas, was administered by the Levy Court, an ancient Maryland institution. The members of this Court, appointed by Congress, had many of the powers conferred upon municipal councils: they could levy taxes, pass local ordinances, make building regulations and issue liquor licenses. They had also the power to appoint trustees to supervise the public schools of the County. Since the population of the area, however, was still so small in 1865, the duties of the Court had been relatively light. Apart from the villages of Tenleytown in the North, Uniontown across the Anacostia and Reno on the northwestern heights, most of the land in the County was occupied by farms and large estates. Some of the wealthiest residents of Washington were also large landowners in the County: the banker, W. W. Corcoran, was the proprietor of "Harewood," the present site of the Soldier's Home, his partner, George W. Riggs, owned "Eckington" in the northeast section, and Chief Justice Chase had purchased another large estate in the same area which he named "Edgewood." The Kalorama and Woodley estates just north of the Washington City boundary had been owned by the Barlow and Walker families for many years.

In both the municipalities of Washington and Georgetown there had been elections held annually to elect city officials. The number of voters in Washington had always been small; no more than 6,000 had voted in the years before 1866, and fewer than 1,000 in Georgetown. Government clerks had seldom bothered to take part in municipal affairs, and were not encouraged to do so by the older citizens. Many of the poorer elements of the community had been disqualified by failure to pay the poll tax which had been imposed in 1858 for the upkeep of the public schools. Women and Negroes were, of course, excluded from the ballot. There was no attempt at this time to preserve the secrecy of the polls, and printed tickets bearing the names of the candidates were openly distributed to voters by party agents. These tickets were of distinctive size and color so that a man's vote could often be determined before it was cast. Such a system often led to brawls at the polling stations, but conditions in the District had been much better than in other cities, New York for instance, where men who voted against the interests of their employers, national group or party boss, were often beaten by hired thugs. In the election of 1857 when the anti-Catholic Know-Nothing Party was at the height of its power, there had been severe disturbances at the Washington polls, but since that time there had been little trouble.

The Mayor of Washington in 1865, Richard Wallach, was a native of the city who had been elected in 1861 after his predecessor, James G. Berret, had refused to take the oath prescribed by the Department of the Interior in his capacity as Police Commissioner. Berret was a Maryland man and suspected by many of favoring the South; Wallach was of New England ancestry and a strong supporter of the Union. In every other respect, however, he was a typical Conservative, who had been a slave-owner and a strong opponent of Abolition.

The division of the city into wards had been indirectly responsible, in the District as in other American communities, for some of the worst features of municipal government. The ward system tended to sectionalize the city and to give great powers to the commissioners of improvements. These ward commissioners competed with each other for funds to be spent in their respective bailiwicks for street and other improvements, and their power was in proportion to the funds which they could secure to provide employment for their constituents. Such a system inevitably led to bloc-voting, especially in cities with large groups of foreign-born voters, such as the Irish and Germans, and to the rise of the city boss, who was no more than a ward commissioner on a larger scale.

From the earliest period of Washington history to the Civil War the division of authority in the District between Congress and the elected city governments had been a source of conflict. Congress had always been niggardly in its appropriations of funds for public works, but had given no authority to the Councils of Washington and Georgetown in their charters for the paving of the principal streets and avenues. The extreme width of these thoroughfares and the consequent high cost of paving made this question a perpetual subject of contention between Congress and the city governments. In 1864 the Councils were finally given permission to pave the streets but little had been accomplished. Provision was also made in 1864 for paying half the cost of street lighting and two-thirds of the salary of the Metropolitan Police, as well as a share of the Washington City sewerage. During the War the Councils had also increased their expenditure; in 1862 a school fund had been inaugurated and the first large schoolhouse, named after Mayor Wallach, had been erected near the Capitol. In order to pay for these improvements the city authorities of Washington had increased the tax on real estate from 60 cents per $100 valuation to $1.00. The floating debt of the city increased from $89,271 in 1862 to $302,284 in 1866, and the funded debt from $943,000 to $1,245,284 in the same period. The indebtedness per capita, however, was still only $11, lower than that of most large cities in the United States.[6]

Now that Washington was beginning to emerge from its long slumber of neglect, attributable to the apathy of Congress and the small-mindedness of its citizens, a new generation of civic leaders was coming to the fore, anxious to make the city really worthy of being the nation's capital. Real estate values, which had been stationary for many years, began to boom as the result of the enormous growth of population during the War, and speculators started to develop new housing projects in different parts of the District. S. P. Brown, a former government contractor, had bought a large tract of land on an eminence above 16th Street and had begun after the War to develop it as the village of Mount Pleasant. Albert Grant, who had served as a bridge-builder in the Union Army, was erecting on East Capitol Street a row of 16-room mansions, obviously intended for Congressional use, with water and gas "laid on." Alexander Shepherd, a native of Washington, who was a partner in the gasfitting firm of John W. Thompson, was engaged in speculative building in the vicinity of Connecticut Avenue below Dupont Circle. Shepherd, born in 1836, had served in the District militia during the War and had served three terms as a member of the Washington Council. He had bought a 300-acre farm out on the Seventh Street Road (now Georgia Avenue) and was in 1865 a member of the Levy Court, one of the wealthiest and most energetic young businessmen in the city.

The largest landowner in the District and undoubtedly its richest citizen was the retired banker, William Wilson Corcoran. A native of Georgetown, Mr. Corcoran had made his fortune by financing the sale of government bonds during the Mexican

War in 1848. With his partner, George W. Riggs, he had founded the banking house which was to become the most important in the city of Washington. In 1854 Mr. Corcoran had retired, however, from the banking business to devote himself to his other interests, especially to collecting works of art. His red sandstone residence, formerly the home of Daniel Webster, stood at the corner of H Street and Connecticut Avenue; he was the owner of "Harewood," a large estate north of the city; and he had just completed in 1862 an elaborate building designed by the architect of the Smithsonian Institute, Alexander Renwick, which was to house his collection of paintings and objets d'art.

In 1862, however, Mr. Corcoran found it advisable to leave Washington for political and family reasons. His only daughter, Louise, was married to George Eustis, secretary to John Slidell of New Orleans, who had been appointed by Jefferson Davis Confederate Envoy to the French Court. A lifelong Democrat and a personal friend of Robert E. Lee, Mr. Corcoran could not bear to remain in Washington during the War; he did not return until it had been over for several years, but remained with his family in Paris, adding to his art collection. His house on Lafayette Square was leased to the French Minister for the duration of the War, "Harewood" was turned into a hospital, and the building on Pennsylvania Avenue and 17th Street destined for his paintings became a warehouse for government records.

Henry D. Cooke, the next wealthiest man in Washington after Mr. Corcoran, had also been a banker and had likewise made his fortune through selling war bonds for the government. He had come to Washington in 1861 for Lincoln's inauguration from Columbus, Ohio, where he had edited a Republican newspaper subsidized by his brother, the famous Philadelphia financier, Jay Cooke. As an old friend of Salmon P. Chase, Secretary of the Treasury during the War and former Governor of Ohio, Henry Cooke was in a position to be of great service to his brother. Chase was a man who had had little financial experience and it was not long before he came to depend upon Jay Cooke for advice upon matters of financial policy. The success of the Cooke brothers in the sale of war bonds led to the formation of the First National Bank of Washington, of which Henry Cooke became president; it soon became second only to Riggs and Company in the Washington banking world. Henry Cooke was no financial genius like his brother, but an affable and likeable man who was personally popular with members of Congress and with such men as General Grant. Henry Cooke lived in a large Georgetown mansion, where he entertained in a regal manner.

The Washington newspapers had their offices on Pennsylvania Avenue; correspondents of the out-of-town papers were located on "Newspaper Row" across from the Willard, on the site of the present National Press Building. The local papers were poorly-printed four-page sheets which could not be compared with the great dailies of New York, Boston or Philadelphia. The *National Intelligencer,* founded in 1800 and for many years a newspaper of national importance under the editorship of Seaton and Gales, had been purchased in 1864 by John F. Coyle. Though opposed to Secession, Mr. Coyle was generally sympathetic to the South, and considered, in company with other Washington Conservatives, that the city should be administered by the larger property-owners. The *Evening Star,* founded in 1852 by Joseph W. Tate as a penny paper with particular emphasis on local affairs, was now edited by W. D. Wallach, a brother of Richard Wallach, Washington's Mayor. Crosby S. Noyes, an enterprising young man from Maine, who had come to Washington in 1847 with only two dollars in his pocket, was the *Star's* business manager, and acknowledged to be the brightest newspaperman in town. The *Star* had fervently supported the policy of Lincoln; it was firmly for the Union but decidedly not Radical in its sympathies. The *Chronicle,* which John W. Forney of Pennsylvania, Clerk of the Senate during Lincoln's administration, had launched, was the organ of the Radical Republicans. The *National Republican,* edited by William Murtagh, represented the middle-of-the-road Republican viewpoint. Among the weeklies were the Democratic *Sunday Herald,* Donn Piatt's lively sheet, the *Capital,* and the *Critic,* which contained theatrical and local news. The *Georgetown Courier* reflected the strongly Southern and Conservative views of that community. *Columbia,* a German-language weekly, published items of special interest to the 12,000-odd residents of German descent, many of whom had come to the capital during the decade preceding the War, and were owners of prosperous small businesses.[7] The German population in Washington was highly organized, with flourishing clubs and societies such as the *Turnverein, Schützverein, Sängerbund,* and literary, patriotic and beneficial organizations.

On the Avenue, or perhaps on Sunday along the suburban roads leading to Rock Creek Park, might be seen a robust figure six feet tall, costumed in blue or grey, moving along at a firm but moderate pace. His broad shirt collar was always open, beneath a curly grey beard. His face was as red as an apple, and his sparkling blue eyes had a look of animal health more characteristic of a frontiersman than a government clerk. Walt Whitman's *Leaves of Grass* was merely a curiosity to most literary-minded Washingtonians, but in Europe it had caused a furore and was being translated into many foreign languages. Whitman had worked for some time in the Bureau of Indian Affairs, where his volume was brought to the attention of his chief, James Harlan, Secretary of the Interior. After he was dismissed in June 1865 by the scandalized Harlan, a pillar of the Methodist Church, Whitman found a place in the office of the Assistant Attorney-General, which he held for several years. Whitman was fortunate in having some enthusiastic friends and supporters. Among them was John Burroughs, a frequent companion on his Sunday hikes, who published in 1866 a passionate defense of his poetry. Another young clerk and admirer was W. D. O'Connor, whose essay, "The Good Grey Poet," printed in 1867, further vindicated the reputation of his friend.

The reading public of Washington was far more absorbed in the novels of Mrs. E. D. E. N. Southworth, a plump little woman who lived in a cottage by the Georgetown Canal. Her turgid romances—*The Hidden Hand, The Fatal Marriage,* and *The*

Maiden Widow, to name only a few of her immense output—sold by the thousands.

Some of the newspaper correspondents in the city were equally popular literary figures. George Alfred Townsend,[8] of the *Hartford Courier,* was writing spirited accounts of life in the capital, later to be collected under the title *Washington Inside and Outside.* Ben Perley Poore,[9] of the *Boston Journal,* who had edited the first edition of the *Congressional Directory,* was on the closest terms with most of the Republican leaders in Congress. The "literary ladies" of the press, Mary Clemmer Ames and Emily Edson Briggs, were keeping the readers of New York and Philadelphia up to date with the gossip of the city. Occasionally Washington would welcome a national celebrity—Julia Ward Howe on a visit to her fascinating brother, Sam Ward, the lobbyist; Gail Hamilton, the most popular women's writer of the day; Anna Dickinson, the young Quaker girl and passionate Abolitionist, who had taken to the stump during the War and who was to publish in 1868 the first novel sympathetic to racial intermarriage, *What Answer?* At Forney's apartment on Capitol Hill they would meet with the Radical journalists and intellectuals. Matthew Brady, the great photographer of the War, was a frequent guest, and there would occasionally be music and recitations. The Democratic literati had their salon in the home of Horatio King, Postmaster-General under President Buchanan, and himself an essayist of distinction. But the most lofty discussions were held in the house of Senator Charles Sumner of Massachusetts, where the New England intelligentsia and such local celebrities as Professor Joseph Henry of the Smithsonian Institute and Ainsworth Spofford, the Librarian of Congress, were regular visitors.

Some of the relics of past administrations were not yet extinct. Peggy O'Neale Eaton, who had played such a glamorous role in the era of Andrew Jackson, resided in the neighborhood of 20th and I Streets, and President Tyler's widow was living in the capital in almost complete seclusion. In the corridors of the Capitol and in the lobby of the old Metropolitan Hotel there might still be seen a rheumatic old gentleman with curly mustachioes, leaning on a cane, a blanket over his shoulder, wearing a spotted tie and a flowered vest which obviously belonged to better days. Beau Hickman had been a landmark in Washington ever since he had arrived from Virginia to take up a minor government position in the '30's. At that time there had been no more elegant gentleman in the city than Hickman, with his broad-tailed blue coat covered with brass buttons, his plaid pantaloons, ruffled shirt, standing collar and top hat with its narrowing crown. But the small legacy which he had inherited vanished after a few years of gambling and frequenting the ladies of the town; for as long as most Washingtonians could remember he had earned his living by telling stories of the great men with whom he had a nodding acquaintance and by introducing hotel guests to them for a quarter or fifty cents. Beau never drank, but had an excellent taste in good "siggars," which he would accept as a substitute for whisky. The anecdotes concerning him were legion.[10]

By 1865, however, conversation in the hotel lobbies and drawing-rooms of Washington was little concerned with Hickman and similar picturesque relics of the past. The main focus of interest in the capital had shifted to the newcomers, and especially to the colored men and women who had flocked to the city during the War from the plantations of Maryland and Virginia. Their presence, more than any other single factor, would determine the future of Washington for the next decade, and would have a lasting effect upon the political destiny of the Nation's capital.

Chapter 2

Freedmen and Refugees

From the earliest days of the District of Columbia its Negro population, slave and free, had always been a considerable element. Free Negroes had been among the first settlers, and one of them, Benjamin Banneker, a mathematician, had been selected by George Washington to serve as assistant to Major l'Enfant at the time the Federal City was planned and laid out. The number of free colored men and women had grown steadily during the years before the War. In 1830 there had been 6,152 freedmen and 6,119 slaves, in 1840 8,361 freedmen and 4,694 slaves and in 1860 11,131 were free and only 3,185 slaves. The statistics of the free represented slaves who had been manumitted by their masters, Negroes born of free parents, and those who had run away from other states.

The legal restrictions of freedmen—or Black Codes, as they were called—had been taken from the regulations in force in Maryland at the time the District of Columbia was created. Every free Negro had been required to give to the Mayor satisfactory evidence of freedom and a fee of $50 for himself and for each member of his family. In addition, he had to secure a bond for $1000, which had to be renewed every year, that he would maintain good behavior and not become a public charge on the community, and this bond required five white guarantors. Freedmen who did not carry their papers upon their person were subject to imprisonment; often these papers were stolen or destroyed and freedmen were kidnapped and sold South. Any person harboring or concealing a freedman who could not exhibit a permit from the Register authorizing him to reside in the District could be punished—and exceptions were made only for transients or those employed by members of Congress. No Negro, slave or free, could testify against a white man. Meetings in private houses could be held only by special permission from the Mayor, under penalty of lashes and imprisonment for unauthorized gatherings. Licenses were granted to Negroes for no business except driving a cart or carriage. Any Negro caught and convicted of playing cards or any other game of chance was subject to a $10 fine, and no Negro, slave or free, could be out on the street after 10 P.M. without a special permit. Slave jails were to be found all over Washington City and Georgetown until Congress put an end to slave-trading in the District in 1850. One of the largest traders in the South, Armfield and Franklin, had their main office in Alexandria.

The white citizens of the District had been alarmed over the rapid growth of the free colored population, and they had been especially concerned that their numbers should not further increase. The severity of the Black Codes had been designed to keep down the number of free Negroes who were generally regarded in the South and in the District before the War as a public danger. Slave owners were worried lest the free Negro set a bad example to his slaves; they feared that they might encourage others to settle in Washington, where they would have to be supported by the taxpayers.

Though the legal restrictions imposed by the Black Codes were formidable, the Circuit Court of the District under Judge William Cranch had been extremely lenient to the freedmen in its rulings. Freed Negroes in the District were able not only to find employment but even to prosper and build up modest fortunes. Often, with the help of white friends and sponsors, free colored men operated small hotels, boarding-houses, restaurants and saloons; the barber trade was almost entirely in their hands, and so was the hacking and carriage business. Negroes were to be found in such skilled trades as printing and cabinet-making, and there were also many colored bricklayers, stonemasons, tanners, millers and wheelwrights, while Negro women were employed as nurses, dressmakers, laundresses and in all forms of domestic work.

The wealthiest colored men had been conspicuously successful in the catering business. James T. Wormley, the owner of a restaurant at 15th and I Streets, was also the proprietor of several houses in downtown Washington, one of which had been occupied during the War by General Winfield Scott.[1] Wormley, who had begun his career as a hack driver, had later been a steward on a Mississippi steamer. By 1868 his culinary skill had become so famous that Reverdy Johnson, whom Andrew Johnson appointed Minister to the Court of St. James, took him to London to supervise the preparation of terrapin for his guests. John A. Gray, formerly a waiter at the Washington Club on Lafayette Square, and whose own house had been the rendezvous of Francis Barton Key and Mrs. Daniel Sickles in the pre-War *cause-célèbre,* also catered to some of the best families in the city. Alfred Jones, a colored feed merchant of Washington, had become wealthy enough before the War to buy a house on H Street which had formerly been occupied by the British Legation, and in Georgetown another feed merchant, Alfred Lee, was one of the most prosperous merchants in town. William Shadd, who rose from hotel porter to become White House caterer under Andrew Johnson, left in 1868 an estate of nearly $100,000.[2] Already by 1860 Negroes paid taxes on real estate worth $650,000 and in one square alone owned property worth more than $40,000.[3]

Among the older colored families the Syphaxes were perhaps the most outstanding. They were directly descended from George Washington Parke Custis, Martha Washington's grandson, who had been brought up at Mount Vernon. Maria, his daughter by a slave, Airy Carter, had been freed upon her marriage to Charles Syphax and given as her dowry fifteen acres from the Arlington estate. During the War, when the estate had been confiscated by the Federal Government for non-payment of taxes, Congress passed a special bill to ensure the colored family's title to their property. William Syphax, Maria's eldest son, occupied a prominent place among the colored men of Washington before the War and had been one of the founders of the 19th Street Baptist Church. Since 1852 he had been a messenger in the Interior Department, a position open to few colored men at the time.

As early as 1807, Negroes had provided for the education of their children in the District, and many men and women had come down from New England to open schools in Washington and in Georgetown. John F. Cook, a minister who had married the daughter of the founder of the first colored school in Washington, was prominent among the early teachers. His two sons, John F. Cook, Jr., and George W. T. Cook, carried on his work. "The sentiment against the education of the colored classes," wrote Professor Barnard in his special report to the U. S. Department of Education[4] "was much less vigorous in the early history of the capital than it was a third of a century later. The free colored people were sometimes even encouraged in their efforts to pick up some fragments of knowledge. They were taught in the Sunday schools and evening schools occasionally, and respectable mulatto families were in many cases allowed to attend with white children in the private schools and academies. There are scores of colored men and women still living in the District who are decently educated and who never went to any but white schools. There are also white men and women still alive who went to school in this city and in Georgetown with colored children and felt no offense."

Following the revulsion of feeling, however, which took place after the Nat Turner Rebellion in Virginia, many of the colored schools were burned in the "Snow Riots" of 1835. John F. Cook was forced to flee to Pennsylvania for two years before public feeling had calmed down enough to permit reopening his school. The institutions maintained by Northerners continued, but under strong opposition from the Washington authorities. In 1851 Myrtilla Miner, a young woman who had come down from New York to open a school for colored girls under the auspices of Harriet Beecher Stowe and a group of Philadelphia Quakers, encountered stern disapproval from the Mayor of Washington,

Walter Lennox. In the opinion of the Mayor, the school would attract to the city a larger number of Negroes than it could support, and it would give them an education "far beyond what their political and social conditions would justify."[5] Nevertheless Miss Miner went ahead with her plans and maintained her school on New Hampshire Avenue until the outbreak of the War.

On April 16th, 1862, slavery was abolished in the District of Columbia, and compensation given by the Federal Government to slave-owners, except to those proved disloyal to the Union. The number of slaves set free was 3,128, and their owners received an average of $300 for each. The measure had been coupled, at the insistence of Abraham Lincoln, with an appropriation of $100,000 to help settle the freedmen in such countries as Haiti and Liberia, but there is no evidence to show that Negroes in the District took advantage of the offer. The Emancipation Bill was highly unpopular with the white citizens of Washington and the Board of Aldermen addressed a memorial to Congress urging it to "provide safeguards against converting this city into an asylum for free Negroes, a population undesirable in any community."[6]

Congress was in no mood, however, to provide assurances of this kind during the War, and the influx of Negroes from the surrounding areas of Maryland and Virginia started immediately. By 1866 it was estimated that there were over 30,000 colored men and women in Washington who had come to the capital during and after the War, many of them under the impression that they would be taken care of by the same government which had set them free. While the newly-formed Bureau of Freedmen and Refugees was attempting to find employment for them in the North as farm workers or servants, it was quite unable to cope with the completely destitute families, for which Congress was obliged to appropriate special relief funds. Few Negroes could be persuaded to volunteer for employment in Virginia and Maryland farms, in spite of references and assurances of good treatment from families in need of labor.[7]

The Freedmen's Bureau had set up tenements at Kendall Green and at the Campbell Barracks, while across the Potomac on the Arlington estate of Robert E. Lee, which had been taken over by the government during the War, a large settlement was established known as Freedmen's Village. But the work of the Bureau was only a minute alleviation of widespread human misery. The refugees were scattered all over the District wherever they could find vacant land or friends with whom they could take shelter. Some set up improvised hovels in alleys, others within abandoned Army fortifications[8], many in the "Island" of southwest Washington, and still others in the vicinity of Boundary Street and across the Anacostia in Uniontown. The very names of some of these communities indicated their condition: Goose Level, Vinegar Hill, Foggy Bottom, Hell's Bottom, Bloodfield, Prather's Alley and Nigger Hill. The worst slums of all were to be found in the very center of Washington near the old canal, the section known as "Murder Bay." Writing of this area in 1867, Major Richards, head of the Metropolitan Police, described it thus in his report to the Board of Common Council:

> Here crime, filth and poverty seem to vie with each other in a career of degradation and death . . . Whole families are crowded into mere apologies for shanties, which are without light or ventilation. During the storms of rain or snow their roofs afford but slight protection; while beneath a few rough boards the miasmatic effluvia from the most filthy stagnant water renders the atmosphere within these hovels stifling and sickening in the extreme. Their rooms are usually not more than six or eight feet square, and not a window or even an opening (except a door) for the admission of light. Some of the rooms are entirely surrounded by other rooms, so that no light at all reaches where persons spend their nights and days. In a space about fifty yards square I found about a hundred families composed of about three to five persons each living in shanties one story in height except in a few instances where tenements are actually built on top of others . . . In one building visited seven families were found on the ground floor, consisting of from two to seven

persons each, a restaurant and a boardinghouse. The second story is a large dance hall where these persons congregate for their amusement. Nearly all these people came from Virginia during the Rebellion.[9]

The suffering of the colored refugees in the District had stimulated the activities of churches in many parts of the North not only to raise funds for their relief but also to establish small schools for their children. By 1864 they had set up in Washington and Georgetown 12 day schools with 25 instructors and 30 day pupils, and 30 night schools with 36 teachers and 1,350 pupils.[10] The Freedmen's Relief Association established a school on M Street, and their example was soon followed by religious groups —the Baptists, Universalists, Unitarians, Catholics and Quakers.

After Emancipation in 1862 Congress had passed a law establishing free education for colored children in the District, but since their financial support was to be derived solely from ten per cent of the taxes paid by colored taxpayers, the amount realized was completely inadequate. In 1864 another law was passed by which the corporations of Washington and Georgetown were required to set aside twenty per cent of their entire school fund for the use of colored schools. This figure was arrived at by estimating the proportion of colored children to the total number of children of school age within the confines of the city areas. Mayor Wallach, however, who had been bitterly opposed to the principle of using white school funds for the education of colored children, whose parents had contributed less than their share of the tax fund, did his utmost to thwart the law. Choosing to interpret the act in a narrow manner, he refused to pay more than ten per cent of the school fund to the colored school trustees, who at this time were under the jurisdiction of the Interior Department.[11] Wallach considered that the colored children "had been forced upon us by the Federal Government" and that it was the responsibility of the Federal Government rather than the District to look after them. The situation developed to a complete impasse, which was aggravated by the fact that Wallach was a Democrat and Congress militantly Republican. This situation continued until 1867 and the arrears in the salaries of colored teachers continued to mount.[12]

The colored school system was fortunate, however, in having as one of its trustees a genuine friend, the Postmaster of Washington, Sayles J. Bowen. Originally a Democrat, Mr. Bowen had come to Washington in 1845 from Pennsylvania to take up a position in the Treasury Department, but lost his job three years later for distributing anti-slavery propaganda. He had been one of the earliest supporters of the Republican Party, and had been rewarded for his campaigning by being appointed Disbursing Officer to the Senate in 1861. From then on his promotion had been rapid. Lincoln had made him one of the first Commissioners of the Metropolitan Police and he was appointed City Postmaster in 1863. For eleven years he had served as a member of the Levy Court, and had been instrumental in the construction of many new roads in this rural area. Bowen had helped to secure for Negroes the right to serve as jurymen, and he was President of the Freedmen's Aid Society, which distributed private charity to the destitute refugees from the South. In 1862, when Congress established public schools for Negroes, Bowen was made one of the first trustees and every law relating to the system came under his personal supervision. In 1866 and 1867 when Mayor Wallach persistently refused to pay to the colored school trustees the amount which Congress had authorized, Bowen advanced $20,000 out of his own pocket in order to permit them to continue.[13]

Bowen had been one of the few white men in Washington before the War who had publicly taken a sympathetic position towards the Negro. Dr. Gamaliel Bailey, the founder of the Abolitionist weekly, *The National Era,* which had published in instalments *Uncle Tom's Cabin,* had been almost killed by an angry mob. A former colleague of Dr. Bailey, Lewis Clephane, had remained, however, in Washington and become one of the founders of the *National Republican.* A man of high moral character and generally respected in spite of his advanced political views, he had been appointed City Postmaster before Bowen, and later served as Collector of Internal Revenue for the District. Several Protestant ministers were also known for their strong anti-slavery views—the Unitarian ministers William Henry Channing, Chaplain to the House of Representatives, and his successor from Virginia, Moncure Conway. Byron Sunderland, Congregational Minister and Chaplain to the Senate, was equally outspoken in his statements on slavery.

But the greatest and most influential friend of the Negro was the Senator from Massachusetts, Charles Sumner, one of the founders of the Republican Party and for several years Chairman of the Committee on Foreign Relations in the Senate. For most of his political career Sumner had devoted his efforts, his great learning and oratory, towards the complete emancipation of the Negro. To Sumner the Constitution represented a charter of human rights, and there was no provision in it for second-class citizenship. The Negro was a citizen by virtue of having been born in the United States, and as such he was entitled to the full protection of the law. Sumner refused from the outset to compromise on the basic principle of racial equality, and he had also realized that the Negro should be freed from his ignorance and poverty as well as from his bondage. He fought consistently for free homesteads and free education for the former slave, as well as for the right of suffrage which he believed to be the inalienable right of every American citizen.

Enemies of Sumner, of whom there were many even in his own party, could not easily understand why a Boston Brahmin who had grown up with Agassiz, Longfellow, Lieber, and who was on intimate terms with the great New England writers and thinkers, could devote himself so singlemindedly to the cause of the lowly Negro. They accused him of intellectual arrogance and playacting. Secretary of the Treasury McCulloch stated in his memoirs that Sumner's "sympathies were for races—too lofty to descend to persons."[14] Yet a perusal of Sumner's immense correspondence reveals him to be a man of warm personal affections and a devoted and loyal friend to men and women of all stations in life. He was a citizen of the world, a man who had been received with open arms by aristocrats and statesmen in England, who had known in his youth Carlyle, Wordsworth and Macauley, was a regular correspondent of the great French political thinker De Tocqueville, and was equally at home in Washington or London, Paris or Rome. Furthermore Sumner's interest in the Negro was by no means theoretical. He had been for many years in close touch with the leaders of the Negro race, men such as Frederick Douglass, George Downing, the New York and Newport caterer, and James Wormley and his brother William, one of the Commissioners for Colored Schools in Washington. It was precisely because Sumner had such personal contacts with individual Negroes that he was able to understand the potentialities of the race to which others, their eyes clouded by prejudice and preconceptions, were totally blind.

Sumner had taken active part in the fight for the rights of the Negro in the District of Columbia. Through his efforts, after he had made a formal complaint to the District Attorney, segregation was abolished on the Washington and Georgetown Railway streetcars. Sumner was also responsible for the enfranchisement of colored people as witnesses in the District. He introduced a bill in Congress to permit Negroes to serve as members of juries and as officers in the government of the District which finally was enacted into law.[15] The District of Columbia was of especial interest to Sumner, since this was an area over which Congress had exclusive legislation, and in 1866 at his own request he was placed on the Senate District Committee.

In the summer of 1865 the leading colored men in Washington had met to consider means for securing the right to vote in local elections. For many years colored property owners in Washington and Georgetown had felt that they had been treated most unfairly by the white population: while they paid taxes like other citizens for the support of white schools, the Mayor and Councils of Washington were refusing to turn over to the Commissioners for Colored Schools the proportion of the fund which had been authorized by Congress. They had many other grievances, such as exclusion from hotels and restaurants on account of color, and segregation in theatres and other public places, which they felt could be settled if they were given a voice in municipal affairs. The same autumn before Congress reconvened, a petition was drawn up signed by John F. Cook, Jr., the teacher and Oberlin graduate, and by 25 other colored property owners of Washington setting forth their grievances and requesting the right of suffrage.

The question of voting by Negroes had become at this time a burning national issue and one on which the Republican Party was by no means unanimous. Even in the North only six states permitted Negro suffrage without restriction. Negroes were not permitted to vote in Pennsylvania, Ohio, Indiana and Illinois, and the State of New York still maintained property qualifications for Negro voters. Abraham Lincoln had been in favor of extending the vote in the South only to those Negroes who had fought in the Union Army and to those who could pass a literacy test. The Radical wing of the Party, led by Sumner and Thaddeus Stevens, was, however, adamant on this issue. It was essential in their opinion that the colored man should be permitted to vote in order to protect himself against the former Rebel. Furthermore the control of the Southern States by the Republican Party could be maintained by the Negro vote, since it was quite inconceivable that the vast majority of Negroes would vote for any other Party than the Republicans who had freed them.

Realizing the difficulties of achieving Negro suffrage in the States, the leaders of the Radical Wing of the Republican Party began to turn their attention to the District of Columbia over which Congress had jurisdiction. If Negro suffrage could be achieved in the District, with its large colored population, that would set the pattern which some of the Southern states might eventually be persuaded or compelled to follow. Thus the municipal politics of Washington and Georgetown were to become a vital issue in the struggle for power between the Radical Republicans in Congress and Andrew Johnson, the Conservative Democrat in the White House.

Chapter 3

The District is Reconstructed

In the spring of 1865 Andrew Johnson was still a popular figure. Although his unfortunate intoxication at the time of Lincoln's second inauguration had not been forgotten, his good qualities were much more in the public mind. The people of the North still gratefully recalled Johnson's services to the Union as War Governor of Tennessee, when his life was in constant danger; they remembered the sufferings of his wife, whose health had been permanently affected as the result of her experiences in Eastern Tennessee. Johnson alone, of all Southern Senators, had remained faithful to the Union, and the nation had shown its gratitude by electing him, although a Democrat, to the second highest public office in the United States government.

In appearance the President was impressive. About five feet ten inches in height, he was strongly built, though his hands and feet were small. His massive head was covered with thick black hair, now interspersed with strands of gray, which he wore long at the back, in the style of the older generation of statesmen. He was inevitably dressed in a black broadcloth coat and waistcoat with black doeskin trousers. Johnson's face was lined with the marks of suffering and conflict, and his manner was usually grave. Charles Dickens, who visited him in 1868, wrote: "He is a man with a remarkable face indicating courage, watchfulness and strength of purpose . . . I should have picked him out anywhere as a character of mark."[1] Henry Adams, meeting him shortly after his return from England, recalled Johnson as the strongest President whom he had seen in the White House.

The behavior of the Vice-President in March had been an unusual incident, as he was known to be a man of temperate habits. Those who knew him best—Secretary McCulloch, Senator Doolittle, his personal secretary Colonel Benjamin Truman, and Colonel Crook, his bodyguard—have all testified that Johnson would on occasions drink a few glasses of whisky, but that he was not given to insobriety, that he never drank champagne or cocktails nor visited barrooms. Many of the excesses attributed to him were actually those of his son, Colonel Robert Johnson, whom his father was forced to send away on a long cruise to Africa, and who died while still a young man from alcoholic debauchery. The President was singularly free of all other small vices; he never visited the theatre, never gambled nor bet on horses; checkers was his favorite game.[2]

Other rumors circulated against Johnson's character at a later date were equally groundless. He was, like all Southerners, courtly in his attitude towards the fair sex, and the wives of Confederate leaders, such as Mrs. Clement Clay and other supplicants for pardons, found him always gracious. If on occasion he was over-indulgent, as in the case of Mrs. Lucy Cobb, who boasted of her access to the White House, and had made the obtaining of pardons her profession, no evidence of infidelity was ever shown. The tenderness and consideration which he displayed towards his wife, Eliza, whose health had been seriously impaired as a result of her wartime ordeals, was indeed one of the few touching features of his stern nature.

More than any President who had sat in the White House since Andrew Jackson, Johnson was a man of the people. He had been almost illiterate when, as a boy, he had crossed the mountains from North Carolina to settle in the small town of Greeneville, Tennessee. Eliza McCardle, who had left her teaching at the age of 17 to become his wife, had to instruct him in reading and writing. From the first politics was Johnson's main interest; he read the speeches of Clay, Calhoun and Webster, and learned the Constitution by heart. His tailor's shop soon became a center for political discussions. Johnson was elected to the State Legislature and in 1835 took his seat in the House of Representatives as member from East Tennessee.

By background and temperament he was a Democrat in the Jackson tradition, bitterly opposed to the slaveholding aristocrats of the Whig Party. Though in his prosperous years he owned a small number of slaves, he was never more than a lukewarm defender of the institution. The small farmers and shopkeepers of his District were mostly hard-working and thrifty people of Scotch-Irish descent, and there were no large plantations. To these people slavery represented a direct economic threat, since many of the plantation owners had made a practice of training their Negroes as artisans and hiring them out at low wages in competition to the white workers. With this background Johnson had come to believe that the enfranchisement of the Southern Negro could only aggravate the bitterness between the races.

Like Andrew Jackson and Jefferson before him, Johnson was concerned with the question of the Western frontier. He had persistently opposed the attempts of Northern capitalists to secure large grants of public land for railroads and similar purposes. In his view the public domain should be allotted to small farmers, and it was his hope that by this means a new class of small holders would grow in the West who would unite with the poor white people of the South whom he represented. Congress had in 1859 passed a Homestead Act which he had drawn up to provide such land for small farmers; it had, however, been violently opposed by the Southern plantation owners, who regarded such measures as likely to lead to their loss of political power. The measure received the veto of President Buchanan, but was passed in 1863.

As the spokesman for the impoverished white class of the South, Johnson had been equally opposed to the aristocracy of wealth which had arisen in the North and to the plantation owners of the South. He had been quick to see that the War had enabled the Northern manufacturers to make enormous profits at the expense of the United States government and the American taxpayers. Most of the bonds issued during the War were now held by Northern capitalists, who were earning interest at six and seven per cent . The high tariffs set up during the War had especially benefitted them, and they were anxious above all else that this protection be retained. Were the Southern states to be readmitted into the Union, the alliance which they would form with the Northern and Western Democrats would once more place the manufacturers of New England in the minority position which they held for so many years before the War. Johnson was well aware that the Northern Radicals would not hesitate to use any means to prevent and delay the readmission of the Southern states—even if this involved increasing the power of the Legislative branch of the government at the expense of the Executive and of the Judiciary. As a devout believer in the sacredness of the American constitution, a well-worn copy of which he carried in his pocket, he was determined to prevent this at all costs.

Johnson had started out as a violent opponent of Lincoln. In 1860 he had voted for Breckinridge and he never professed to be any other than a Democrat. Yet his devotion to the Union was so strong that he was willing to undergo the bitter antagonism of his party in the South for denouncing secession in the Senate in 1861; he was even brave enough to return to Eastern Tennessee before the outbreak of hostilities to throw all of his influence against the dissolution of the Union. His wartime services as Governor of Tennessee, when he was besieged for two months in Nashville, were considered so outstanding that in 1864 the Republican Convention showed little hesitation in selecting him to be Lincoln's running mate. In his letter of acceptance, however, Johnson made his position clear, indicating that he had not departed from his principles as a Democrat, but that "the higher duty of first preserving the Government" was his primary concern.

Once elected Vice-President, Johnson showed that he was entirely in accord with the plans for Southern Reconstruction which the President was formulating. He approved the theory under which Lincoln had created provisional governments for Arkansas and Louisiana, a theory which Congress had rejected in 1864 by a narrow margin. After Lincoln's assassination he made no changes in the Cabinet and saw no necessity to call a special session of Congress. He believed like Lincoln that it would be possible through the exercise of persuasion and goodwill to lead Southern men of influence into accepting the defeat of slavery as inevitable, and that their ideas and policies would change accordingly.[3]

To those, however, who had been responsible for Secession, Johnson maintained his bitterness and contempt. "I shall go to my grave with the belief that Davis, Cobb, Toombs and a few others of the arch-conspirators and traitors should have been tried, convicted and hanged for treason," he wrote to his former secretary, Benjamin Truman.[4] "I'd show coming generations that, while the rebellion was too popular a revolt to punish many who participated in it, treason should be made odious and arch-traitors should be punished." Such strong opinions had made many of the Radical Congressmen who had been associated with Johnson in the Committee on the Conduct of the War, including Wade and Sumner, confident that he would endorse their theories of Reconstruction and they felt hopeful that he would declare himself in favor of Negro suffrage. They did not or could not understand that it was his deep sense of personal loyalty—his Tennessee mountain heritage—which made him condemn so fiercely the conduct of those men who had deserted the Union.

In the Cabinet Seward, for whose opinion Johnson had the greatest respect, stayed on as Secretary of State. Stanton, the Secretary of War, had always maintained an ambiguous position; by nature an intriguer, he had changed sides many times during his political career. Lincoln had found him the most difficult of all his Cabinet to get along with, yet Stanton's energy and his devotion to the Union were so great that he had felt constrained to retain his services. Welles, Secretary of the Navy, was temperamentally more akin to Johnson than any other member of the Cabinet. A former Democrat from Connecticut, he was a man of bluff nature, outspoken, with little use for pretexts. Through Welles's diary, the most revealing single document of Johnson's administration, the problems and personalities of the times stand out in clear relief. With Hugh McCulloch, the Secretary of the Treasury, an Indiana banker and moderate Republican, Johnson was on indifferent terms. He publicly approved of the Secretary's program to reduce the national debt and high interest payments, but personally leaned to the inflationary views favored in the West that the circulation of money should be increased. James Harlan of Iowa, the Secretary of the Interior, James Speed of Kentucky, the Attorney-General, and William Dennison of Ohio, the Postmaster-General, who were inclined to the Radical doctrine, were seldom favored with his intimacies. The President had, indeed, few close political advisers; during the early part of his administration the men close to him were Preston King of New York and Senator Doolittle of Wisconsin, both moderate Republicans. During his entire career Andrew Johnson had been a solitary figure, and he had become accustomed to making decisions upon what he believed to be right rather than on the shifting basis of political expediency.

During the first months of the new administration, life at the White House assumed a more settled and domestic air than had been seen for many years. The President's routine was simple and regular. He rose at seven (six in the summer) and read until ten. Between ten and noon he received callers and after a mid-day meal met with the Cabinet and other important callers. At three o'clock he would take an hour's walk, and after an early dinner retire to his study until midnight to work on his papers. Six secretaries were kept busy, and his correspondence is one of the largest and best-preserved among the presidential files.

Owing to the illness of Mrs. Johnson, who spent most of her time in a rocking-chair in the upstairs sitting-room with her needlework, the household duties devolved upon the President's two daughters. Mrs. Patterson, the elder, whose husband was Senator from Tennessee, was a quiet young woman with a remarkable capability for her task, in which she was assisted by her sister, Mrs. Stover, whose husband had been killed in the Union Army. The Executive Mansion had been sadly abused by the hordes of visitors during the War, who had cut pieces from the draperies and trampled with muddy feet on the fine carpets. During the six weeks after her husband's assassination, Mary Todd Lincoln had been in a state of collapse, and there had been no steward to protect the White House, which was open to everyone. Valuable silver, china and gold spoons, worth altogether more than $22,000, had been removed, and it was common knowledge in the city that they had been sold. In February 1866, Congress was forced to appropriate an additional sum of $46,000 to replace them and to permit further necessary purchases for the household.

The initial appropriation of $30,000 made in 1865 shortly after the Johnson family moved into the White House enabled Mrs. Patterson to make only the most essential repairs. The old furniture of the East Room, the sofas which had been used as beds by the soldiers on guard, were replaced, as well as the carpets, and the Blue Room was also redecorated. There was insufficient money to replace its expensive paper, but panelling and gilt ornaments were added to give it a brighter appearance. Mrs. Patterson's chief outlays were for the State Dining Room, for which she purchased thirty new chairs, a tapestry Brussels carpet, and a Solferino dinner service and glasses. The state dinners which she gave were on a generous, "almost a princely scale"[5] a surprise to many who had commented on the "Republican simplicity" of the establishment. "We are a plain people, Sir, from the mountains of Tennessee, and do not propose to put on airs because we have the fortune to occupy this place for a little while," Mrs. Patterson had once remarked to newspaper reporters; they were surprised that when the dignity of the Presidential office demanded, Andrew Johnson and his family could rise to the occasion.

During the spring of 1865 until the end of May harmony reigned between the White House and Congress. Johnson had shown exemplary tact and patience in listening to the arguments on the Reconstruction of the Southern states from many different sides. Some of his former associates of the Committee on the Conduct of the War, Senator Benjamin Wade of Ohio and Senator Charles Sumner of Massachusetts who had maintained their contact with him, were of the opinion as late as May 12 that the President was sympathetic to Negro suffrage and that he would use his personal influence to persuade the Southern states to adopt it. They were to be sadly disillusioned when Johnson issued on the 29th his North Carolina Proclamation. The Provisional Government set up under Governor Holden made no provision for the extension of the suffrage, leaving the matter to be decided by the voters of the state under a new constitution for which a statewide convention was to be called. Only those who had voted before May 20, 1861, and who had taken the oath prescribed in the Amnesty Proclamation, would be entitled to take part in this convention. On June 13 a similar Proclamation was issued for the State of Mississippi, and during the next month for Georgia, Texas, Alabama, South Carolina, Virginia and Florida.

At the time when the North Carolina Proclamation was issued, only six states in the North and West had granted suffrage to Negroes. Even in New York colored voters were required to own $250 worth of property as a condition of being permitted to register. Lincoln had recognized provisional governments in Arkansas and Louisiana from which Negroes had been excluded as voters. Logically, therefore, Johnson's position was sound, and in conformity with the principle of States' Rights in which he so ardently believed. His great mistake was in omitting to take into consideration the temper of the people of the North, who feared with some reason that the Southern states would return to Congress the same type of men they had elected before the War. Such men, with their allies, the Northern and Western Democrats, might form a coalition strong enough to undo what the War had accomplished. The enfranchisement of the Negro, for which they showed little enthusiasm at first, might at least change the balance of power in the South, and enable good Union men to be returned to Congress. To permit a state of affairs by which Jefferson Davis, Robert Toombs, John Slidell, and other Confederate leaders would be re-elected to Congress was as unthinkable and shocking to the leaders of the Republican party as would have been to the Allies the return to power in Germany of Goering, Von Ribbentrop and Goebbels after the Second World War.

The Constitution of the United States had made no provision for secession, and the question of readmission of states into the Union was completely without precedent. Johnson, after hearing the arguments on all sides, had come to the conclusion that the Union had never been dissolved, that while "individuals" had declared the secession of the Southern states in 1861 and had organized governments on an independent basis, such action had been unconstitutional and ineffective. Since the Union could not be dissolved, such actions were null and void; the states had never ceased to be members of the Union, and the Federal Government should not deny them admittance to representation, nor seek to impose conditions for the readmission of their representatives.

Among the Radicals many different theories of constitutional procedure had been discussed during the course of the War. Thaddeus Stevens of Pennsylvania had repeatedly urged that the South be treated as a conquered nation. He had advocated that the property of those men who had participated in the Rebellion be seized and that compensation be made to the Northerners who had suffered loss during the War. The land of all Confederates owning more than 200 acres should be confiscated and distributed to freedmen in 40-acre lots, the remainder sold to provide pensions for Union soldiers and to pay the cost of the national debt. He had as yet not enunciated his plans for the readmission of the Southern states into the Union, but it was clear that unrestricted Negro suffrage would be a prerequisite.

Charles Sumner, less concerned with revenge, was more interested in the constitutional questions involved. According to his views, the seceding states had "committed suicide" and no longer existed as legally organized governments. He had declared that it would be contrary to the Constitution to readmit these states on their pre-war basis. Congress alone had the right to decide the conditions under which representatives would be accepted among their ranks, in exactly the same capacity as it possessed the right to admit new territories to statehood and national representation. The right of the Negro to suffrage had in his opinion been won in the War, and to exclude them as voters in the South would be a betrayal of their cause and of the principles for which the war had been fought.

Once Andrew Johnson had declared his hand, the Radical Republicans abandoned all attempts to influence him further. Whitelaw Reid describes the host of Confederates who descended upon the capital during the summer of 1865:

> Every day the White House presented the same scene. Passing through the ante-room to the public staircase one always encountered a throng of coarsely-dressed, bronzed Southerners carrying heavy cases, tobacco-ruminant and full of political talk. The unfurnished, desolate-looking room in which visitors gathered while waiting their turns for interviews was crowded. One day I saw two or three Rebel generals, and as many members of the Rebel Congress and at least a score of less noted leaders. In a corner, occupying the only chair which this room contained, sat a former Secretary of War of the Rebel Confederacy . . . . From 7 until 3 the President sat in the room adjacent conversing with one or another as the doorkeeper admitted them. Pardons were discussed, policies of reorganization were canvassed. The pardon-seekers were the counsellors for reorganization; there were none others with whom to consult.

Thus the weary day passed with a steady stream of Rebel callers. At 3 o'clock the doorkeeper's hands were full of cards not yet presented to the President and the ante-room was thronged; then the doors were thrown open and the crowd rushed in, as if scrambling for seats in a railroad car. The President stood by his desk; to his left at another table stood General Mussey and Colonel Browning, his two private secretaries. On a table in the center of the room lay a pile of pardons a foot high watched by a young major in uniform.[6]

Not a few of the pardons granted were to residents of the District of Columbia for having "left a loyal district" during the War for the South. The Archives of the War Department concealed until 1953 the names of those to whom pardons were granted, though an Executive Document published in January, 1867, listed those of 25 residents of Washington and Georgetown pardoned by the President. Among them were Richard Cox, whose estate in Georgetown Heights, "Berleith," had been converted into a home for colored orphans during the War, D. J. Castleman, member of a wealthy land-owning family in Washington, W. D. Cassin and Lloyd J. Beall, members of the most prominent of Georgetown families, and Charles Wallach, a brother of the Mayor of Washington. The number of District residents disenfranchised during the War was considerably higher, and their voting privileges were not fully restored until 1870.[7]

Many of the Radical Republicans, especially Charles Sumner, were apprehensive concerning the number of pardons granted by Andrew Johnson to the Southern sympathizers in the District. In the comprehensive plan for the enfranchisement of the Negroes in the Southern states which Sumner and his fellow Radicals had drawn up, the District was to have the first place in the timetable. Sumner considered it particularly shameful that in the national capital men should be denied the vote, which in his opinion was guaranteed to every American irrespective of racial origin or color. It seemed especially unfair to him that "rebel sympathizers" should receive pardons while colored men, some of whom had fought and suffered for the Union, should be denied the opportunity to defend their own interests at the polls.

In the fall of 1865 the issue of Negro suffrage in the District came into the open. A month before Congress was due to assemble, Mayor Wallach had been empowered to call a special session of the Councils in order to make provision for a plebiscite on this issue, should Congress decide to pass legislation enfranchising the colored District residents. When the 39th Congress reconvened in December, Senator Wade immediately proposed a Bill to extend the suffrage to all male Negroes in the District over the age of 21, and on December 5 Representative Kelley of Pennsylvania introduced a similar Bill in the House. The referendum which followed showed that the voters of Washington were opposed to Negro suffrage by a vote of 6,591 to 35, and those of Georgetown by 712 to 1.

After the result Mayor Wallach wrote in a letter to the President of the Senate, Lafayette Foster of Connecticut:

> This vote, the largest with but two exceptions ever polled in this city, conclusively shows the unanimity of sentiment of the people of Washington in opposition to the extension of suffrage to that class. No others in addition to this minority of 35 are to be found in this community who favor the existence of a right to suffrage for that class and in the manner proposed excepting those who have memorialized the Senate in its favor and who, with but little association, less sympathy and no community of interest with the city of Washington, receive here from the general government temporary employment, and, having at the national capital a residence limited only to the duration of a Presidential term, claim and invariably exercise the right of franchise elsewhere.

The colored people of the District, however, were not deterred by the result of the referendum, from which they, of course, had been excluded. They had every reason to count upon the support of Congress, which considered the question as a national rather than a purely local issue. While in 1865 such Northern states as Wisconsin, Connecticut and Minnesota had rejected the extension of suffrage to Negroes, the District, over which Congress possessed the supreme legislative authority, might be placed in a different category especially since it was linked to the larger issue of granting the political franchise to the colored population in the Southern states. In January, 1866, when the debate on the District Suffrage Bill opened in the House, Representative Kelley read into his speech the following petition signed by John F. Cook and by 25 other colored property owners in the District:

> We are intelligent enough to be industrious, to have accumulated property, to build and sustain churches and institutions of learning. We are and have been educating our children without the aid of any school fund and until recently had for many years—unjustly as we deem—been furnishing a portion of the means for the education of white children in the District.
>
> We are intelligent enough to be amenable to the same laws and punishable alike with others for the infraction of said laws. We sustain as fair a character on the records of crime and statistics of pauperism as any other class in the community, while unequal laws are continually barring our way in the effort to reach and possess ourselves of the blessings attendant upon a life of industry and self-denial and virtuous citizenship.
>
> Experience likewise teaches that debasement is most humane which is most complete. The possession of only a partial liberty makes us more keenly sensible of the injustice of withholding those other rights which belong to a perfect manhood. Without the right of suffrage we are without protection and liable to combinations of outrage. Petty officers of the law, respecting the source of power, will naturally defer to the one having a vote, and the partiality thus shown will work much to the disadvantage of the colored citizen.[9]

In the debate which followed Representative Kasson of Iowa declared himself in favor of qualified suffrage for colored veterans and also favored a literacy test for prospective voters. Wilson of Iowa contended that many men who could not read "loved their country, loved justice and had made a better record . . . for liberty and humanity than have some of the most learned men in the land." He feared that the men who opposed Negro suffrage would be the ones who would administer the literacy qualifications. Boutwell of Massachusetts, attacking the proposed limitations, declared "Property qualification is not only unjust in itself, but it is odious to the people of the country to a degree that cannot be expressed. Everywhere, I believe for half a century, it has been repudiated by the people." The literacy test required in Massachusetts was a very different proposition, in his opinion, from that proposed for the District, since for two centuries his state had provided free public education. "Why should the example of such a state be quoted to justify refusing suffrage to men who have been denied the privilege of education and whom it has been a crime to teach?" The Bill was finally passed without either the educational or property qualifications by a vote of 122 to 56. William Owner, a Washington resident whose diary affords much insight into the sentiments of citizens whose sympathies during the War had been with the South, bitterly commented:

> Yesterday the white nigger members of the House of Representatives proposed their nigger suffrage bill, thereby reducing every white man in the District to the level of the nigger. The galleries of the House were crowded with the niggers, and at the announcement of the vote the niggers stamped and shouted and the white niggers on the floor joined in the chorus. A more humiliating scene was never witnessed.

Since Republican leaders were uncertain of being able to muster a two-thirds vote in the Senate to override the expected veto of the President, no further action on the Bill was taken, however, during this session of Congress.

On the same day on which the Suffrage Bill was introduced in the House, Lot Morrill of Maine, head of the District Committee in the Senate, brought forward a bill reorganizing the District government. Under this proposal the franchise was to be abolished except for such offices as Comptroller, Register, Tax Collector and Assessor. Three Commissioners to be appointed by the President and confirmed by the Senate were to administer the government of the District. The bill had the approval of many prominent men in the District, and the Board of Trade at a meeting the previous November had endorsed a similar resolution drawn up by Alexander Shepherd. Many property owners favored the Morrill Bill, hoping that it would put an end to the agitation for Negro suffrage, and that it would simplify local administration by abolishing the separate bodies which were delaying and cramping the improvement of the District. Senator Morrill's measure, however, was premature, and its sweeping abolition of representative government aroused no sympathy in Congress.

On February 7, 1866, the President accorded an interview to a delegation of eleven Negro leaders, among them the great Abolitionist orator, Frederick Douglass; the wealthy hotel owner, George T. Downing of Newport, Rhode Island; and John F. Cook of Washington. Downing opened the interview by saying, "We desire you to know that we come feeling that we are friends meeting a friend," and Douglass added, "Your noble and humane predecessor placed in your hands the sword to assist in saving this great nation, and we hope that you, his able successor, will favorably regard the placing in our hands the ballot which will save ourselves."

While maintaining the same friendliness of manner Johnson indicated to the delegation his fear that a "war of races" would ensue if the poorer white man and the Negro were placed in competition with one another at the ballot box. He reminded his audience that Ohio had recently declared against Negro Suffrage and asked why Southern states should be forced to change their system while Ohio and other states in the North and West were opposed to similar changes. Such decisions, Johnson said, should not be forced upon the white population of the South against its consent, and he urged the emigration of Negroes to Africa and Latin America as a solution of the problem. The colored delegation had little opportunity to express its views, and as Douglass turned to leave he said, "The President sends us to the people and we go to the people." "Yes, Sir," Johnson replied, "I have great faith in the people. I believe they will do what is right."

Shortly afterwards the members of the delegation published in the Northern papers a reply to the various points which the President had raised and which they had had no opportunity to discuss. They were especially concerned over Johnson's theory that hostility would result between the Negroes and the poor white class as a result of the extension of the franchise. This hostility, they stated, was artificial and had been the result of the institution of slavery; besides, even if it were true, justice should permit the Negro to defend himself.

A few days later, on February 13, Douglass was invited by the ladies of the Freedmen's Relief Association to address a meeting for the benefit of destitute colored women and children. By this time the suffrage issue had become so controversial that the committee, even though it was composed of the wives of leading Republicans in the House and Senate, encountered the greatest difficulty in finding a suitable hall for the lecture. Through the efforts of the Rev. Byron Sunderland, a former Senate Chaplain, the First Presbyterian Church was made available. Chief Justice Chase presided at the meeting and more than $500 was raised. Douglass spoke in his most eloquent vein, reminding his listeners that the reaction in favor of the defeated South was already beginning to be felt, and warning them lest in the process of Reconstruction "they do not leave in the soil the same sort of root or fiber from which may spring other assassinations than that of Lincoln." Such a speech inevitably caused a severe dissension among the church trustees and the temporal church committee, several members of which resigned in protest.[10]

In the fall of 1866 the congressional elections revealed the strength of the Republican Party. Andrew Johnson, who had taken the stump through New York and the Middle West, had done his cause much more harm than good. Many waverers, even though they were not convinced regarding Negro suffrage, preferred the Radical candidates to the former enemies of the Union. All of the mid-western states plus Missouri and West Virginia were lost to the Democrats by large majorities. The 40th Congress would contain 143 Republicans in the House to 49 Democrats, and in the Senate 42 Republicans and only 11 Democrats, since, of course, representatives from the former rebel states were still excluded. Thus the Republicans, solidly entrenched behind a two-thirds majority in both Houses, would be in a position to carry out their own policy of Reconstruction and to disregard completely all future presidential vetoes. Johnson's sole remaining strength lay in his power of appointment and in the delaying tactics still at his command.

When the 40th Congress convened in December one of the first bills to be considered was the measure enfranchising the Negroes in the District. The debate on the bill was short, and it was passed by a majority of 118 to 46 in the House and by 32 to 13 in the Senate. In its final form the following provisions were enacted into the District Suffrage Bill:

SECTION 1. Elective franchise was to be conferred upon all citizens over 21 without distinction of race or color who had resided in the District one year preceding the election. Only minors, felons and "those who may voluntarily have given aid or comfort to rebels in the late Rebellion" were excluded.

SECTION 2. Maximum penalties of a $5,000 fine or a year in jail or both were established for election officials rejecting the vote of any person enfranchised under the Act.

SECTION 3. Persons wilfully disturbing electors in the exercise of their franchise were liable to penalties for misdemeanor. A fine not exceeding $1,000 and 30 days in jail or both could be imposed.

SECTION 4. The Criminal Courts of the District were to give the Act in special charge of the Grand Jury of the Common Circuit of each term of the Court.

SECTIONS 5 and 6. Voting lists were to be prepared by the mayors and aldermen of the cities of Washington and Georgetown on and before the first day of March each year and to be posted in public places ten days before the annual election.

The Act by implication abolished the poll tax which had been established to create revenue for the school fund and the requirement that voters pay their personal tax before being allowed to cast their vote.

On January 4, 1867, Andrew Johnson, who had by this time prepared his veto message of the Bill, called together a meeting of his Cabinet to discuss the situation. The message which he read was calm and considered. The President pointed out that in New York Negroes were obliged to comply with property requirements not necessary for white voters before being permitted to vote; in other Northern states, such as Pennsylvania and Indiana, they were completely excluded from the franchise. "It seems hardly consistent with the principle of right and justice," ran the message, "that representatives of states where suffrage is either denied the colored man or granted to him on qualifications requiring intelligence or property should compel the people of the District of Columbia to try an experiment which their own constituents have thus far shown an unwillingness to test for themselves . . . The original purpose of placing the seat of government under the exclusive jurisdiction of Congress was to secure the entire independence of the General Government from undue state influence and to enable it to discharge without danger of interruption or infringement of its authority the high functions for which it was created for the people." It was never contemplated that by so doing "it would afford to propagandists or political parties a place for an experimental test of their theories."

While residents of the District were denied a vote in the electoral college, in all matters concerning their domestic affairs their wishes should be consulted and respected. The President stated his fears that the Negroes "with all the facility of a nomadic people" might flock to the District in such numbers as to take control of the city government and the powers of taxation over property in which they had no interest. The Act "would engender a feeling of opposition and hatred between the two races which, becoming deep-rooted and ineradicable, would prevent them from living together in a state of mutual friendliness." He also considered that the Bill discriminated against naturalized citizens, who not only required a five-year period of residence to receive the right of suffrage, but had also to give evidence of their moral character and loyalty. "To give suffrage indiscriminately," the President concluded, "to a new class wholly unprepared by previous habits and opportunities to perform the trusts which it demands is to degrade and finally to destroy its power, for it may be safely assumed that no political truth is better established than that such indiscriminate and all-embracing extension of popular suffrage must end at last in its destruction."[11]

The Cabinet was impressed with the message and overwhelmingly sympathetic to the sentiments which it expressed.[12] Seward stated that while he himself had always advocated Negro suffrage in New York, the situation was so different in the District and in the Southern states that he doubted the wisdom of extending the franchise immediately to the colored population. McCulloch and Stanbery, representing Indiana and Ohio which had recently refused to accord the suffrage to Negroes, opposed such a measure for the District, as did also Browning and Randall. General Grant, who was present by special invitation, was very emphatic against the Bill, not because it disenfranchised rebels, but because he thought it a contemptible business for members of Congress whose states excluded the Negroes to give them suffrage in the District. Welles read some rough notes which stated that the Bill, by giving the franchise to the blacks and excluding the rebels, was contrary to the Constitution. "If suffrage is claimed for the blacks," he stated, "on the ground that they are rightfully entitled to it as citizens of the United States, then to deprive the white citizens of that right which they now enjoy is to inflict a punishment upon them and to subject them to a forfeiture, and it is proposed to do this without due form of law—that is without trial or conviction, they by an *ex facto* law are to be condemned. The Constitution would thus be violated in two of its most important provisions deemed essential to the preservation of liberty, and the Act, if sanctioned, will stand as a precedent for any violation hereafter."

The only Cabinet member who took a dissenting view was Stanton, who took from his portfolio a brief and carefully written statement to the effect that he had examined the bill and could perceive no constitutional objection to any of its provisions; therefore he hoped that the President would give it his approval.

Congress lost little time in overriding the veto message received on January 7, the Senate by a vote of 29 to 10 on the same day, and the House by 113 to 38 votes. When the Speaker of the House announced the result there was "such profound silence that a pin dropping might have been heard. There were several hundred Negroes present, and scarcely had the echo of the Speaker's voice died away before such a tumultuous cheering, waving of hats and clapping of hands arose from the colored portion of the assemblage that all the efforts of the Speaker, rapidly using his gavel, could not restrain them."[13]

The occasion was indeed a historic one. Not only was the national capital to become the testing-ground for the principle of universal male suffrage in the United States, but the first battle had been won in the conflict between the President and Congress. Comment in the local press was mixed. The *Star* and *Chronicle* supported the Bill, the former in moderation and the latter with jubilation. The *Intelligencer* denounced it violently and the *National Republican,* which had as yet not aligned itself completely against the President, considered the measure premature. William Owner in his diary wrote a characteristic jeremiad, "Every dog has his day, and the niggerites, the descendants of nigger stealers at the North, are having theirs, but the indications are that the pall of night is about to fall on them with a darkness as black as their beloved nigger—it cannot come too soon for the good of the country."[14]

Chapter 4

The Rise and Fall of Sayles J. Bowen

Shortly after the passage of the District Suffrage Bill new regulations were issued by the Supreme Court of the District laying down provisions for future elections. Voters were required to have resided for more than three months in a city ward prior to the date of registration; if they changed their residence in the interim they were to lose their vote. Five judges of election were appointed in Washington and three in Georgetown to hold office for a period of two years. They were to sit in open session preceding the election to receive evidence of qualification by prospective voters. The lists which they subsequently prepared were to be posted in public places for at least ten days previous to the election date, and a period of from two to five days was allowed to correct any omissions. Three commissioners of election were to be appointed in each precinct to hold office for two years, with the duty of supervising the balloting and seeing that only voters with certificates of eligibility deposited their votes in the ballot boxes. They were then to declare the polls closed and announce the result of the election.[1]

In spite of the apprehensions of many citizens the first municipal elections in the District under the new law were conducted in a remarkably calm and orderly manner. Both Republicans and Democrats were represented on the board of election commissioners, and the Superintendent of the Metropolitan Police, Major

A. C. Richards, a former school teacher, whom Lincoln had appointed in 1864, kept a strict watch on the polling stations. The *Evening Star* commented on the Georgetown elections held on February 25, 1867:

> The colored voters exercised their new privilege with becoming modesty and quietly withdrew to their homes after voting, and the white voters most warmly opposed to Negro suffrage evinced a purpose to maintain order and ensure a fair trial of the experiment. The result is shown in the election of the candidate of the Negro suffrage party for Mayor, Charles D. Welch, and seven out of eleven of the councilmen supported by the same party. It must be conceded by their opponents that the colored voters, whether acting from their own prompting or under judicious advice, voted for and elected good men, men of integrity and capacity. Their action and bearing of yesterday will certainly go far in dispelling the prejudice against Negro suffrage, and if they act always as discreetly and temperately, will doubtless in time do away with it altogether.[2]

The *Georgetown Courier*, reflecting the prevailing Democratic sympathies of the town, was concerned lest the election results might lead to undue support for Negro suffrage. Attempting to forestall such comment as the *Star* editorial, the editor stated:

> We desire in advance to inform our contemporaries of the press that the probable defeat of the ostensible white man's candidate for the mayoralty of this city must not be attributed to the Negro vote . . . the candidate of the so-called Negro party is regarded by hundreds in the Conservative ranks as a martyr, having recently been removed from the office of city collector, while his opponent (Henry Addison) is unscrupulous, reckless and about as unpopular as any man could be.[3]

The following week, however, the editor was forced to concede:

> Though less strange results have frequently caused much harm, yet there has been no violation of the laws. Beyond the excitement visible in the countenances of our citizens,

no overt act has been committed, and the city during the past week has been as quiet as could be expected.[4]

The passage of the Negro Suffrage Bill served to give fresh support for the Morrill Bill introduced the preceding year which proposed the abolition of representative government in the District. At a meeting of the Board of Trade on February 25 a resolution was passed asking Congress to repeal the charters of Washington and Georgetown, and that the two cities be governed as one under Commissioners appointed by Congress. On March 5 the *Star* reported at a second meeting of the Board that the idea had been endorsed by George W. Riggs, the banker, W. W. Corcoran, Henry D. Cooke and George Plant, a prominent business man. Though no further action was taken, the necessity for a drastic change in the government of the District was beginning to gain popular support, and in time was to become acceptable to the taxpayers in the two cities.

The registration of voters in Washington which followed the Georgetown elections was 70 per cent greater than in the previous year. In some areas, however, the white voters were reluctant to "lower themselves" by voting alongside the Negroes. The *Star* commented editorially on March 20:

> We regret to see this spirit manifested and are satisfied that, if persisted in to any extent, it can only serve to put the people of this city in a wrong attitude as being disposed to resist the action of Congress or to receive it in a sullen mood. Every consideration of propriety and of interest in our city's welfare requires that we should not even by implication put ourselves in antagonism to the will of Congress deliberately expressed in regard to District matters over which that body has supreme control.[5]

When the final figures were counted, 9,792 white voters were registered and 8,212 Negroes. Only 14,049 of the 18,000 registered, however, actually voted, and it would appear that many of the white voters registered could not bring themselves to go to the polls under the new conditions. The colored men, on the other hand, turned out in force. In the seventh ward the colored people came out at two A.M. with bugles and horns calling on all voters. By four A.M. some 700 or 800 colored voters were in line at the 1st precinct and by 10:30 the number had increased to about 1,000. At that time not one white man was in line at the precinct and only about 25 white votes had been received. Itinerant sutlers carrying stands and tables with kegs and pails of crude lemonade, homemade pies, pigs' feet, pickles and candies, carried on a brisk trade.[6] Major Richards was on hand with his police to see that no coercion was used by either side, and he refused to permit the separation of the races at the polls by the forming of two distinct queues. When the final results were announced, the Republicans could claim 16 out of 21 members of the Board of Common Council and five out of eight of the aldermen due for election. The *National Intelligencer* immediately complained of fraud, Republican inspectors having passed along the lines at the polls to see that none of the fake Republican tickets which the Democrats had printed to confuse the illiterate voters were actually used. The *Star* commented on the fact that there was little drinking, and that the number of arrests in the District on election day was not much above the average.

Mayor Wallach now found himself in a position analogous to that of Andrew Johnson vis-a-vis the Republican Congress. All that he could do was to obstruct the course of affairs which he knew to be inevitable. He had strong support, however, from the surviving Democrats of the councils. On June 6 Colonel W. W. Moore, President of the Board of Aldermen and a leader of the "Jackson Democratic Association," made a violent attack in the Board on Negro suffrage. Quoting the report made by Major Richards on slum conditions among the colored population he estimated that about one-third of the freedmen who had come to the District between 1863 and 1866, were already dead.

> But the vote of Monday last has shown that enough of the pauper class remain to enable them, with the aid of the

> existing population of the same race, marshalled under political demagogues who use them for selfish purposes to control the municipal affairs of this city regardless of the health, the comfort or the interests of the white race, who, as the owners of nearly all the property within its limits, should according to every principle of justice have a controlling interest in its taxation and municipal government.[7]

He complained bitterly that the "better-informed portion of the African race residing in this city" should have united with the stranger refugees for the purpose of overthrowing the white race. "The American People," he continued, "will not permit their capital city to be thus placed under the dominion of an uneducated race so destitute of the material qualities necessary to the enlightenment and exaltation of men." Colonel Moore endeavored to show that, on the basis of prewar elections, some kind of fraud must have taken place in the registration. Before the war, when the white population numbered 60,000, no more than 7,000 (12%) used to vote—which was approximately the same ratio as in the recent election. On the same basis the 8,212 colored voters registered would represent a population of 70,388, which was more than double their present number. He concluded by giving the tax figures paid by colored property owners in 1864 and by pointing out that colored soldiers represented less than ten per cent of the total number of District men who had fought in the Union Army. This speech was later reprinted in pamphlet form and widely distributed throughout the city.

Colonel Moore's arguments, though forcefully expressed, did not carry much weight except among those who already had preconceived objections to Negro suffrage. Not one colored candidate had been put forward in the election; the only positions which had been given to colored men in the new municipal government were minor ones. John F. Cook had been appointed to a clerkship in the office of the new tax collector, and the Board of Common Council had chosen colored men to fill the positions of reading clerk and messenger. His arguments, moreover, failed completely to take into consideration the enthusiastic response of the colored voters to their new privilege, as well as the disinclination of many of the white voters to attend the polls. Although the amount paid in property taxes by Negroes in 1864 had amounted to only $36,098.98, this sum represented, however, at the prevailing rate of taxation ownership of more than $600,000 worth of property.

Later during the year the conflict between the Mayor and the new councils became increasingly acute. In December the Republican City Register, Frederick Boswell, a shrewd politician with a keen sense of the trend of public opinion, openly voiced his defiance of the Mayor. In a communication to the Board of Common Council read on the 30th he refused to draw a check for payment of the salaries of white teachers. As a reason for the unprecedented action he cited the Mayor's failure to sign the school bill giving equal payment to colored teachers. Furthermore, the Mayor had disregarded the Act passed by Congress on July 23, 1866, requiring Corporation officers to make immediate payment of the full amount due to the Colored School funds, which were in arrears for more than two years, and which Bowen had paid out of his own pocket. A further reason was the fact that an order of the District Supreme Court which required the immediate payment of the colored school fund had been disregarded.

> "It has been my desire from the first," wrote Boswell, "to pay those (white) school teachers, but I must not forget that we owe to all classes alike, male and female, who are employees of this corporation, and you will not forget that I was elected on the platform of equal and exact justice to all men without regard to race or condition, therefore it would not be justice or law or to pay one class of our teachers and take chances for the other. Let the Mayor comply with the law, and neither the Councils nor School teachers will have cause to grumble with the Register. Until the law is complied with I positively assert I will not sign a check for school purposes under the late law unless your honorable Board shall pass an explanatory act with the con-

current action of the Board of Aldermen. Let the responsibility rest where it belongs. The Mayor is responsible and no one else."[8]

Colonel Moore, infuriated, offered a bill on January 6, 1868, to remove Boswell as Register. However, in the meantime the District Supreme Court had granted a petition of mandamus made by the white teachers for their salaries, and Boswell was forced to yield. The Board of Common Council nevertheless re-affirmed their approval of his action by a vote of 15 to 4 on February 10.

The municipal charter of the Corporation of Washington, which was to expire in June, 1868, was altered in several significant respects by the Act of Congress of May 28. At the suggestion of Charles Sumner, who had been placed on the District Committee at his own request in 1866, the power of the Mayor to appoint all subordinate officers of the Corporation was transferred to the councils, sitting in joint session. This move, analogous to the Tenure of Office Act directed at Andrew Johnson by the Republican Congress, was planned to restrict the power of Mayor Wallach, if he were to be re-elected. The section of the charter requiring property qualifications for city officials was also repealed. By another provision introduced by Representative Martin Welker, an Ohio Republican, the three months' period of residence within a city ward previously required for registration was reduced to 15 days. Welker claimed that a large part of the population frequently changed their boarding-houses, and that the 15-day period was in conformity to that of other municipalities. Service men in the city were specifically excluded from the polls unless they could prove a year's residence in Washington, and property qualifications for all Washington City officials were removed.[9] These changes were bitterly attacked by the Washington Conservative newspapers, which claimed that Union soldiers were being discriminated against at the expense of the Negroes, and that the "pauper vote" was being deliberately encouraged by Congress at the expense of men of substance and property.

Seeing the triumph of the Radicals in Congress, Wallach declined the Democratic nomination. "The dignity, importance and usefulness of Mayor of this city," he declared, "had been sacrificed to insure for a time in this community a supremacy of those in political sympathy with a majority of that body."[10] In his place John T. Given, a prominent business man, was selected by the Democrats, and a violent campaign followed.

The political climate of the 1868 Washington municipal campaign was very different from that of the preceding year. Since March the Impeachment Trial of Andrew Johnson had excited the entire nation, and his acquittal in the Senate by the margin of one vote had infuriated the Radical Republicans. Congress had passed its Reconstruction program over the repeated vetoes of the President, Federal soldiers had been sent to the South to maintain order, and partisan feeling throughout the nation was at a boiling point, especially in Washington.

In the 1868 registration the numbers were even larger than in 1867. The white voters totaled 12,011, more than 2,000 in excess of the previous year, and the colored 7,996, a falling off of slightly more than 200.[11] On this occasion Negroes stood for the first time as candidates for city offices. John F. Cook was nominated as Alderman and Carter A. Stewart, the proprietor of the hairdressing salon at the Willard Hotel, to the Board of Common Council.

On May 16 the *National Republican,* which had hitherto displayed little enthusiasm for Negro suffrage, published an editorial warmly endorsing the candidature of Sayles J. Bowen for Mayor.

He was, the editor claimed,

> a gentleman who is thoroughly identified with the interest of this city and who will make, if elected, every exertion and use all the influence in his power to build up, improve and render this city what it was intended to be by its founders . . . he is a business man . . . and thoroughly identified with all those questions of improvement which have been projected and, when carried out, will make this city second to none in the world.

In the editorials which followed during the coming weeks the *Republican* defended their candidate against the violent attacks of the *Intelligencer* and the weekly Democratic papers.

On the 26th the editor wrote:

> The election of the Republican candidate for Mayor will be evidence to Congress that we have at last consented to consider our business interests and respect the authority that controls us, and it will be no doubt followed by liberal appropriations for the benefit of our city.

The *Star,* recently acquired by C. S. Noyes along with four other business and newspaper men—Alexander Shepherd, Samuel Kauffmann, George W. Adams and Clarence Baker[12]—also endorsed Bowen's candidature, and the *Chronicle,* representing the Radical viewpoint, was wholeheartedly behind him. The contest was more than usually significant, since this was also the year of the Presidential elections; the election of a Republican mayor would clearly indicate to the entire nation that Washington, so long controlled by the Democrats, was also following the Republican trend.

The contest between Bowen and the Democratic candidate, John T. Given, was the most hotly contested one the city had experienced. Only 1,730 of the registered voters failed to show up at the polls, compared with almost 4,000 the preceding year. As a result of the unprecedented white vote Bowen's majority was only 83. The Republicans moreover lost control of the Board of Common Council, to which 12 Democrats were elected and only nine of their party. The Board of Aldermen was equally divided, each side having elected seven members. Bowen received 9,170 votes to Given's 9,087, and four out of the seven city wards were in Democratic hands. Both John F. Cook and Carter A. Stewart, the colored candidates for office, were elected.

The aftermath of the Washington election was marked by considerable violence. The Conservative newspaper, the *Evening Express,* claimed in an article headed "Carnival of Blood" that colored men had run riot in the streets, murdering one white man and wounding another, and that several restaurants had been forcibly entered and much property damaged. The *Georgetown Courier* in its issue of June 6 claimed that the election was a Democratic triumph, since Given had carried a majority of the wards, and that "the change may or may not have been effected in the *Chronicle* office where, of all places, it was found necessary to deposit overnight the ballot boxes belonging to an entire precinct." "This election," continued the editorial,

> has developed a feeling at which we would fain hope even the most ultra Radical would stand aghast. The races are now pitted against each other in deadly animosity and but very little added excitement is required to drench the streets of the capital with human blood. However abhorrent to our feelings may be the idea of giving to an inferior and degraded race such undue influence in politics as that which enables them today to hold the balance of power in the Republic, yet the collisions of the past few days and subsequent loss of life should give pause to all and admonish those who can allay by every possible means the embittered passion so painfully aroused.

The Democrats claimed that boatloads of Negroes had been imported from nearby Maryland and Virginia before the election and "colonized" in Washington to vote the Republican ticket. This argument was given great prominence in the Democratic newspapers, despite the fact that the registration of Negro voters had actually declined since 1867, and although Democrats were represented on each of the registration boards. They were especially incensed at the action of the City Register in declaring illegal the votes of more than 150 service men, who had been registered prior to the passage of the new Washington charter in May.[14] Mayor Wallach declined to recognize Bowen as legally elected, and refused to surrender to him the keys and papers of his official post. Five days after the election Bowen, acting upon legal advice, had the door of the Mayor's chamber broken open by a locksmith and took possession.

The refusal of the Democrats to acknowledge the election of Bowen was based upon what they termed the illegal actions of Register Boswell. Not only had he invalidated the soldier votes, which would have effected a Democratic victory, but he had also declared void the election of two soldiers to the Council in the Fifth Ward in favor of Republican candidates who had received fewer votes. Boswell had furthermore recognized the election of John F. Cook and Carter A. Stewart to the Councils, although the Bill passed by Congress to permit public office to Negroes had not yet received the President's signature.[15] By these actions the Republicans would gain one member in the Board of Aldermen and three in the Common Council, thus giving them a majority in both Councils. The Democrats called repeatedly upon the Register to deliver the ballot boxes to the Councils, in order that duplicate certificates of the election results could be made out as provided in the Charter. They were desperately anxious to procure this evidence, which they believed would show the boxes had been tampered with. On his refusal the Democratic members of both councils left the City Hall and set up a "rump" council at the Columbian University Law School building on 5th Street directly across from the City Hall. Thomas E. Lloyd, one of the Democratic Aldermen, was named temporary Mayor, and he promptly called for Boswell's resignation for not declaring Given to have been elected. By June 12 the deadlock had reached such a point that a Bill was introduced by the District Committee of the Senate providing that the Register's certificate, based upon satisfactory evidence furnished by the Election Commissioners be made *prima facie* evidence of election, and establishing a procedure for submitting contested elections to the Supreme Court of the District. The Bill passed the Senate and on the 16th was sent to the House, which also gave it approval and passed it on to the President for his signature.[16]

Lloyd in the meantime had sent a letter to Bowen stating that he had been appointed Mayor and asking him to vacate his office. He called in person at the City Hall, but Major Richards, who had thrown a police detail around the building, refused to grant him entrance. On the 17th Judge Fisher of the District Circuit Court declared the election of Bowen to be legal on the ground that Given, his opponent, had not contested it, and treated Lloyd's appointment as Mayor *ad interim* unworthy of consideration. The Conservatives attempted to vent their spleen on Major Richards for having helped Bowen to force an entrance into the City Hall, but the charges were dismissed immediately by the Court.

On June 30 in his inaugural speech to the Councils Bowen outlined his ideas for the improvement of the city. "Probably no city government in this nation," he said, "has been longer or more persistently misruled than this; and none certainly has been made the object of such generosity on the part of the people's representatives." He spoke of the contract system which, in his opinion, had wasted hundreds of thousands of dollars by the use of inefficient materials, and he indicated that in the future the city would hire its own laborers. In the Board of Aldermen which met the same day, a contest arose over the chairmanship between Colonel Moore and Zalmon Richards, a Republican and brother of the Superintendent of Police, which ended in Moore's yielding under protest.

The deadlock in the city government had led to the revival of activity among those seeking to move the national capital to the Middle West. On June 15 John A. Logan of Illinois gave notice that he would offer a resolution providing for the removal of the capital to St. Louis, which was now the geographical center of the United States. A book by L. U. Reavis of that city setting forth the claims of St. Louis had appeared a few months previously and the movement was strongly endorsed by such influential men as Joseph Medill, publisher of the *Chicago Tribune,* and Horace Greeley, who had always detested Washington. The neglected condition of the District, its close proximity to the South, and Lincoln's assassination were all used as arguments by the capital-movers. Although the St. Louis advocates finally decided that the time was not yet ripe, their activities had sufficiently frightened the business men of Washington to make them realize the need for extensive and immediate improvements in the city.

Bowen's administration began under serious difficulties. His majority in the Councils was only a nominal one, and any increase of the funded debt, which required a two-thirds majority of the voters, would have been out of the question. In order to conciliate the voters he had therefore to carry out the improvements to the streets through the employment of day laborers, most of whom were Negroes.

Much progress was made during the first year of his administration in opening up new areas of the city. Two hundred twenty-three squares were graded and gravelled, and many streets in the northwest section were extended to the city boundaries. In Southwest Washington a new thoroughfare, 9th Street, was cut through the high bluff which shut out the view of the Potomac, and a new road was built along the river front. However, contract work was not undertaken on a large scale, and by June, 1869, only ten squares had been paved. Bowen was finding that the cost of running the city was exceeding his expectations. Although he himself had been largely responsible for having increased the pay of members of the councils from $250 to $600 per annum, and of having raised the salaries of ward commissioners, clerks, members of the fire department and other city employees in 1869,[17] the Mayor found during that year that there were insufficient funds in the city treasury to pay them. To keep all of his constituents and fellow-Republicans contented was a far more complicated business than running the City Post Office, and Bowen was no professional politician.

He was, however, favored by the turn in the national tide of politics. General Grant had been inaugurated as President in March, 1869, and it was becoming increasingly clear to the business men of the District that, if they wished to secure from Congress larger and more generous appropriations, it would be necessary to jump on the Republican band-wagon. The trend was reflected even in Georgetown, traditionally Democratic and Conservative, where the Republican candidate for Mayor, Dr. C. H. Craigin, was defeated by Henry M. Sweeney, running on a "Citizen's" ticket, by the narrow margin of 37 votes.

After their experiences the previous year the Democrats had grown despondent over their chances of carrying the 1869 municipal elections in Washington, and had begun to grasp at straws. The *National Intelligencer* endeavored to place upon Bowen's shoulders the failure of the District to receive appropriations for new railroads, and it accused him of a lack of cordiality on receiving official visitors to the city; previous Mayors, the paper claimed, had drawn from their own purses for that purpose.[18] Boswell's accounts were also attacked and large discrepancies cited. The Negroes, it was said, were at the mercy of white demagogues who incited them "to invade white society and invade theatres and restaurants."[19]

On June 2, 1869, a few days before the election, Bowen made an address in which his achievements of the past year were reviewed. He promised that by the end of the fiscal year $200,000 of the floating debt of the Wallach administration would be paid, as well as the interest on the funded debt when it fell due. More public schools had been built, better wages paid to teachers, and more work done on the city streets than in any other one year in the history of the city. He made a special appeal to his "newly enfranchised friends" to stand by the party which first gave them the privilege of voting and which was defending their rights in the South.

The Washington municipal election of 1869 was also a bloody one. In the Second Ward a group of anti-Bowen Negroes headed by a contractor, Charles Stewart, and calling themselves the "Colored Citizens Movement" were attacked by Negro Republicans, who attempted to prevent them from voting. In the disturbances which followed Major Richards was struck by stones thrown by the mob, and the police were obliged to fire into the crowd to disperse it, killing one Negro and wounding a score of others. Bowen hastened over to the scene, and order was eventually restored. The same evening, however, Stewart's house was ransacked by the angry crowd, and he was forced to take refuge in a police station for the night. Deprecating the outbreak of violence, the *Star* commented, "The impression will go abroad that the election would have resulted differently had the 'Colored Citizens' voters been permitted to deposit their ballots unmolested, whereas we do not believe that fifty colored people in the whole city would have voted that way."[20] This excess of zeal among his supporters was to plague Bowen for many years, and was a major contributing factor in the subsequent change in the administration of the District.

The 1869 election resulted in almost a clean sweep for the Republicans. The registration had fallen off by more than 5,000 and it was obvious that many Democrats had abstained from voting. Boswell was elected Collector, John F. Cook, Register, and R. Donegan, the Republican nominee, Surveyor, by majorities of more than 5,000 over their Democrat rivals. Only Colonel Moore and two other Democrats were left on the Board of Aldermen, which now contained eleven Republicans. Carter A. Stewart became the second colored man elected to the Board. In the Common Council none of the Democrats gained a seat. A Negro was elected on each of the seven wards. Of these Robert Thompson and Frank B. Gaines had been slaves; John T. Johnson, for the past year reading clerk of the Board, was a former attendant in the cloakroom of the House of Representatives; A. B. Tinney was a brick-layer employed at the Navy Yard; George Hatton, a former sergeant-major of a colored regiment, was a laborer. Henry H. Piper, a watchman in the Treasury, was a man of some education who had won the confidence and esteem of his superiors in his previous work for the Navy Department. Sampson Netter, the seventh member, was a preacher.

With so large a representation on the Councils—though not in excess to their proportion of the city population—the colored members lost no time in drafting a bill to achieve equal treatment for Negroes in places of amusement and other public entertainment. It had long been the practice in Washington, as it is today in most parts of the South where separate houses are not available to the colored population, to restrict Negro spectators to the upper galleries. The bill which became law in June, 1869, prohibited such distinction on the part of the theatre proprietors and stated that any person willing to pay the regular price of admission and whose conduct was orderly should be admitted to any part of the house under penalty of a fine not less than $10 and not exceeding $20 levied on the theatre if discrimination were practised.

At the time the theatre bill was passed, Mr. Spalding, one of the proprietors of the National, was considering a plan to set aside a portion of the theatre for the use of the better class of colored patrons who did not wish to mingle with the riffraff of the upper galleries.[21] The action of the city council made him fear that he would be in danger of losing the bulk of his white patrons if the bill were to be enforced. John F. Cook made it clear in a letter to the *Chronicle* on June 8 that the compromise suggested would not be acceptable to him and that he would insist on the law being obeyed to the letter. In October the proprietors of the National Theatre were served with a warrant for ejecting three colored men, one of them James T. Wormley, from the dress circle. Justice Olin issued on the 14th a writ demanding that the papers be sent to the District Supreme Court where the case would be tried. No record, however, can be traced in the files of the Court, and it is likely that strong pressure was placed upon Wormley by the Justice to abandon the suit in favor of the suggested compromise. In this instance, as in subsequent cases, the Court appears to have taken the attitude that it would be more prudent not to force the issue and risk stirring up further racial antagonism.

During the mayoralty of Sayles J. Bowen the Washington City councils also passed an act "to regulate admission and accommodation in licensed houses and places of amusement."[22] This ordinance made it illegal for proprietors of hotels, taverns, restaurants and saloons to refuse service to "any quiet and orderly person" on account of race or color, and imposed a fine of not less than $50 for the offense. A sum equal to half the amount of the fine could be paid to the informer in such a case. In the same act the penalty of $20 imposed by the act of June 10, 1869 with reference to places of public amusement was increased to $50. Whether this second act was any more effective than that which applied to theatres is, however, extremely doubtful. No record can be found of a successful prosecution under it, and subsequent District governments found it apparently necessary to re-enact a similar law.

The thorniest of all racial problems was that of the public schools. In 1868 Mayor Bowen had stated in his inaugural message that the mixing of white and colored children in schools was impracticable:

> The colored people are opposed to it, and so strong is the prejudice of many of our white citizens that they would prefer their children to remain in ignorance rather than to send them to school where children of color would be permitted to attend. At present, therefore, I would advise separate schools for each class.[23]

However the following year Bowen's views as expressed in his annual message had entirely changed. With so large a majority in both councils, he doubtless felt it no longer necessary to tread warily and conceal his sentiments. This time he declared:

> In my judgment the time has arrived when these (colored) schools should be incorporated with our other public schools, placed under the same management, be conducted on the same system and share impartially in all respects the same advantages. The Board of Trustees of Public Schools should consist of both white and colored members in due proportion, and no difference should be allowed in the qualifications of teachers on account of the color of the pupils. The exigency which required the temporary creation of a separate board of Trustees for colored schools has now happily passed away . . . The distinction of color is now no longer

> recognized in our charters, nor at the ballot box, in the Courts of Justice, the lecture room, the hall of public amusement, the public conveyance, nor the city councils. It should be eliminated as soon as possible from our school system. The breaking down of all caste distinctions is one of the great missions of the American people, and the sooner all classes conquer their prejudices and accept the situation, the better for all concerned. All children should be educated as the children of American citizens, the future sovereigns of the Republic, and should be taught to ignore all class distinctions. Nowhere can this be done as effectively as in the common school, by the daily exercise of the schoolroom, where merit and achievement only give precedence. And, on the other hand, by no method will the animosities and peculiarities of race and caste be so surely perpetuated and intensified as by the keeping up of separate systems of education in our schools.[24]

The Mayor referred to the bill which had been introduced at previous sessions of Congress by Charles Sumner, which provided for the abolition of the dual school system in the District. This bill had twice passed in both Houses, but owing to the failure of Andrew Johnson to sign it before adjournment, had never become law. The bill provided for the complete integration of the white and colored schools, imposing penalties on any school officials who refused to accept either colored pupils or teachers upon an equal basis.[25] The President's action had been influenced, the Mayor said, by the "misguided efforts of a few of the very class for whose benefit it was intended." The separate school system provided lucrative employment to a number of educated Negroes who feared that they would be placed at a disadvantage in an integrated establishment.

There was some evidence to show that the prejudices against the integration of public schools were not universally felt in the District. On September 20 at a meeting of the Board of Aldermen a petition was read from the heads of 34 white and 27 Negro families residing in the fourth ward at which a primary school for the common education of children of both races was requested, and this was later followed by another representing 23 white and one colored family who resided in the same area. A. E. Newton, chairman of the Committee on Congress and the Councils, reported that he had investigated the matter and was fully satisfied that the petitions were genuine, although admitting that there were many other white families in the neighborhood who opposed the idea. He considered that the petition was a reasonable one and should be granted, in order to demonstrate the feasibility of maintaining mixed schools in the capital. The denial of this request, would, he stated, "indicate an extreme of unreasonableness bordering on fanaticism" and would call forth prompt Congressional intervention. J. Ormond Wilson, the Superintendent of Education, had also endorsed the proposal as a private citizen.[26]

A few weeks later the question of the dual school system was put to the test in a sensational manner . . . The Rev. Sella Martin[27] of the 15th Street Presbyterian Church, in an attempt to test the law, sent his nine-year-old daughter to a white public school, having previously secured a ticket of admission from Professor George Vashon[28], one of the colored school trustees. Since both the girl and her mother who accompanied her were of extremely fair complexion, the girl was admitted without question, and it was some time before her racial affiliations were recognized. When the news spread, angry parents promptly removed their children from the school, and a heated argument took place between the Rev. Mr. Martin and Miss Noyes, the school principal.

In the company of General Balloch of the Freedmen's Bureau, Miss Noyes called upon the Mayor, who referred the matter to a Sub-Board for its decision. The question was aired in the Board of Aldermen on November 29 by Colonel Moore, who introduced a resolution of censure towards Professor Vashon for having obtained a ticket for the colored girl and stating that the law of 1869 which abolished the word "white" in the Washington city charter could not be construed as referring to the school system. The resolution, however, was tabled.

William A. Cook, the Corporation Counsel, whose opinion in the matter had been asked by the Sub-Board of School Trustees, gave a somewhat ambiguous answer. He supported Mayor Bowen's view that the Martin girl, having been given a ticket of admission to Miss Noyes's school by one of the school trustees, was legally entitled to be admitted as a pupil. He refused, however, to be drawn into giving an opinion on the principal issues involved: what degree of Negro blood required a child's being placed in the colored schools, and what should be done to divide the school fund, should mixed schools be established in the city. "If the question of the power to establish mixed schools in this city or the admission of different races into the same school comes properly before me," he wrote, "I will endeavor to give them the consideration which their importance may demand. But it is possible that Congress, which will shortly assemble in the exercise of its acknowledged power, will by plain and legitimate legislation settle the entire subject and thus prevent protracted discussion and legislation." Following his reply, J. Ormond Wilson, the Superintendent of Schools, issued an order not to permit colored children of any shade of complexion into white schools until Congress had passed the necessary legislation changing the existing District school laws.[29]

When Congress assembled in December 1869, Charles Sumner reintroduced his Bill in the Senate, which referred it to the District of Columbia Committee. Since no immediate action was forthcoming, Professor Vashon, doubtless hoping to needle the Committee into more prompt consideration of the subject, again took the initiative by giving a ticket of admission to Charlotte Carroll, a girl only slightly darker in complexion than Sella Martin's daughter, to the school of Miss McGhee. When the parents discovered the situation, seven of the white children left. Mrs. Carroll was persuaded to withdraw her daughter by the school principal.

Shortly afterwards, on March 14, George Hatton introduced a resolution in the Board of Common Council calling upon members of the School Board not confuse the issue. "Whereas

Professor Vashon, claiming to be a colored gentleman himself . . . has on several occasions admitted to the schools under his care, children who by some strange freak of nature happened to be somewhat bleached, and yet their parents believe they are certainly colored, and thus reckoned with the whole number of colored children in the District, and whereas we believe that God is no respecter of persons and to admit those half and three-quarter blood mulattoes and quadroons or octoroons to the public or white schools . . . is, in our opinion dangerous . . . opening up a new and more dangerous avenue of distinction, that the Board of Trustees of Public Schools (Professor Vashon particularly) be . . . requested by this Board on behalf of the pure blacks, not to make any distinction on account of race or color in the admission of children to the schools under their jurisdiction." The resolution was agreed to by a vote of 17 to two, with only two of the colored members of the Council abstaining.[30]

The following month Henry Piper introduced a bill in the Council which requested the Senate Committee on the District to pass as soon as possible a bill for the reorganization of the Washington public schools into one common system under which all children could be educated regardless of race or color. After Hatton had moved unsuccessfully an amendment requesting the Mayor to remove all colored children from the public schools until Congress would have passed a law consolidating the District schools, a vote was taken. The Piper resolution was read for a third time and passed unanimously by the 18 members of the Council present.[31]

George Hatton, who had been called by the *Star* "a natural orator and politician and ready debater," was proving to be a thorn in Mayor Bowen's side. Hatton had never been an admirer of Bowen, and had opposed his candidacy at a meeting of the Fourth Ward Republican Club the preceding year. At the beginning of July shortly after the election, he had accompanied the Mayor and other members of the councils on a trip to the field of Gettysburg. Refused service in the dining-room of a hotel en route, he was incensed at what he called Bowen's failure to defend his rights, and made much ado of the matter on his return to Washington. Bowen pointed out in rebuttal that Hatton had borrowed money from him, and that he was indulging in bluster to avoid having to make repayment. But the damage had already been done; Hatton was now Bowen's enemy, and his defection was a serious blow to the Mayor's prestige among many of his colored supporters.

On his return from Gettysburg, Bowen, endeavoring to raise more money for the prosecution of street improvements, raised the property tax from $1.00 to $1.40, the highest figure it had reached in the history of the corporation. He was constantly harassed by the conflicting demands of the ward commissioners, who each demanded that they receive their share of the improvements as a reward for their political services in mustering voters. Bowen discovered that the very efficiency of the political system through which he had come to power constituted an unforeseen problem. The Democratic opposition could always be relied upon to attack him as a matter of principle; his fellow Republicans on the other hand fought him because they considered that they had not received their fair share of the spoils. Had he been a different type of man, a hard-boiled big city boss, he would doubtless have been able to handle the situation more effectively. But Bowen was an idealist, and he found it difficult to make the necessary political compromises. Dr. William Tindall, his secretary for two years, has referred to his suspicious nature, and it is probable that he had become embittered as the result of his long devotion to the Negro cause. In many respects his temperament was similar to that of Charles Sumner, whose political views he so largely shared. Bowen counted, however, on the cooperation of the public and of the daily press, which still supported him. The *National Intelligencer* ceased publication at the end of 1869, having lost its lucrative government printing contracts.[32]

On August 31, 1869, the bitter factionalism within the Republican ranks was publicly exposed. John H. Crane, Commissioner of the Fourth Ward, accused the Mayor of fraud, claiming that Donovan, a contractor, had been overpaid by Bowen. He claimed moreover that Donovan had received a contract for graveling and grading certain city streets at a time when many corporation day laborers had remained unpaid for three months owing to lack of funds. A committee of three Aldermen was immediately appointed to examine the charge, which involved a supposed loss to the city of over $1,300. Crane was dismissed from his position as ward commissioner, but he refused to hand over to the Mayor his official books and papers. On September 29 a "serenade" was given to Register Boswell at his home by a group of disaffected Republicans at which Hatton made a violent and personal attack on the Mayor. Boswell, who fostered higher political ambitions, refused, however, to ally himself to the outspoken opposition, though he managed to insinuate in his reply that Bowen was not a "temperance man."[33]

On October 4 the Committee of Aldermen studying the Crane charges held public hearings at which ample opportunity was afforded to all the Mayor's personal and political enemies to vent their grievances. Bowen had penned a note on the back of Donovan's bill, asking the First National Bank cashier, W. S. Huntington, to advance $3,000 out of the current taxes due to the corporation in payment. While the practice of paying contractors on work in progress after it had been certified by City inspectors was long-recognized, Bowen's action in anticipating city revenue was decidedly unorthodox. The contract had, moreover, been awarded before ten days' notice had been given to all prospective bidders, in violation of a section of the law. Nevertheless, the Investigating Board voted by a two-to-one majority to dismiss the charges, with which both the city councils concurred. The report of the investigating committee vindicated the Mayor's action, stating that part payment on work uncompleted according to contract could not be considered a violation of the law. Alderman Champion, one of the three members of the Committee, refused to sign the report.

Three days later on November 12, Bowen was accorded a political serenade and formally endorsed as Republican candidate in the mayoral election to be held the following year. The procession was led by Perry Carson, a gigantic Negro, mounted on a white horse and wearing a black velvet hat with a white plume and a yellow sash with orange and white rosettes. Following him were 5,000 men, most of them colored, bearing 200 torches and placards. Bowen, replying to the addresses, spoke of the discontented and grumblers in the local Republican party and gave the reasons for their attitude—they had either been removed from lucrative office or had failed to receive contracts for themselves or their friends. He spoke of his achievement in funding the floated debt of the previous administration and pointed with pride to the grading and improvement of the streets and to the laying of gas and water mains throughout the city. Much of this labor had been performed by workmen who received $2.00 per day from the Corporation instead of $1.00 or $1.50 paid by contractors who attempted to skimp on materials. The Republican party, he maintained, should be given full recognition for inaugurating the day's work system and for other reforms of equal benefit to the laboring masses.

Though the charges against Bowen had been dismissed, the precarious state of the city finances was rapidly approaching a crisis. On January 4, 1870, the furniture of the Mayor's office was seized after a judgment had been granted to a local firm on a bill for furnishing goods to the District Asylum. The officers proceeded to levy on a green rep sofa and five office chairs, while the Mayor called upon the messenger not to let the goods out of the room. The officers carried the articles to the East Wing of the City Hall, posting a bill offering them for sale, but a writ of replevin was quickly obtained by the Corporation Attorney in the Circuit Court and the furniture was eventually returned to the Mayor's chambers.

Such a disgraceful incident, though by no means unprecedented in the municipal history of the United States at this period, served to fan the smoldering dissatisfaction with the political administration of the city. On January 13 a meeting was held in the offices of the real estate offices of Kilbourn and Latta which was attended by a number of prominent citizens interested in a more efficient form of city government, among them S. P. Brown, Crosby S. Noyes and Alexander Shepherd. Shepherd spoke in favor of a modified form of Territorial government in which the upper branch would be appointed by the President and the lower branch made elective, an idea which met with general approval. Two days later Shepherd presented the draft of a bill designed to provide such a form of administration for the entire District. It called for a House of Assembly containing 25 delegates with legislative powers embracing those conferred by charter upon the corporations of Washington and Georgetown, and a Governor to be appointed by the President. Bills were to be presented to the Governor for his signature, and his veto could only be overridden by a two-thirds majority. Congress still retained the right to repeal any law passed by the Assembly. A Delegate representing the District was to sit in the House of Representatives.

The proposed change of government was naturally opposed by the ward commissioners and other individuals such as Boswell, whose position as Register was worth about $20,000 per annum.[34] Some of the Negro politicians also saw in the proposed bill, under which the Upper House was to be appointed, the loss of some of their new privileges. On February 2 a meeting was held at Union League Hall by opponents of the measure; William A. Cook, the Corporation Counsel, voiced his fears that under a joint administration the Republican vote in Washington would be offset by the Conservative element in Georgetown and in the county.

Meanwhile the anti-Bowen movement was gathering momentum. On January 23 a group of Reform Republicans had met to consider an alternative candidate as mayor. Bowen was bitterly attacked as a tyrant, and his methods of distributing patronage and contracts and of paying claims were roundly condemned. The meeting was blockaded by some of the Bowen partisans, who failed, however, to break up the proceedings. On the 29th the *Star* published an editorial castigating William A. Cook for a reference he had made to the Washington taxpayers, and the heavy artillery of Crosby Noyes was now turned around and trained for the first time on the Bowen administration.

Bowen received the mayoral nomination on May 5 from the Republican General Committee, but only after a severe split had occurred in which Major Richards was supported by one wing of the party. The *Star* bitterly attacked the Bowen administration on the 7th, referring to it as a "Ring" and claiming that his extravagance had cost the city $43,800 more per annum to run than under his predecessor. Part of this sum, it claimed, had been expended on the rental of offices for the ward commissioners. The *National Republican* also followed the lead of the *Star;* personal differences had arisen between Bowen and Murtagh, the editor, who had been greatly disappointed in the Mayor's failure to secure increased Federal appropriations for the District. The majority of the weekly papers turned against Bowen, leaving him with only one daily in his favor—the Radical *Chronicle.*

On May 13 a "Regular Republican Convention" nominated as opposition candidate Matthew G. Emery, a native of New Hampshire who had resided in the capital for many years. Emery was by trade a stone mason, and had received many important government contracts, including the Capitol building and the Washington Monument, of which he had laid the cornerstone. In 1855 he had been elected Alderman for the 4th ward and during the War he had served as Captain in the District Militia. A Union man, but never a violent partisan, Emery was an excellent choice for the Reform Republicans. He had openly broken with Bowen in February when he accused the Mayor of malfeasance in office and had refused to retract his statement, though threatened with a libel suit. Emery was exactly the kind of man who could be expected to unite the business interests in the city among the ranks of both political parties. He was particularly endorsed by Shepherd, who feared that a prolongation of the Bowen regime would handicap the District's chances of further Congressional aid and that it would strengthen the position of those who wished to remove the capital to the West.

In order to overcome the powerful machinery of the ward commissioners supporting Bowen's candidature, Emery's followers realized that it was necessary to form a coalition with the Democrats and also to capture the colored vote. Such a campaign was a delicate one to handle, but the Washington newspapers made an all-out effort. Every day in the *Star* and the *National Republican* editorials appeared inveighing against the inefficiency and corruption of the "Bowen Ring," which was compared to Tweed's notorious machine in New York. The previous accusations of Negroes being imported from Virginia and Maryland for voting purposes and "colonized" in the city before election day were revived; it was even claimed that men had been brought from as far distant places as Port Tobacco in Southern Maryland and that circulars had been placed in Negro churches in the vicinity of Washington urging men to come to work in the city at $2.00 a day at a time when the wages of many of the resident colored laborers were still in arrears.

Repetition of such allegations in the Republican newspapers was eventually to have the effect of dividing the Negro vote. On May 12 the *Star* reporter at a meeting in the 7th Ward counted 83 Bowen voters to 80 Emery supporters in an area previously a Bowen stronghold. "It is a fact beyond dispute," stated the editor,

> that the best and most effective speaking on either side has been made by colored men like Hatton and Henry Johnson in open denunciation of the Bowen rule . . . The great mistake of the Bowen ring has been in underrating the intelligence and self-respect of the colored people. Nothing could be more contemptuous and insulting to the colored man than the theory openly avowed and acted upon by the Bowen party that there is so much merchandise voting material to be treated with supercilious neglect for eleven months of the year and then bought by the droves by a few days' work at gutter-cleaning just before the June elec-

tion. The colored citizens feel keenly this insulting estimate of their morals and self-respect. They realize that their interests are identical with those of the business men of Washington and that their permanent prosperity must depend on that of the city in which they live.

The *Chronicle* defended Bowen's record as Mayor, and printed a statement in which he blamed the sad state of the city's treasury on the fact that $500,000 of current taxes were still unpaid. This figure was disputed by Colonel Moore in the Board of Aldermen, who showed a statement that the amount still to be collected was less than half of the stated sum.

On May 25 a giant Emery meeting was held, at which Shepherd was the principal speaker. He referred to the election promises which Bowen had not been able to fulfill and to the disgraceful state of the city finances. Three days later the Senate passed the bill which Shepherd and his colleagues had drafted providing a territorial administration for the District.

On the 31st, Registration Day, the *Star* made a special appeal to colored voters to follow the dictates of their own conscience rather than listen to race agitators.

> Any man, whoever he may be, that appeals to the colored people as a class to take part in this or any other election is an enemy of that race . . . Our faith is firm that they will fulfill the best expectations of their true friends. No race could have acted better during the War or since peace has been proclaimed. But we would wish to see them as independent citizens, thinking and acting for themselves, following their own convictions and exercising the ballot for the public good. There is no slavery as base as that which prostitutes the high privilege of suffrage to the venal use of demagogues, such as now seek to again betray and defraud the colored people of Washington to their own selfish ends.

The following day Boswell addressed a rally in the 7th Ward and announced that he had joined the Emery forces. He produced a letter from his candidate stating that "If elected to the office of Mayor of this city it will be my pleasure as well as my duty to give the colored citizens of Washington a fair share of the patronage under the municipal government." The meeting was also addressed by W. A. Taliaferro, a colored resident, on Bowen's behalf. The final registration figures released by the press showed a total of 18,490, of which 10,955 represented white and 7,535 represented colored voters. The total was only 1,517 less than the record set in the 1868 mayoral elections.[35]

The District Committee of the Senate on June 3 investigated the financial status of the corporation and heard testimony by Shepherd, Clephane, Moore and others regarding the city's overdraft. Bowen had estimated the floating debt of the corporation at $300,000, of which $200,000 was overdrawn at the bank and $100,000 in dishonored checks. Those familiar with the city finances claimed, however, that this figure was far too low, and that the actual amount of the city debt, including the salary arrears of the teachers, police, laborers, and the employees of the Fire and Gas departments, was twice as large as the Mayor's estimate.

As Election Day drew near the newspaper editorials became increasingly impassioned and banner headlines appeared for the first time in all the city sheets. The *Star* announced on June 4 that the corporation laborers, most of whom had not been paid since the beginning of the year and had been forced to sell their scrip at a heavy discount, were now given $5.00 each on their overdue accounts and they were told no further work would be forthcoming if Emery were to be elected. The *Star* also claimed that circular letters had been written by William A. Cook to various government clerks asking them to report the names, positions and places of residence of all those who voted against Bowen.

On Election Day, June 6, all drinking places were closed and extraordinary precautions were taken by Major Richards and the Metropolitan Police to watch out for illegal voting. The *Star* reported that several "colored toughs" had arrived from

Baltimore on an early train with the purpose of voting for "Boss Bowen," but that they were escorted to jail and none of them were able to get near the polling stations. The afternoon election returns showed that Emery had won a sweeping victory —10,096 votes to Bowen's 6,877. Of the registered voters all but 1,507 had gone to the polls. In the wards the results were much closer, but only four Bowen followers were returned to the Board of Common Council and only in the 1st and 2nd Wards were the Bowen candidates for Aldermen successful. Only two colored supporters of Bowen were elected—Henry Piper and the Rev. Anthony Bowen.[36] F. D. Gaines had been returned, having switched to the Emery ticket. Three new colored Emery candidates—Benjamin McCoy, a school teacher, Thomas A. Gant, a messenger, and William A. Freeman, a government clerk—were returned. The *Star's* headlines were memorable:

VICTORY!!!! VICTORY!!!! VICTORY!!!!
EMERY ELECTED BY 3800 MAJORITY!!!!!!
CARRIES EVERY WARD IN CITY!!!!!
FAREWELL, BOWEN!!!!!
BY-BYE, COOK!!!!!
BY-BYE, MORSE!!!!!!
A LONG ETERNAL ADIEU TO THE WHOLE SWINDLING RING!!!!!
GRAND SHOUT OF THE NATIONALITIES
HALE KERLUMBAY!!!!!
YAH YAH YAH!!!!!!!!
ERIN GO BRAGH!!!!!
GROSS SIEG!! VIVAT HOCH!!

The following day Crosby Noyes printed an editorial Te Deum:

We have never seen Washington looking so happy as to-day. There is a sort of beatific, millenial, glorious blaze of content on the face of everybody you meet delightful to behold. We say *everybody,* because the Bowen crowd have retired to such strict seclusion that not a man of them has been seen to-day.

Thus the first phase of Washington's Reconstruction came to an end, and a new era which was to see the establishment of Territorial Government for the District had begun. The unsuspecting citizens of the capital were little aware of the troubled times which lay ahead, and of the coming scandals, compared with which the alleged malpractices of the "Bowen Ring" would prove petty and insignificant.

Chapter 5

The District Becomes a Territory

During the latter part of Mayor Bowen's administration Congress had begun to show a considerable degree of interest in District affairs. Statutes were passed modernizing the District laws, many of which were still based upon the ancient Maryland code. A Married Women's Act brought District property laws into harmony with those of the other states. Deeds which had required acknowledgment before the two Justices of the Peace might henceforward be brought before one only. The old usury laws, long evaded, were amended to provide for a special contract rate of ten per cent, while six per cent remained the official rate. Charters were granted to the Washington Market, the Zoo, the Corcoran Art Gallery, the Georgetown and Columbia Street Railroad. A Police Court was added to the other Courts of the District. Temporary relief was given to the poor. Municipal authority was given to set aside portions of the broad streets and avenues for parks, for beautifying Franklin Park and Thomas Circle, for enclosing Lafayette Park with an iron fence. In the fall of 1870, following a petition signed by prominent Washington citizens, Congress made provision for the paving of Pennsylvania Avenue from the Capitol to the Treasury Building. The cost was to be divided between the Federal Government, the corporation of Washington and the individual owners of abutting property. The appropriation was not sufficiently large to permit a concrete surface, but even the wooden blocks would be a great improvement of the Avenue, which was covered with potholes for most of its length.

In May, 1870, the Senate, following the memorial which had been presented by Alexander Shepherd on behalf of the Citizens Committee, and disturbed by the desperate financial condition of the corporation of Washington, had passed a bill which placed the District under a quasi-Territorial régime. The bill was introduced by Hannibal Hamlin, a former Vice-President of the United States and now Senator from Maine. Under the Hamlin Bill the corporations were to remain intact and the new government was given only general powers. Such a government, as the *Star* pointed out on February 23, was top-heavy on the administrative side, cumbersome and expensive. When a similar bill was later introduced in the House by Representative Cullom of Illinois, it was promptly tabled.

Congress was not prepared at this time, however, to abolish completely all representative government in the District, as had been suggested by Senator Morrill in 1865. To have done so would have undermined the Southern policy of the Republican Party, and laid the party leaders open to the charge that a commission form of government in the District was but a device to eliminate the Negro vote. Since Negroes held the balance of power in the newly reconstructed Southern states this was a risk which Republicans could not afford to take. It was necessary for them to find a formula whereby the District administration could be more efficiently coordinated, the authority over the national capital strengthened, and yet sufficient popular representation retained by the electorate to stifle any possible complaints. The first session of the 41st Congress ended without such a plan having been formulated, and it was not until the next session in January, 1871, that the matter was again considered.

The new President was even more concerned with the improvement of the national capital than most of the members of Congress. Having resided in Washington a few years before his election, he had become acquainted with some of the men who had been most active in the development of the city. Among his intimate friends was Henry D. Cooke, President of the First National Bank of Washington, and brother of Jay Cooke, the financier who was one of the largest contributors to the Republican Party coffers. It is also probable that through Henry Cooke the President became acquainted with Alexander Shepherd, since Cooke had been one of the prominent citizens associated with Shepherd in the Citizens' Committee and in the Board of Trade. With a new President in the White House, Shepherd was eager to enlist the support of his Administration in his plans for the large-scale improvement of the capital.

Shepherd was exactly the kind of man with whom Grant could feel on easy terms. He was without academic pretensions, a business man, a former Union Army soldier, a Republican but not a Radical. Big in stature as well as in his ideas, he was an extrovert, with a winning and engaging personality. "I have never heard another male voice that was his equal in richness and fullness of tone as an instrument of conversation. If he had studiously applied his talents to public speaking he would readily have attained distinction as an orator," recalled William Tindall.[1] Shepherd's determination to make Washington into a capital city worthy of the United States appealed strongly to the President. Here was an objective to be gained: the very difficulty of the obstacles involved made the idea still more attractive. It was not long before the improvement of the national capital became, like the annexation of San Domingo, a top-ranking project on his calendar. For Shepherd as a man he conceived a warm friendship, and he soon became a member of his most intimate circle, "the Kitchen Cabinet," as his enemies were to call it.

Ulysses S. Grant, who had been a failure in the Army until his spectacular rise during the War, and had been unsuccessful both as a farmer and in business in the West, was particularly susceptible to self-made men. As a youth he had known extreme poverty—after the Mexican War he had been earning $50 a month in his father's store in Galena, Illinois, and his life at "Hardscrabble Farm" near St. Louis had been a gloomy one. A man of modest personal habits, apart from his weaknesses for fine cigars and horses, and of an undemonstrative and introspective nature, he felt himself irresistibly drawn to dynamic extroverts like Shepherd. With men of inherited wealth he had little in common, and in the presence of such intellectuals as Sumner he felt ill at ease. Politically Grant was no Radical, and had been careful not to identify himself with their theories. On the other hand, he had little political philosophy of his own, except a vague belief in the will of the people as expressed through their representatives in Congress. Had he possessed able advisers such as those who had helped Andrew Johnson during his administration, Grant might have avoided his worst pitfalls.

In his inauguration address in 1869 he had expressed his desire to achieve national unity, and the beginning of his administration had been marked by greater harmony between the Executive and Legislative branches of the government than had existed in Washington for many years. His cabinet appointments had also reflected the same desire for harmony. Hamilton Fish, the Secretary of State, was a former Senator from New York, a patrician Conservative; Attorney-General E. Rockwood Hoar of Massachusetts and Secretary of the Interior Jacob D. Cox of Ohio were men generally esteemed for their ability and integrity. On the other hand, he had startled Washington by appointing two of his millionaire friends, the department store owner A. T. Stewart, of New York, and Adolph E. Borie, of Philadelphia, to the secretaryships respectively of the Treasury and of the Navy. Neither man possessed political experience and Stewart was constitutionally disqualified for the position. Some men, such as Rutherford B. Hayes,[2] might be sympathetic, but more felt like Henry Adams, who remarked that "a great soldier might be a baby politician."[3]

Grant's private secretary, Colonel Orville E. Babcock, who became Commissioner of Public Grounds and Buildings, was destined to play an important part in the improvement of the

District. Babcock, a stout, black-eyed man with a ruddy complexion, wearing an imperial in the style of Napoleon III, had an insatiable appetite for high living which rendered him an easy tool to special interests desiring the private ear of the President. As Commissioner, Babcock was a failure; the scanty records of his five-year term reveal how little time he devoted to his duties outside the White House. His chief interest appears to have been in animals; he was responsible for placing two deer and a pair of prairie dogs in Lafayette Park and an eagle in Franklin Park.[4] Babcock also undertook to refurnish the White House, and found Congress much more generous in its appropriations than it had been towards Andrew Johnson. The bills from one New York house alone amounted to $8,784.25, including such items as "2 sets of Drawing-room curtains $360.00, walnut Book Case $530.00 and 3 Rose du Var Mantels at $975.00 apiece."[5]

With the Grant family in occupation the White House took on a more cheerful aspect than it had for many a year. Mrs. Grant, the daughter of Judge Dent of St. Louis, was a simple, kind-hearted soul, whose absent-mindedness and faux pas were the source of innumerable family jokes. "She squints like an isosceles triangle," wrote Henry Adams, "but is not more vulgar than some Duchesses."[6] Mrs. Grant dressed plainly and employed no social secretary, answering personally her vast correspondence. Family routine was regular; the President rose at seven and read a newspaper until 8:30 when breakfast was served. He took a short walk and returned to his office at 10. In the morning he received callers, members of the Cabinet and of Congress. Luncheon was served at one. At three o'clock he would close his office and either stroll along the Avenue or visit his stable, selecting one of his favorite horses for a brisk drive. Mrs. Grant was occupied in the unending task of leaving cards and paying social calls. Sometimes two of the finest horses from the White House stable would be brought out for a drive to Soldiers' Home or in Rock Creek Park. Albert Hawkins, the tall black coachman, who sat in his box "like the statue of a grenadier" and the equally impressive footman Jerry Smith would drive with great dignity.[7] Whenever A. J. Drexel, the Philadelphia banker, would be driven to the railroad station after a stay at the White House it was his custom to tip each of the coachmen $20, saying that a ride in so splendid a carriage was worth the price.[8] The four wonderful horses dancing and chafing at their bits, the gleaming harnesses, the great polished carriage and Albert, his white teeth glistening through the smile that all his struggle for dignity could not banish from his ebony face made a picture that held every eye.[9] Family dinner at the White House was at five; after receiving friends the President would always retire by 11.

The basement of the Executive Mansion was converted into a playroom for the boys. Fred, the eldest, was away at West Point. Buck and Jesse attended the Emerson Institute on 14th Street, where they were driven each morning by an orderly in a cart drawn by a pair of Shetland ponies. Jesse had made friends with Albert the coachman and had a large collection of pets—dogs, gamecocks and an ill-natured parrot given him by the Mexican Minister. Nellie, a handsome girl in her teens, had a room on the second floor. She was a sophisticated and spirited young lady, who loved dancing and was the favorite of the younger social set. In the Spring of 1872 she was sent to London by her mother, where Adam Badeau, then consul, entertained her handsomely and arranged for her presentation to Queen Victoria.

The President's two favorite forms of recreation were fast horses and billiards. At his request a billiard room was installed in the White House and the stables in the rear were enlarged to accommodate his string of fine animals. The coach house contained a tandem, barouche, top buggy, pony phaeton, road wagon and a sulky. For the first time in White House history a professional housekeeper had been provided by Congress. Mrs. Mullen took care of the furniture and looked after the servants, thus permitting Mrs. Grant to devote more time to her social duties. A set of elegant new china was ordered for state dinners, each plate having painted on it a different flower, as well as the official eagle, shield and stars. On such occasions Melah, the

Italian steward[10], would prepare a banquet of some thirty dishes, and different wines were served at every third course. The guests sat at a horseshoe-shaped table with a large flower-decked mirror in the center which the President would have arranged to hide from his view the guests whom he was not anxious to see. Grant's own preferences in food ran to simple dishes, such as pork and beans and rice pudding, and he usually left many courses untouched. The hospitality of the White House was bountiful according to the customs prevailing at the time. Half a dozen extra places were always laid at dinner to take care of unexpected guests, and the spare rooms in the Executive Mansion were seldom unoccupied. Almost every penny of the President's official salary of $25,000 and much of his personal savings were consumed in official entertainment during his first term of office. During his administration the White House was completely open to the public; the Levees held during the sessions of Congress were free to all who wished to attend, as were the weekly Saturday afternoon receptions.

The course of municipal politics in Washington after the great upheaval of June, 1870, was running smoothly. Mayor Emery, who had taken office on June 13, began his term with the enthusiastic support of the great majority of citizens. His inaugural address to the Councils displayed an earnest desire to conciliate the many groups of voters who had endorsed him. "I am a Republican," said the Mayor, "but my republicanism is based on principle and not pure partisanship. I claim no rights as an American citizen which I am not willing to accord to all Americans without regard to race or religion . . . Those opposed to the extension of the franchise must now see the wisdom and necessity of accepting the situation and, whatever the reasons for their opposition, it now only remains for them and for us to do our whole duty in providing for those who hold the mighty power of the ballot in their hands, and for all in our midst the most ample means of true education and improvement. If there are any among us who are blind to these truths, who will not accept even unchangeable facts and who seek to make war upon the vested and constitutional rights of our citizens, I have no political sympathy for such persons and no political favors to bestow on them. I fully concur in the great settlement of right, now a part of the Constitution; and I as fully concur in the statement that the attempt in this city by the use of worn-out party cries to keep alive the enmities originating in the combat over past issues, and by party discipline to array one race in perpetual and useless hostility to one another, is an insult to intelligence and a betrayal of true Republican principles. I am equally opposed to the attempt to form a white man's party or a black man's party. Both are alike uncalled for and injurious to the interests of the people."[11]

When Emery took over the city government the treasury was empty, and the amount of floating debt still to be determined. By July it was ascertained that the funded debt had risen to $1,314,785.47 and that the floating debt was close to $1,000,000. Policemen and school teachers, as well as corporation laborers, had not been paid in months.[12] Emery suggested on June 27 settling the claims on the corporation by issuing certificates of indebtedness for all taxes payable in 1870, 1871 and 1872, the last two classes of which would bear six per cent interest. An immediate loan of $150,000 was necessary to pay the back salaries of teachers and District officials. In September he was forced to raise the property tax rate from $1.40 to $1.80, though the school tax was reduced at the same time.

In accordance with the spirit of his inaugural message some patronage was given to the colored men who had supported Emery: George Hatton was rewarded for his campaign speeches by a clerkship at the Center Market and Perry Carson, a powerful political figure among the colored population, known on account of his size as "the tall black oak of Anacostia," was given a post at City Hall. Some of Bowen's former supporters were still convinced, however, that they were being discriminated against. A. M. Green, a former ward commissioner in a petition to the Superintendent of Public Buildings, complained that the Emery government was giving Negroes less than their fair share of work, although they composed two-thirds of the laboring force of the District. The reformers had at first wished to prosecute some of the members of the "Bowen Ring" especially Major William Morse, the City Engineer, but the evidence for prosecution, the contract bids, had disappeared from City Hall. Moreover, with six holdovers from the Bowen administration left on the Board of Aldermen who could have voted against the confirmation of municipal employees, such a move would have been distinctly unwise.

In the fall of 1870 Washington, which had been without a Democratic newspaper since the demise of the *National Intelligencer* in 1869, welcomed a new journal, the *Daily Patriot*. Financed by George W. Riggs, by W. W. Corcoran who had recently returned from Europe, and other wealthy Washington Democrats, it had also received considerable financial support from New York's Democratic boss, William M. Tweed—though this was at the time unknown to the public. The sponsors of the new daily doubtless hoped it would regain for the party some of the national prestige which the *Intelligencer* had exercised for so many years. James G. Berret, the former Mayor of Washington, was made a member of the editorial board, and James E. Harvey, a newspaper man who had served as Minister to Portugal during Andrew Johnson's administration, was appointed managing editor.[13] Well-printed and forcefully edited, the *Patriot* made an excellent impression upon the Washington public; though its circulation was small compared with that of the other dailies, it was well supported by advertisers and widely read by those who wished to form a more balanced picture of national affairs than could be obtained from its three Republican competitors.

The question of the colored schools, which had raged so hotly during Bowen's administration, continued to agitate the citizens of Washington. On May 6 Charles Sumner again introduced in the Senate a bill "to secure equal rights in the Public Schools of Washington and Georgetown," by which the colored school board would have been abolished, and both teachers and students integrated into a common system.[14] Henry Piper again brought up the matter in the Board of Common Council on December 19 in an able speech, pointing out the inconsistency of the present situation. "Gentlemen do not hesitate to enter this Council chamber and occupy seats in close proximity to colored men. Why should they then set an example which they are not willing that their children should follow?" Such arguments, however, appear to have carried little weight even with the majority of white Republicans; the *Star* and the *National Republican,* so loyal to party discipline on other matters, continued steadfastly to oppose a common public school system.

Within the Board of Colored School Trustees all was not well. The echoes of the Bowen-Emery conflict had not yet died away, and a division of opinion had begun to take place among the influential colored men of Washington. The *Star* so persistently ridiculed in its reports of the Board meetings Syphax and Wormley, two of the trustees who had been supporters of Bowen, that its reporter was finally excluded altogether. On August 16 Octavius V. Catto, of Philadelphia, was named Superintendent, and shortly afterwards a protest meeting against Syphax and Wormley was held and a resolution passed asking that they be removed by the Secretary of the Interior. The resolution also called for the number of trustees to be increased to nine—seven from Washington and two from Georgetown. Catto complained in October that he was unable to find the school records and pointed out a discrepancy of $1859.77 between the expenditures of the trustees and the amounts as issued in the vouchers. On December 8 the Senate asked the Trustees to prepare a report on the District Colored Schools. Syphax and Wormley in their statement stressed the need for further legislation.

> It is our judgment that the best interests of the colored people of the capital and not theirs alone, but those of all classes, require the abrogation of all laws and institutions creating or tending to perpetuate distinctions based on color . . . The laws creating the separate schools for colored children in this District were enacted as a temporary expedient to meet a conjunction of things that has now passed

away . . . . A system is now fully recognized at the Capital to the seating side by side of white and colored people in the railway car, the jurybox, the municipal and government offices, the city courts, even in the Halls of the two Houses of Congress . . . If fathers are fit to associate, why are the children not equally so? It is worthy of note that in this context some of the most distinguished men in literary, social and political circles in this section of the country have recently, in standing for their claims to be considered the best and truest friends of the people of color, take pains to inform the public that they were reared with colored children, played with them in the sports of childhood and were even schooled by colored nurses in infancy, hence that no prejudice of color exists on their part. If this be so, then with what show of consistency can they object to the children of both classes sitting side by side in school?[15]

The third member of the Board of Trustees, Charles King, filed a separate report, showing some difference of opinion:

In reference to the schools of mixed races, I think that a real difference of opinion may exist among friends of the colored people; but the time is rapidly approaching when this discrimination must be obliterated all over the country, and I know no better locality in which to make a beginning than the District of Columbia and no better time than the present. Let all discrimination on account of color be avoided in the public schools of Washington. Let them be amply provided for in the respect of funds and teachers, and a very few years will see the example followed all over our free country. The colored race will feel the stimulating effects of direct competition with the white race, their ambition and self-respect will grow under its influence and add dignity to their character and rapidly develop a type and style of manhood that must place them on an equality with other races of the world.[16]

No consideration, however, was to be given to any changes in the District school system until February 8. In the meantime Burton C. Cook, of Illinois, Chairman of the House District Committee which had been discussing various proposals for the reorganization of the District government, proposed a new Bill, which with little debate was accepted by the House.[17]

The theory of the Territory Bill, as Cook explained it to the House, was to secure a proper Conservative influence in the District government by the appointment of a portion of its officers by the Federal government. Actually, the Bill as passed represented a half-way stage to the government by commission proposed by Senator Morrill, and the authority given under it to District authorities was considerably less than that of any Territory. Besides providing for a Governor to be appointed by the Executive with the sanction of the Senate, the Bill provided for an eleven-member Legislative Council (of which two were to be Georgetown residents and two were to be from the County of Washington) who were also to be appointed by the President. Five members of the Council were to be named for one-year and six for two-year terms. Popular election was provided for the House of Delegates, which was to consist of twenty-two members. The District was to be divided into eleven new voting areas; a year's residence in the Territory and 30 days in the voting district were required of prospective voters.

The Territorial Legislature was forbidden to extend credit to both public corporations and individuals, or to grant them special privileges. It was prohibited from passing laws regulating divorce, the procedure of the Court of Justice, the remittance of fines, the sale of real estate belonging to minors, and the terms of public officials. All officers disbursing money were to be bonded. The salary of the Governor was fixed at $3,000 and that of the Secretary of the District at $2,000. Members of the Legislature were to receive $4.00 per diem for their services.

In Section 18 of the Bill Congress made it clear that the laws of the Legislature should at all times be subject to its final authority and that "nothing shall be construed to deprive Congress of its power of legislation over said District in as ample manner as if this law had not been enacted." Furthermore, while maintaining its authority, Congress was still not prepared to acknowledge the obligation of the United States towards the District on account of the land which it owned within the confines of the new territory. While provision was made in Section 36 for a valuation of Federal property every five years, no fixed contribution or proportion of the District budget was mentioned in the Bill. The same safeguards which had been established in the Washington City Charter of 1868 on the amount of debt which could be raised by bond issues were continued: five per cent of the assessed value of the real property of the District was to remain the limit, and such a loan, moreover, required the ratification of both Houses of the Territorial Legislature and the assent of the Governor. The city charters of Washington and Georgetown were to remain in force, but only temporarily and for the purpose of collecting money due to the Corporations and of meeting claims against them. The Mayors of Washington and Georgetown were to remain in office until the first of June, when the officers of the new Territorial Government would take over their duties.

But the most important provisions of the Bill were contained in Section 37 in which a Board of Public Works was to be created in the Territory. The Board was to be composed of five members, each of whom was to receive a salary of $2,500 per annum and to be appointed by the President for a four-year term. All of its members were to be bona-fide residents of the District: one member was to be a resident of Georgetown and one of the County, and the Board was also to include a civil engineer. According to the wording of the Bill, the Board of Public Works "shall have entire control of and make all regulations which they deem necessary for keeping in repair the streets, avenues, alleys and sewers of the city and all other works which may be entrusted to their charge by the Legislative Assembly or Congress. They shall disburse upon their warrant all moneys appropriated by the United States or the District of Columbia, or collected from property owners, in the pursuance of law, for the improvements of streets, avenues, alleys, sewers, roads and bridges." The cost of the improvements was to be met in part by levying one-third against the owners of property which adjoined the improved areas. All contracts to be entered into by the Board had to be made following appropriations made by law, and no payment was to be made on any contract in which a member of the Board was personally interested.

The lack of documentary evidence makes it impossible to know what part, if any, Alexander Shepherd played in the establishment of the Board of Public Works. The original bill which he and the Citizens' Committee had drafted in 1870 and introduced in the Senate by Hannibal Hamlin shortly afterwards had made no such provision. In view, however, of Shepherd's close association with President Grant and of his cordial relations with influential members of Congress it is not beyond the bounds of possibility that the concept of a Board of Public Works was his suggestion. Whether the wording of Section 37 was also suggested by him is also a matter of conjecture, since the ingenuity which he was to exercise in by-passing its restrictions was truly remarkable.[18] It is also apparent that Shepherd was far less interested in a permanent form of government for the District than in securing a means for the carrying out of his plans for large-scale improvement of the national capital. The Board of Public Works, being composed entirely of members appointed by the Executive, afforded an ideal means for such operations with the minimum amount of opposition. Once the city improvements had been completed, he was to display remarkably little enthusiasm for the continuation of the Territorial Government and for the preservation of local suffrage.

The Territorial Bill met with the general approval of almost all residents of the District. On January 21st the Board of Trade passed a resolution which declared, "We hail with joy the passage of the Bill for the Government of the District of Columbia by the House of Representatives this day, believing that it will be the beginning of a new era in the development and progress of our best interests."[19] The only opposition was expressed by a small group, consisting for the most part of the former supporters of Sayles J. Bowen. On January 2nd a meeting was held under the chairmanship of Dr. Charles Purvis, one of the physicians of Freedmen's and a trustee of Howard University. John R. Elvans, a prominent business man, was among the few white citizens present. The resolution adopted by the meeting claimed that the changes in the District government would reduce the laboring classes to serfdom, and that the advocates of the Bill were the large property-owners. Mayor Emery announced his opposition to the measure on the grounds that the public would have no representation on the Board of Public Works or in the Legislative Assembly. "If the people of the District are not capable of self-government," he declared, "popular government will be considered a failure in the nation's capital. I am not ready to make such an admission. We do not wish to be responsible for misgovernment we cannot correct. It would be better to have commissioners at once."[20]

Such protests, however, had little influence upon the Senate, which passed the Territorial Bill in the early hours of February 21 with but little debate, and the measure was signed the same day by President Grant. The new Legislature was to be elected in April and on June 1 would take over the entire administration of the District. The corporation governments of Washington and Georgetown were to continue in operation until that date, but principally to complete existing assignments rather than to make provision for new contracts.

February 21 was indeed a notable day in the history of the District. On that day Pennsylvania Avenue, the paving of which had just been completed, was to be the scene of a great carnival, planned by Shepherd and a committee of Washington business men. The date not only preceded George Washington's Birthday but fell upon the Tuesday preceding Lent, when carnivals were traditionally held, so that the occasion was in the nature of a three-fold celebration.

Shepherd's offices on the Avenue at 11th Street were the headquarters of the festivities, for which $40,000 had been raised among local merchants. The whole Avenue from the Treasury to the Capitol had been decorated with flags and bunting, and emblems and "transparencies" had been strung up outside every store. Attracted by the special half-price excursion tickets issued by the railroads, more than 10,000 tourists flocked to the city. School children were dismissed to attend the carnival, and one of the largest crowds which Washington had ever seen thronged the sidewalks of the Avenue.

The new wooden pavement was christened by parades of civic organizations, led by Mayor Emery and Alexander Shepherd, the police and the fire companies in red and brass, with their engines sparkling and bright. Then followed the horse races, a mule race, a wheelbarrow race, a goat race, and a display of vehicles and horses. "Beau" Hickman mounted on a grey mare, wearing a beaver hat and his Sunday clothes, drew a burst of laughter from the spectators. On 6th Street the dashing Dr. Helmbold, who had arrived with a large retinue at the Arlington Hotel, appeared with a three-horse tandem with a gold plated harness, attracting much attention and praise for his feats of horsemanship. The Marine Band played all day. In the afternoon as the natural light grew dim the Avenue was illuminated by strings of Chinese lanterns, and the Capitol dome was specially lit for the occasion.

On the same evening the Corcoran Gallery, which had not yet been opened to the public, was the scene of the most magnificent ball ever given in the capital. The occasion was to raise funds for the still uncompleted Washington Monument as well as to celebrate the Father of his Country. The gentlemen of the press, and in particular the "literary ladies" who had been called in to assist them in the description of feminine toilettes, were in ecstasy. The arrangements also represented a great improvement upon the hurly-burly of Washington receptions, "no feeling the hilt of the General's sword in your favorite rib," no "strange oaths" and "modern instances," as the reporter of the *Patriot* put it. The ballroom at the top of the grand staircase, with its crimson-carpeted steps, was a blaze of lights; three immense chandeliers had been added to the long lines of electric jets. At the extreme right a carpeted dais with chairs and couches of crimson and gold were set aside for the President and his party, surmounted by a triumphal canopy of flags and the American eagle.[21]

The following day, though Ash Wednesday, was the occasion for further celebrations on the Avenue, attended by an estimated 70,000 spectators, and a tournament was held in European carnival style. A masked ball at the National Theatre marked the climax of the most brilliant public festival which Washingtonians could remember.

The era of good feeling which the Carnival had engendered was, however, of short duration. At the beginning of March the President gave to the press the names of his nominees to positions in the new District Government—all of them Republicans. Henry D. Cooke, Grant's intimate friend, was named Governor and President ex-officio of the Board of Public Works. Shepherd was made Vice-President of the Board to which were also appointed S. P. Brown, the former contractor and builder, and James A. Magruder, a former Army engineer. A. B. Mullett, the architect of the Treasury Department, was named in an advisory capacity.

The property holders, many of whom looked with suspicion at Shepherd's own real estate speculations, were disturbed by the partisan nature of Grant's appointments. They foresaw that men such as these would not hesitate to increase the funded debt of the District and that higher taxation would inevitably follow. Nor were the President's selections for the Legislative Council calculated to win Conservative support. They included three Negroes and other men not considered by the older residents of the District to be completely representative of the community. The *Georgetown Courier* complained on April 15th, "Not one old resident, nor a Democrat, nor a Catholic, nor an Irishman nor a man of Irish descent among the nominees, and yet we have three darkies—Douglass, Gray and Hall, a German (Miller), two natives of Maine and one of Massachusetts. And this is the banquet to which the Democrats have been invited! This is the work of the consummate statesmen who by false representation succeeded in obtaining the support of Democratic congressmen to carry through both Houses their bastard offspring!"

The Democrats could find little satisfaction in Grant's other appointments, especially that of William A. Cook, one of their chief targets of attack during Mayor Bowen's administration, as Corporation Counsel for the District. The newly-created Board of Health, which had been established in the Organic Act to regulate the sanitary conditions of the District, was composed of two well-known doctors, Bliss and Verdi, and a colored lawyer and Republican politician, John M. Langston. The Secretary to the District, Norton P. Chipman, was also an ardent Republican, who had risen from private to Brigadier-General in the Union Army. As assistant to the Adjutant-General he had taken a prominent part in the prosecution of Major Wirz, the Confederate officer charged with the atrocities of Andersonville Prison, who was executed for his cruelty. After the War Chipman had set up an office in Washington as a patent attorney. His friendship and popularity among Republican members of Congress was regarded, no doubt, by the President as an effective means of securing for the District the larger appropriations which would be soon needed for the improvement of the national capital.

On March 29th the Republican Central Committee met to select their candidate for the District's Delegate to Congress. On the first ballot Chipman received 43 votes, Frederick Douglass 27, Boswell 21 and Bowen eight. It is interesting to note that on this occasion the colored delegates were divided in their sympathies: Anthony Bowen, Perry Carson, J. T. Johnson, W. A. Taliaferro and A. B. Tinney cast their vote for Chipman, while Col. N. J. Ordway, T. C. Connolly and several of the white Republicans voted for Douglass.[22] A few days later the Democrats selected as their candidate Richard T. Merrick, a prominent member of the District Bar, and member of a distinguished family from Maryland, where he had served as State Senator.

The election campaign, though short, was a violent one concerned with only one issue—that of the public schools. The Senate, in which Sumner had brought up on February 8 his bill for an integrated school system, had not yet taken action, but the fear that Congress, which had passed similar bills under Andrew Johnson's administration, might take some step to amalgamate the white and colored school systems, was widespread. The *Patriot* on April 1 stated in its editorial, "We will go as far as the furthest in providing means of education for colored children . . . But while standing ready to concede a fund proportionate to the colored population for this purpose and to be taxed for it, we shall not consent on any terms that our children shall be forced into companionship at the school board with the children of contrabands, who have all the vices of slavery coursing in their veins and its diseased infection inflicting their bodies." On April 6th it violently attacked William A. Cook, Bowen's Corporation Counsel, who had been appointed to the same position in the Territorial Government, and comparisons were made between the Legislative Council of the District and the Legislature of South Carolina. Merrick challenged Chipman to a public debate on the mixed school issue, but he prudently refused to become involved.

The claims of Negro "colonization" were again revived in the Democratic press of Washington and Baltimore. The *Patriot* reported on April 10 the drowning of Tom Bowie, a well-known colored henchman and ward-heeler. It was claimed that he had been sent by General Chipman to bring back boatloads of colored men from Maryland and Virginia who were to flood the polls on Election Day, men who had never resided in the District and never voted except during the Bowen regime. "The station-houses," the same paper reported, "were crowded with Negroes seeking lodging, many of the same men who had voted for Republican candidates in Fairfax County, Alexandria and in the Fifth Maryland District." The *Patriot* pointed to the registration figures as evidence of fraud: out of a total white population of 90,549, there registered 17,746, a percentage of 19.5, while out of a colored population of 41,138 the Negro registration had amounted to 10,774, or 26 per cent. This percentage, the editor contended, was only accountable by illegal registration of Negro voters. The editor claimed on the 18th that 3,000 such illegal votes had been exposed and that Governor Cooke had unfairly appointed the Judges of election by naming Negroes instead of Democrats to the Board.

That the colored voters were fully aware of the importance was indicated in a letter published by Frederick Douglass in the *Chronicle*. Merrick, he wrote, represented the "good old days of slavery"; Chipman, a "new era in American civilization." "I say shame, eternal shame on any colored voter who supports Richard T. Merrick, and withered be the black man's arm and blasted be the black man's head who casts a vote against General N. P. Chipman."[23] This was to be no fight between rival Republican factions as in 1870; it was to be a fight between the old Democracy and the era of equal rights which Grant had initiated.

Only in two Districts, however, did the colored men put up their own candidates. Solomon G. Brown, who stood for the First District in the former County, was a Washington resident of more than twenty years' standing who had served as a messenger at the Smithsonian Institute and later became a member of the Board of Trustees for the County Schools. The *Republican* described him as a "gentleman of intelligence who has the respect of all his neighbors."[24] The colored candidate in the 7th District was the Rev. James Handy, a native of Baltimore and Minister of the African Methodist Episcopal Church, who had resided in Washington since 1862. Neither of the two candidates had previously been active in local politics.

The elections, as was predictable at the outset, resulted in a complete Republican victory. Chipman received 15,195 votes to Merrick's 11,104, and in the House of Delegates 15 Republicans and only seven Democrats were returned. Even in one of the strongest Conservative Georgetown districts John E. Cox, the Republican candidate, was elected. The Democrats had endeavored to the last to bring the school issue to the fore; on their election tickets was printed "Opposed to Mixed Schools," with an engraving of Franklin School on the back. They had also made counterfeits of the smaller Republican ticket in a desperate but vain attempt to deceive illiterate colored voters.[25]

The *Patriot,* commenting on the results, was particularly bitter in its denunciation of government clerks, who, they claimed, had been given a day off by the heads of their Bureaus and compelled to register. It claimed that 3,500 of such employees had voted, most of them for the first time since their residence in the District, and that the election had been won by their votes.[26] The *Chronicle* retorted that no one had been "compelled" to vote, but that blank circulars had been given to each employee to fill up with the name of his state and the number of his congressional district, similar to those distributed every four years before the Presidential elections. "A number of clerks who have not voted in several years but who are housekeepers here and are deemed to have forfeited the privilege of voting elsewhere have concluded they have a right to vote, and that they ought to defeat Merrick," the editorial added. The same paper later answered the *Patriot's* contention that since the colored male population over 21 stood at 10,149 according to the 1870 Census, and the registration of colored voters in April, 1871, was 10,774, fraud must have taken place. "There are scores of colored men working outside the city," the *Chronicle* stated on April 17, "whose families reside here. The home is where the family is. The right of these men to vote is perfectly clear. The statement that they have voted in Maryland and Virginia is a simple unvarnished falsehood. If it were not, these men would have been arrested at once."

In the 1870 elections, when the colored voters had been divided in their allegiance, none of the old charges that Negroes had been imported for voting purposes had been made, and on the only instance of such an attempt recorded by the *Star,* Major Richards had put the would-be voters in jail. In the election of April 1871 besides the usual precautions Justice MacArthur of the District Supreme Court had issued additional instructions to the Superintendents of Election, ordering them to deliver the sealed ballot boxes to the Governor before they were counted, providing for open ballots to be folded in order to conceal the name of the voter, and declaring scratched or pasted ballots to be void. The *National Republican* reported on the 18th that William Dickson, one of the Democratic candidates, had congratulated the Board of Registration on its "fair play," and even the *Patriot* was forced to admit after the election that there were few incidents and little drunkenness.

On May 15 the new Legislative Assembly held its first meeting in the recently redecorated rooms which had been leased in Metzerott's Hall. The new offices of the Territorial Legislature had been lavishly furnished. The Council Hall floor was covered by a Brussels carpet of a handsome pattern and solid walnut desks were furnished for the members and officers of the Council, and numerous committee rooms were equally well-equipped. The offices of the Territorial Government and of the Board of Public Works on John Marshall Place had been remodelled at the cost of $57,000, and yet another office for the Governor had been leased at the corner of 17th Street and Pennsylvania Avenue across from the Corcoran Gallery. After the inauguration of the Legislature a grand parade of all the District Republican Clubs, the civic associations, the Fire Department, the "Pioneer Club" and the "Ordway Guard" as the new District Militia commanded by Col. N. J. Ordway was called, marched by way of Louisiana Avenue and along Pennsylvania past the White House, where President Grant reviewed them, to the residence of Governor Cooke in Georgetown. In front of the mansion brilliantly illuminated and festooned with flags, the Governor stood to receive them. At his side General Chipman, Judge Fisher, General Dent, Alexander Shepherd and W. S. Huntington, the banker, stood up while the band struck up "Hail to the Chief."

The Councils met for their first business session on May 21 before the Washington and Georgetown Corporations had passed out of existence. Little had been accomplished by the old Councils during the past few months except for the winding up of previous contracts. Mayor Emery had been forbidden by an official injunction of the Board of Public Works from letting further contracts for the duration of his term; he had retaliated by refusing to levy taxes in Washington for the fiscal year ending in June, claiming that this was the responsibility of the new government, though Georgetown made its collections as usual.

At the first session of the Legislative Council Frederick Douglass was elected Vice-President. He did not keep the seat long, however, resigning on June 20 in order to accompany the San Domingo Commission, to which he had been appointed secretary. His seat was later filled by Lewis Douglass, his eldest son, a printer by trade and publisher of the Negro weekly, *The New National Era*. John T. Johnson, a former cloak-room attendant at the Capitol and proprietor of a refectory there, was made Treasurer of the Board of Public Works and several colored men were given positions as clerks in the various branches of the District government.[27] The Democratic newspapers were particularly incensed by the appointment of Charles Douglass, the youngest member of the family, who had been General Howard's secretary and had supervised the construction of Howard University, to the position of Commissioner of Schools in Uniontown. The *Patriot* remarked, after one of the white teachers in the area had resigned rather than serve under a colored Commissioner, that "the Radical demagogues" were merely interested in using the Negro to stir up hostility between the races and that they had little interest in what became of him afterwards.[28] O. S. B. Wall, who had served as Captain of a colored regiment during the War and who, as Justice of the Peace, had administered the oath to the Legislative Assembly, was shot and severely wounded in an argument with a white army officer. At the beginning of June the colored laborers went on strike for a wage of $2.00 per diem, which they were able to obtain through the personal intervention of Governor Cooke. This action of the Governor did not endear him to the Democratic press, which accused him of weakness and partisan politics.

While the new government had not announced its plans for the improvement of the District, its opponents were becoming increasingly apprehensive. The *Patriot* warned on May 17 that before making new loans the government should establish a commission to determine the amount of the floating debt. "Our policy is not to borrow a dollar until our finances are put in order and a sinking fund established for the extinction of the existing debt. If that simple and straightforward course be pursued, the credit of the city will immediately revive and a mighty impetus given to its prosperity. But to start with loans is to end with loans and to make dissatisfaction and corruption inevitable."

Governor Cooke's inaugural message to the Councils on May 15 had stated that the ratio of taxation of the city of Washington in previous years had been $13.26 per capita, which was below that of all but four of the largest cities in the United States. The aggregate debt of these cities was also much higher than that of Washington, with reference to population and taxable property. Such a statement had naturally caused alarm on the part of the large property-holders in the District that their taxes would be raised in a short space of time. They were well aware of the extent of the speculations of Shepherd and S. P. Brown in the real estate market; the fact that both of these men were members of the Board of Public Works, the lavish furnishing of the new offices of the District government and the hiring of a large staff of employees had made them fear that the District was to experience what New York had undergone during the rule of Boss Tweed. They had no illusions regarding Governor Cooke. "Why is the Governor like a gentle lamb?" the *Patriot* jested, "Because he is led by A. Shepherd." It was obvious that, with such men in control of the District, the city improvements would be executed on no niggardly scale, and that "something big" was being planned.

Chapter 6

"Boss" Shepherd and His Works

The opponents of the new District government did not have long to wait for the fulfillment of their worst expectations. Only three weeks after the inauguration of the Territorial administration the Board of Public Works announced its "comprehensive plan of improvements," which it submitted to the Legislature.

The improvements proposed by the Board were of an heroic scale. The original plan of Major Pierre l'Enfant, which for decades had remained a dream, was actually to be realized. The chief emphasis of the Board's proposals concerned drainage, grading and paving. The unsightly Tiber Creek was to be covered over by arches and to be made the principal sewer of the District, draining the water from the northwest areas of Washington and Georgetown into the Potomac. In addition, many miles of sewerage were to be provided in order to take care not only of the present but also of the future requirements of the urban areas.

The plan called for uniform grades to be established on the principal thoroughfares and avenues of the city in order that the vistas and perspectives of the L'Enfant plan could be realized. The pavements were to be of various materials: wood, asphalt, stone and macadam. In order to reduce the width of the larger streets trees were to be planted, and owners required to create large gardens in front of their houses facing the street. The cost of these improvements, the Board estimated, would be $6,000,000; one-third of this amount was to be assessed to the owners of property adjacent to the areas which were to be improved, and the balance of $4,000,000 to be raised by a bond issue. An unusual feature of the Board's plan was its proposal to establish a scale of fixed prices which would serve as a basis for contracts. It was claimed that both the previous systems, that of taking lowest bids from contractors and that of employing day laborers, had proved equally unsatisfactory.

To the vast majority of Washington residents, who had been used to the piecemeal and half-hearted street improvements of previous municipal administrations, the magnitude of the operations proposed by the Board was astonishing. Although the "magnificent distances" of the earlier decades had been partially filled, no attempt had yet been made to achieve a uniform grade in the streets. With the exception of Pennsylvania Avenue none of the major boulevards had been levelled to permit the noble perspectives originally planned for the Federal City. L'Enfant's plan had always seemed a remote and distant project, something which few citizens reckoned on seeing fulfilled in their lifetime.

Shepherd, while aware of the sentiments of the property owners and of the opposition that might be anticipated, was determined to waste no time in carrying through his plans. He was doubtless anxious to finish the work during the four years of his term as Vice-President of the Board. Under another administration it would be unlikely that conditions could possibly be more favorable than they were in 1871, and if the improvements were not carried out immediately, many years might pass before another such opportunity occurred. Even if the cost of the improvements exceeded the estimated figure and the District debt were carried beyond its legal limit, he could be sure that Congress would never repudiate the financial obligations of the capital of the United States.

The plan immediately became a political issue. It was attacked by the *Patriot* on the ground that the new contract system would result in a one hundred per cent profit for the contractors. The sum of $4,000,000, which it was proposed to raise by bond issue, would, it was claimed, exceed the authority given to the District authorities under the Organic Act. There was already in existence, the editorial pointed out, a funded debt of over $3,000,000 from the old corporations and county which the Board's plan failed to take into account; this sum, added to the new loan proposed, would greatly exceed the five per cent of real property valuation which Congress had authorized.[1]

On July 7 the Legislative Council gave its sanction to the Board to negotiate the loan, with the stipulation that contracts would be entered upon at twenty per cent less than the estimates. Disbursements to the contractors were to be made by warrants on the Treasurer of the District; such warrants were not to be drawn until the completed work was ten per cent in excess of the warrant. They authorized the sale of $1,500,000 worth of bonds in 1871 and $2,500,000 worth in 1872. Four days later the Board, of which Shepherd had been elected Executive Officer, announced the selection of an Advisory Committee. General Humphrey Meigs, one of the best Army engineers, General Babcock, Superintendent of Public Grounds, and Frederick L. Olmsted, Engineer of New York's Central Park, had been invited to serve as advisers to the Board. A Parking Commission was also appointed, consisting of some of the leading landscape gardeners in Washington: William R. Smith, superintendent of the Botanic Gardens; William Saunders, superintendent of the Department of Agriculture, and the horticulturist, John Saul.

As soon as the loan had received the approval of the House of Delegates, Governor Cooke hastened to New York to raise the necessary funds. On July 22 the *Star* announced that $1,500,000 had been secured at 96½ per cent with six per cent interest. Such terms were exceptionally favorable, considering that the bonds of the Corporation of Washington were selling greatly under par at 80; the loan reflected the confidence of Wall Street both in the credit of the new government and in the personal standing of the Governor and the Cooke dynasty.

The larger property owners of the District lost little time after the Legislature had approved the Loan Bill in organizing to oppose it. Many of them feared that the taxes which they would have to pay for the improvements adjacent to their properties would be so large as to prove confiscatory, and the fact that the government of the District was entirely in the hands of the Republicans caused many of them to become alarmed that assessments might be made on a partisan basis. On July 24 Walter Cox[2], one of the leading attorneys in the city of Washington, met with Governor Cooke together with some of the large property owners whom he represented—among them George W. Riggs, William H. Claggett and George H. Plant. The conditions of the loan, Cox told the Governor, were not satisfactory to his clients. The aggregate District debt, he claimed, amounted already to $3,349,124.00, while the total assessment of District property totalled only $77,191,941.37. Even the $1,500,000 already raised as the first installment of the loan would, he declared, cause the statutory provision of the Organic Act to be greatly exceeded. Furthermore, the bond issue would be illegal unless ratified by a majority of the voters at a special election, as provided by the Territorial Act.

Governor Cooke, however, refused to postpone the bond issue, and the following day, acting on a plea from the property owners, Justice Wylie agreed to consider an injunction in the District Supreme Court. All contract work was immediately halted by the Board pending the decision of the Court.

At the hearings, which began on August 1, Governor Cooke replied to the injunction, stating that the assessed values of property in the District amounted to $84,630,074.37—a figure greatly in excess of that given by Walter S. Cox. The indebtedness of the District, said the Governor, apart from the old corporation debts which he claimed were to be excluded, amounted to only $200,000. On this basis there could be no doubt, he claimed, that the $4,000,000 loan came under the statutory provisions of the Organic Act and was entirely legal. Mr. Cox argued in rebuttal that it was impossible to disregard the existing funded debt of the District, and he also stated that the Board of Public Works, which had been set up as a branch of the District Executive government, had assumed legislative powers.

The case of the District was argued by Caleb Cushing, a former United States Attorney-General, and one of the nation's most brilliant lawyers. Cushing argued that the loan was favorable to the taxpayers as a whole, but contended that the individuals who held large quantities of the old corporation bonds and certificates of indebtedness had special reasons for opposing the new loan, which might further depreciate the value of their holdings by creating an additional lien upon the assets of the District.

Nevertheless Justice Wylie decided to grant the injunction the following day, giving as the grounds for his decision the fact that under the Organic Act the District was a corporation which could sue and be sued. The figures which had been introduced by the contending parties as representing the amount of taxable property in the District were, he maintained, mere guesses, as no new assessment of real estate had been made since the injunction had been filed, and neither estimate could be relied upon.

Seeing that for the time being further action was hopeless, Governor Cooke asked the Legislature to approve a loan of $500,000, pending a decision from a higher court and the special election which the injunction had made necessary. The amount was the equivalent of the amount of the new bonds which had already been sold after the loan had originally been announced. William A. Cook, the Corporation Counsel for the Territory, asked the Court that the injunctionists should give a bond by which the District would be protected against possible suits by the bondholders, and his request was granted by Justice Wylie.

Shepherd had meanwhile taken the opportunity of the lull in the improvements of the District to make a brief tour of other cities in order to inspect the methods of paving which they employed. In the company of a group of District officials and engineers he visited New York, Brooklyn, Philadelphia and Buffalo. Shepherd wished to see for himself which forms of pavement had stood up best in these cities, in order to determine what would be best suitable to local conditions in the District and to form an idea of their cost. Conferences were held with the park commissioners in these cities, and much useful information was collected.

On August 7 a large meeting was held at Lincoln Hall by citizens to protest against the injunction and to press for the prosecution of the improvements. The speakers included General O. O. Howard, General Chipman and Shepherd. "The question really is whether the people of this District—aye the people of the whole country—shall . . . control the seat of the whole government," Shepherd said in a rousing speech, "or whether seventeen very respectable gentlemen shall say to the hundred and fifty thousand souls here 'thus far and no farther.' You shall continue the same old patchwork system which has rendered the nation's metropolis a disgrace and an eye-sore at home and a by-word and reproach abroad. You shall continue to drive over unpaved streets and exposed ravines and be as successfully lost in the blinding dust as was Elijah of old in the clouds which enveloped him as he ascended into the sky. Their timid souls shall say that at least they were to stand taxation like others and that although rascally figures that did not lie showed they represented but a thirty-fifth part of the taxable real estate and but a seventeenth part of the whole property of the District, still they must assert the hereditary prestige which had enabled them heretofore to rule, and must stretch out their arms to crush in one strong embrace the (to them) devastating spirit of progress." Claiming that under the old system contractors sold their certificates at a twenty per cent discount, he concluded, "The crime committed by the Board of Public Works has been simply this, that in the disbursement of the four or five millions which were to have been entrusted to them, the tribute of twenty per cent heretofore paid to this disinterested class was to be withheld and applied to the benefit of the taxpayer. Let me in this connection say that the policy of the Board will be 'millions for improvements, not one cent for tribute.' "[3]

The signers of the injunction petition,[4] seeing the approach of the contest at the polls, began to organize their own campaign. On August 26 a meeting was held at which they constituted themselves "The Citizens Association of the District of Columbia," announcing as their objective "to secure by all honorable and legal means equal, honest and economical administration of the government of the corporation of the District of Columbia." George W. Riggs was elected President, and the Vice-Presidents included William H. Tenney and Enoch Totten, wealthy merchants who had once been associated with Shepherd in the Citizens Committee of 1870. Albert G. Riddle, a former Ohio congressman and one of the leading attorneys in Washington, was also named Vice-President. John H. Crane, the sewer inspector dismissed by Bowen in 1869, was made Secretary and Dr. J. B. Blake, of the Metropolitan National Bank, an old Washington resident whose father had been Mayor of the city, elected Treasurer. The Executive Committee was under the chairmanship of T. J. Durant, a Democratic attorney, and included W. S. Cox, W. H. Philip, a wealthy property owner, the patent attorney Columbus Alexander, and Henry S. Davis, George H. Plant, J. Van Riswick, Francis Mohun, Albert Grant, Esau Pickrell and William B. Todd, important local business men, merchants, property owners and attorneys. While the predominating political complexion of the Citizens Association was Democratic, sufficient Republicans were represented on the Committee to make it a cross-section of the wealthier financial groups in the District affiliated with both political parties.

On August 16 the House of Delegates had announced a special election to be held on November 22 for the purpose of ratifying the Loan. Arrangements were made to advertise the election in the District newspapers; on a motion by Colonel Moore, the *Patriot* was included in the list by a vote of nine to six. On previous elections announcements had never been placed in more than three of the daily papers, and the move of advertising in all was clearly calculated to buy the favors of the District press. Most of the newspaper editors were, with the exception of the *Patriot,* already sympathetic to the Loan; even the *Georgetown Courier,* so strongly opposed to the national administration, had on July 15 censured the *Patriot* for its opposition.

On September 2 the Citizens Association held another meeting at which a long list of grievances prepared by the Executive Committee were read. The Board of Public Works was attacked on the ground that it had been appointed by Congress and not elected by the people, and specific objections were raised as to its operations. It was charged that favorite contractors were being given work to the exclusion of others, and that the provision by which bidders were required to lay down a deposit of $1,000 was denounced. It was charged that many downtown sections of Washington and Georgetown had been excluded from immediate improvement, and that remote and sparsely settled areas bordering on land owned by members of the Board were to be improved first. This last accusation may well have been framed by Albert Grant, who, as the owner and developer of property in the area east of the Capitol, resented the efforts of Shepherd to improve the west end of the city in which he had personal holdings.

The support of the colored voters, by whose aid Bowen had been defeated in 1870, was again sought by the opposition. The *Patriot* on August 18 appealed to those of them "who by thrift and industry have acquired a little property which would be swept away under the prodigal and plundering system which has been initiated in this District." On September 15 at a meeting of the Citizens Association, George Hatton spoke against the Loan, and F. D. Gaines, another former councilman, predicted that "as a general thing the colored people will vote against it." The situation was, however, vastly different from that of the preceding year, when the contest was between two Republican factions. Not only was the prestige of the new District government, a Republican administration, at stake, but also at stake was the opportunity of unlimited new jobs for the colored laborers through the improvements proposed by the Board. As the *New National Era* remarked on July 27, the colored people, though disappointed in not receiving a larger share in the disposition of offices, were nevertheless strongly in support of the loan. The officers of the new government, wishing to keep in the good graces of W. W. Corcoran, sent him a letter on September 9 inviting him to be their guest of honor at an official dinner before his imminent departure for Europe. However, the old gentleman, whose sympathies were irrevocably committed to the Democratic opposition, declined on the grounds of ill health and absence from the city.

The *Patriot,* which only a few weeks before had complained of the prodigality with which newspaper advertising had been distributed by the District government[5], itself published on September 23 a two-and-a-quarter column advertisement of the special election. As a result of this apparent inconsistency an outcry went up from the subscribers, and two days later the Managing Editor, James E. Harvey, resigned, giving bad health as his pretext. He was succeeded by Gen. Noah L. Jeffries, a moderate Democrat, with the assistance of James G. Berret, a member of the Board.

The Citizens Association on September 30 put out a new daily, *The Citizen,* as its official organ. It proclaimed itself neutral in politics, and in favor of improvements, but opposed to the wasteful expenditures of the Territorial Government. The *Citizen,* which had been financed by George W. Riggs, was patterned on the sheet bearing the same title which had been launched in New York by the opponents of the Tweed Ring, and represented a bid for support of Conservative citizens of both parties. On October 9 the *Patriot* was bitterly denounced in its editorial for having accepted the advertising of the District government, although on the same day the new editor of that journal had made clear that its opposition to the Loan had not changed, arguing that the advertisement had been accepted in the general course of business.

The *Citizen* published on October 11 an interesting interview with Sayles J. Bowen, who had lent his support to the signers of the injunction. It revealed that William A. Cook, who had previously asked him to stand as Republican candidate for Delegate, persuaded him to stand down in favor of Chipman, who he assured him was not Shepherd's choice. As a result Chipman had been elected and Bowen had lost his chances of a political comeback. Speaking of the proposed loan, he cynically commented to the *Citizen's* representative that he would vote for it "under the assumption that not more than half would be stolen." On the 18th another article was published claiming that the assent of Mayor Emery to the Territorial Bill had been obtained under similar false assurances that he would be named Governor. A clause providing for the taxation of Federal government property in the District had originally been inserted in the Bill, but stricken out at the last moment in order to obtain congressional support, and the measure had passed in the early hours of morning with but a bare quorum present in the Senate. The same article violently attacked Democratic business men who had been given contracts by the Board to buy their support. Apart from the *Citizen* only the insignificant weekly, the *National Standard,* stood out uncompromisingly against the Loan.

The District Republican Central Committee was again having difficulty in preserving unity among its various factions. Colonel N. J. Ordway, Commander of the District Militia, resigned as President in October in a feud over patronage with William A. Cook. A violent and unseemly altercation took place between them at a public meeting of party members on October 30, at which Ordway accused Cook of having pocketed $600 given by the Committee for election expenses. The Chairman of the meeting, J. W. LeBarnes, a conservative Republican, tried in vain to preserve order, but finally "his cane being entirely broken and his voice altogether gone, he was obliged to leave the chair and let the meeting take its course."[6]

The Republicans could, however, count on the support of one of the best speakers in the party, a man outside the realm of petty feuds. General Chipman, speaking at a mass meeting to ratify the nomination of Peter Campbell for re-election in October, made a passionate defense of the District government and its policy. The Loan, he said, was necessary in order to convince the Congress of the importance of the national capital. Previous governments in Washington and Georgetown had never dreamed of legislating for the welfare of the United States, and as a result, the Federal government had little interest in them. However, under the new system, the District had a chance of making up for lost time. "I am one of those," he continued, "who regard the District of Columbia as belonging in common to the whole people of the United States. We are not here simply to pursue our own business and pleasure; we are not here solely to make this a place of barter and sale, but we are here to make this capital city exemplify the civilization of our country. We are here to make it an exponent of American character; we are to become a place of pleasure and resort for all our citizens who may seek to visit their capital; we are to send them home feeling that they have a personal interest in our welfare and that the money of the General government expended within the District is in part for them and not wholly for our personal advantage; and we are to illustrate to those who visit us from foreign lands something of the power, wealth, intelligence and the business capacity of our people."

Referring to the loan as "the Gettysburg of our struggle for the permanent seat of government and the future greatness of the capital," General Chipman defended the plan of the Board against attacks that it was too vague. "It would be almost impossible," he said, "to carry out improvements on so large a scale without variations which a detailed plan, one voted by the people who did not possess sufficient technical knowledge to understand the details in any case, would prevent." He warmly supported the character of Shepherd against the attacks which had been made upon him, quoting Dr. J. B. Blake who, though an opponent of the Loan, had testified as to Shepherd's honesty and business integrity. The Board was also defended against charges of extravagance, pointing out that it had laid pavements at a lower rate than the work done by Mayor Emery, and calling attention to the reduction of the property tax from $1.80 to $1.70.

The Delegate ended his speech by appealing for support of the loan as a Republican measure. "Democrats can honestly vote for it," he added, "consistently with their party loyalty on its general merits. Republicans cannot vote against it without giving direct aid to the party seeking ascendancy in this District and which we believe at this time could not come into power without impairing seriously the interest of our people."

On October 31 the Citizens Committee held a further meeting at which it was decided to appoint a committee of twenty-five to approach the President and Congress with "the facts" about the Board of Public Works. It was becoming increasingly clear what would be the outcome of the special election, and the Citizens had little faith that Chief Justice Cartter, before whom the injunction appeal was to be taken, would sustain Justice Wylie's decision. The preliminary registration figures made public on November 2 revealed a drop of over 7,000 from those of the preceding April, of which more than 5,000 represented a loss in the number of white voters. On November 7 the *Citizen* had ceased publication.

Chief Justice Cartter on November 11 made known his verdict on the injunction appeal. The theory which had been advanced by the counsel for the District government that the Territory was not responsible for the previous debts of the corporations and of the county was accepted, and all legal obstacles to Shepherd's plan for city improvements were now removed.

The Board, nevertheless, delayed resuming work until the 22nd, when the results of the special election were announced. The Loan was endorsed by a sweeping majority—12,748 against 1,202—and the Republicans captured all but two of the 22 seats in the House of Delegates. Five colored men were returned to the House, the new members including O. S. B. Wall, the Justice of the Peace who had administered the oath to the first Council, and Henry Piper, who had been a member of the Washington City Government. At the same time, a $500,000 subscription to the Piedmont Railway, which was to connect Washington with the West by way of Virginia and West Virginia, was endorsed by an equally large majority. The means by which the railroad subsidy had been tacked on to the Loan were certainly questionable; even the *Star,* which had so consistently supported the improvements, suggested that the company be investigated by the Legislature and that proper security be given by it to the District government.

The *Patriot* now found itself out on a limb without support from even its Democratic colleagues. On November 20 James G. Berret had severed his connection with the paper, and the administration was placed in the hands of a committee composed of prominent Democrats: Col. W. H. Philip, J. C. McGuire and R. T. Merrick. A. G. Allen was made Editor-in-Chief, and Louis Bagger, a young Dane who had worked on *Le Gaulois* of Paris, made City Editor. On the 23rd the new editor found himself obliged to refute charges that the *Patriot* had become financially embarrassed which had been rumored after the interest of William M. Tweed in the newspaper had become known. Tweed's stock was purchased by W. W. Corcoran after the "Boss" had fallen from power in New York, but the publicity, coming at this time, must undoubtedly have caused a shock to the respectable subscribers to the *Patriot.* Such a revelation confirmed many citizens in their belief that the District government was being attacked in order to embarrass the national Administration, and that the opponents of the Board of Public Works were themselves in very questionable company.

The *Patriot's* new editor promptly launched a series of election post-mortems, claiming that the results indicated corruption and the ignorance of the colored voters. The vote in favor of the Loan Bill was broken down:

Colored voters	7,302
Imported farm hands	3,000
Editors and parasites	50
White laborers of the Board of Public Works	2,000
Corporation officers and hangers-on	600
Contractors	100
Murder Bay thieves and pickpockets	200
Sneaks and time-serving cowards	950
Merchants and speculators who expect immediate advantage from the Loan	117
	14,319
Taxpayers, honest men of all shades, colors and nationalities, who cannot be bought, duped or frightened into support of the Ring who registered and voted, registered and didn't vote, and who didn't register or vote at all.	14,681
Total voting population of the District, including 3,000 farm hands imported	29,000
Majority of our voting population against the loan, which comprises 9/10 of our taxpayers, after deducting from the other side 3,000 farm hands from Virginia	3,362

Such highly imaginative statistics were not endorsed by the *Patriot's* Democratic contemporary, the *Georgetown Courier,* which commented the same day, November 25, "As Democrats we cannot but deplore the utterly absurd course which the self-constituted leaders of the opposition saw fit to pursue. The grand work upon which the District Government so laudably entered need not have been made a party issue, because we all along have held that there was no need for it . . . Talk not of colonizing colored men to influence the election or ascribing to anything but 'the logic of events.' The result as demonstrated in the Third District, the Sevastopol of Democracy, and the 13th District, always strongly Democratic, where Mr. Harkness, a well-known opponent of improvements, was defeated by the decisive majority of 324 votes."[7]

In his message to the new Legislature Governor Cooke dealt at some length with District finances. He suggested that the $500,000 which had been appropriated as a temporary loan should be returned out of the $4,000,000 to reimburse the District Treasury, and announced the appointment of a Board of Commissioners to create a Sinking Fund for the old Corporation debts, consisting of W. W. Corcoran, H. M. Sweeny, Moses Kelly and Lewis J. Davis. He urged that the laws of the District, which had never been codified, should be put into a unified form at an early date.

The cold weather now set in before the long-delayed improvements could be effectively resumed. The *Patriot* bitterly complained[8] that "Three quarters of the streets are torn up and will not permit of travel. Mudholes and mantraps, dangerous alike by day and by night, swarm in all directions as thick as the leaves of Vallombrosa, a putrid stench comes from all sections of the city, offensive to the sense and dangerous to the public health. Idle and poaching colored men imported from the neighboring states for political purposes are being paid with the people's money. The streets have been converted into workshops, for on many of the most travelled mammoth saw mills and tar-boiling establishments are to be seen in prominent conspicuousness." Carl Benson, a Washingtonian who had witnessed the large-scale improvements of Paris under Baron Haussmann, complained in a letter to the same paper that the work, instead of being confined to one area as in France, was pursued in all portions of the city. This state of affairs, so exasperating to the citizens of Washington, was a result of the regulations of the Board of Public Works. Once a contract had been given by the Board the contractor felt obliged to stake his claim by immediately tearing up the street, even though he knew that he would be unable to complete the work for several months.

On January 23, 1872, the delegation chosen by the Citizens Committee presented to Congress a memorial signed by a thousand property owners in the District asking for an investigation into the activities of the Board of Public Works. The memorial dwelt on the extravagance of the new government and in particular on the expense of advertising the special election. The House District Committee, impressed by the charges, decided to hold a full-scale investigation beginning on February 1.

General Chipman had meanwhile made his first speech as District delegate, an eloquent appeal on behalf of the public schools of the Territory. Pointing out that Congress had not appropriated an acre of public land for the District schools, he asked that 2,000,000 acres be given for a permanent school fund and 500,000 to be used as a source of building income. Of the school age population in the District between six and seventeen only 7,719 of the white children out of 21,177 were provided for and 4,615 of the colored children out of 10,494. Even allowing for the considerable number of white children attending private schools, it was evident that only half of the children of the District were being given public education. Mr. Ritchie, a Maryland Democrat, tried to pin him down to an opinion on Sumner's Civil Rights Bill, which provided for a single school system for children of both races. The Delegate refused, however, to become involved in this controversial issue, though admitting that he would vote for the Bill if he should be able.

As for the colored people who had come to the District during the War he said, "These people cannot leave us nor would we have them. They are industrious, frugal, law-abiding, good citizens, but they came among us, many of them in a condition of illiteracy and poverty which had been enforced upon them by the nature of our laws, and being directly responsible for their condition as the general government is, it is plainly its duty to make provision for their education."

General Chipman further pointed out that since the establishment of the Internal Revenue Board the District had paid to the Treasury of the United States the sum of $4,434,695.80, compared with taxes collected from the other ten Territories of only $3,252,675.51. Congress, however, had allotted 35,000,000 acres of public land for the endowment of public schools in these Territories, while the District had received nothing.

The Chairman of the Committee investigating the conduct of the District administration, Representative H. H. Starkweather, of Connecticut, was a Republican in complete sympathy with the party. He was also a friend of the Washington banker, W. S. Huntington, who had advanced to him considerable sums of money; Huntington was in turn closely linked to the operations of the real estate firm of Kilbourn and Latta and one of the directors of the Metropolitan Paving Company in which Shepherd had been financially interested. The Committee was composed of six Republicans and three Democrats, the most notable of the latter being Representative Eldridge of Wisconsin and Robert B. Roosevelt of New York. Mr. Roosevelt had played an important part in the defeat of the Tweed machine the preceding year, and he was inclined to look upon the administration of the Board of Public Works as similarly disposed to use public money for personal profit.

The investigation opened with a plea by A. G. Riddle on behalf of the memorialists. He claimed that the plan of the Board was not sufficiently accurate and raised objections to the quality of the work which it had performed. The property owners of the District, he claimed, were not fundamentally opposed to improvements, but they could not tolerate the extravagant and partisan maner in which the Board had operated. In the testimony which followed the situation at the "West End" of Washington, the vicinity of F and G Streets between 17th and 21st northwest, was discussed at length. The charge was made that Shepherd, who owned several houses in this area, was concerned in cutting down the grade of the streets in order to benefit his own property, and that the protests of other property owners in the area, among them Columbus Alexander, had been completely disregarded by the Board. This charge was skilfully answered by the counsel for District government, and the memorialists turned their attention to other matters. Ben E. Green and J. J. Coombes, acting as counsel on their behalf, submitted a list of questions with reference to the expenditures of the Board to be answered by Governor Cooke.

P. H. Reinhardt, the chief clerk of the House of Delegates, appeared before the Committee on January 23, and was questioned regarding the colored vote. He stated that it had become the practice for Republican voters to go to the polls at night in groups and to sleep there until morning, since it would sometimes take a man two hours before he could get to the window at the polling station to deposit his vote. As for "repeaters," he had been told that one colored man whom he saw voting later in the day had previously voted, but could produce no evidence to substantiate this statement.

The charges that voters opposed to the Loan were unable to secure anti-Loan tickets at polling places and of other irregularities was next taken up. John F. Cook appeared on the 27th to deny charges that threats were made by contractors to remove men who voted against the Loan. Another witness, James W. Barker, testified on the same day that he had gone to the office of William A. Cook to procure anti-Loan tickets, which were refused him, but that he secured a pile from a colored man leaving the office. The unsuccessful candidate for the 15th District, Jesse B. Wilson, stated that he had been unable to procure any anti-Loan tickets, and claimed that some of the colored property owners in his district who were against the Loan were accordingly unable to register their vote. John H. Crane, who followed, categorically stated that the Loan Bill had not been carried by a majority of the voters in the District and that many of the old citizens like Mr. Corcoran had not registered[9]. Voting had not taken place on party lines, since many of the contractors who were Democrats had supported the Loan. He believed that editors had been corruptly purchased, even the *Patriot* falling into line after his paper had received the advertising of the District government. There were at least 13,000 men working for the Board, he said—which was approximately the number of the vote in favor of the Loan. Later, under cross-examination by the District counsel, William Chandler, he was more vague concerning the actual numbers on the payroll.

The newspaper editors were next called to the witness stand to explain their relations with the District government. Crosby S. Noyes admitted that Alexander Shepherd owned one-quarter of the *Evening Star* stock. John M. Morris, manager of the *Chronicle,* stated that he had borrowed $4,000 from F. A. Boswell, the Collector of Taxes, to assist in his purchase of the paper from John W. Forney. William Murtagh, the owner of the *National Republican,* testified that Arthur Shepherd, Alexander's brother and newly-elected member of the House of Delegates, was the managing editor of his paper.

On March 2 James G. Berret was called to answer questions regarding the *Patriot.* He admitted that William M. Tweed had been the largest stockholder of the newspaper. Mr. Green, the counsel for the memorialists, had endeavored to pin the blame for the paper's acceptance of District government advertising on Tweed; Berret said, however, that the editor, James Harvey, had undertaken to accept it on Col. Moore's suggestion while he was away in New York. Asked his opinion, as a previous Mayor of Washington, regarding the financial state of the city, he stated that the public debt of the District could be increased up to $10,000,000 without raising taxes by one penny, but only if this amount were judiciously expended. He favored a change to make the Upper House of the Legislature elective, but with the Governor retaining his power of veto.

The testimony of James E. Harvey on March 4 was of particular interest. He had left the *Patriot,* he said, because his health had broken down and for no other reason. While "Boss" Tweed was a majority stockholder, he had never exercised any direct or indirect influence on the paper's control. He did not know what had happened to the Tweed interest, but believed it had been bought either by Col. Philip or by Mr. Corcoran. He attacked the District government, which had been established as non-partisan, and was supposed to obviate the importation of Negroes to override the votes of taxpayers; he claimed that it had shown itself to be exclusively partisan and despotic. Asked by General Chipman for a direct statement regarding the importation of Negro voters, he evaded the question, replying that "they had been driven to the polls in great flocks and had camped there from early morning on election day," but he could not say definitely whether they had been organized and he admitted that they had been well-behaved. Chipman next asked him whether it was not natural that colored men, having been denied their rights for so long, should be zealous to vote at the first few elections. This Harvey freely admitted, adding that "the colored man Gray was a very highly respectable man —even better than some of his associates."

Like his former colleague Berret he was also of the opinion that the District could carry a maximum debt of $10,000,000 "if a scientific plan for improvements drawn up by competent engineers were to be presented. To say, however, that improving a few streets will bring a great influx of population is absurd; the only factors which will bring people to this city are the social and political attractions of the town. Wealth will settle itself gradually around these attractions." He was anxious to abolish the power of the Board of Public Works and in favor of completely ending the Territorial form of government.

Harvey was followed as a witness by N. H. Miller, an Assistant District Attorney for the District government, who also edited a German-language newspaper, the *Täglicher Washingtoner Anzeiger*. He claimed that there were about 15,000 of German descent residing in the District, many of whom were ignorant of English, and that one-third of the taxes of the area were paid by the German population. Captain Albert Grant, he said, had approached him with an offer of $20,000 to buy his paper and turn it into an opposition organ of the District government, which he had refused.[10]

On March 11 Col. W. W. Moore took the stand to testify regarding the extravagance of the Territorial Government. In a letter which the *Patriot* had published on January 30 Moore had previously calculated the total amount spent on government advertising since June 1, 1871 at $113,357.35; this sum did not include the miscellaneous advertising of executive and ministerial offices nor that of the Board of Public Works, the Board of Health, nor the publication of the laws of the Territory estimated at $20,000. The cost of advertising during the special election alone had amounted to more than $10,000. In all the other major cities and Territories of the Union two newspapers were considered sufficient for official advertising. Col. Moore dealt at some length with the general expenses of the Territorial government during its brief existence. Under the Corporation of Washington there had been about 71 salaried officers and 66 officials dependent upon fees. The annual expenses of both city corporations and of the Levy Court amounted in the last year of the old form of government to $423,004. Under the Territory the number of salaried officers had increased to 244, and those dependent on fees to 128, while the cost of the Legislature and all other salaries had risen to $719,813.

On the 12th Governor Cooke appeared to give the information which had been requested by the memorialists regarding the sale of the new District bonds. Not only had these been sold at a satisfactory rate, he stated, but the old Corporation securities had increased in value owing to public confidence in the Territorial government. He regarded the current investigation as extremely damaging to the credit of the District and expressed the hope that it would soon be concluded.

Shepherd, called to the stand the following day, defended some of the expenses of the District government which had been attacked by the memorialists. The City Hall, he said, had but eighteen rooms, of which only eight were habitable, while the Morrison Building, which had been taken over by the Territorial administration, had forty-five. He answered criticism that the members of the Board of Public Works were not financially responsible men, stating that he personally owned property in the District worth $500,000, and that he paid taxes on an assessment of $300,000. His stock in the Metropolitan Paving Company, which had been referred to during the course of the investigation, had been sold as soon as he had been appointed to the Board.[11]

On March 20 Henry Piper, one of the colored members recently elected to the House of Delegates, revealed some interesting facts during the course of his testimony. Standing for the 9th District, in which the white voters had in the April registration outnumbered Negroes by almost 300, he had, as official candidate of the Republican Central Committee, defeated Hallett Kilbourn, an Independent Republican. Both he and Kilbourn had been in favor of the loan. O. S. B. Wall, another colored member elected in the 2nd District, who had likewise received the endorsement of the local Republican Club, had been elected over a white Republican opponent, Joseph T. Hall. In this District also the white voters had been in a majority—786 to 603—in the previous election registration.

As the investigation dragged on and the weather became more favorable for resuming the interrupted work, the supporters of the District government began to agitate for an early close of the proceedings. On March 15 a group of property owners had already sent a memorial to Congress asking that the hearings be concluded, and on April 2 the *Star* reported another request signed by such prominent business men as C. C. Willard, the proprietor of the Ebbitt House, Lansburgh & Co., S. H. Kauffmann, Don Piatt, the editor of the *Capital,* and Kilbourn and Latta. This last firm had reported a few weeks earlier that the number of real estate transfers for the year 1871 had exceeded those of 1870 by twenty per cent, and that the aggregate amount of the transactions which had taken place was $7,447,437 as against $4,927,000.

On April 7 A. B. Mullett took the stand to testify regarding the F Street grades. As Architect of the Treasury as well as of the Board of Public Works, and being engaged upon the construction of the new State, War and Navy Building which adjoined the improvements of the Board on 17th Street, he had been deeply involved. He refused, however, to be pinned down regarding the amount spent on the grading of streets in this locality, and was equally evasive when asked by the counsel for the memorialists to testify about the cost of the sewer system, which critics had complained was amounting to many times the original estimate in the "Comprehensive Plan." Mullett proved to be a difficult witness, and the session while he was on the stand was stormy.

The position of the Board was unequivocally stated by Shepherd, who was recalled on the 10th. "The Board of Public Works," he said, "when they entered on their duties concluded that they had either been created for something or nothing and that if, for anything, it was to devise and carry out as rapidly as possible some system of improvements in order that in this respect the capital of the nation might not remain a quarter of a century behind the times . . ." Speaking of the grading system, on which so much of the fire of the memorialists had been concentrated, he continued: "The streets of Washington up to the time the Board came into power was a combination of bastard grades . . . If one man had a house which happened to be a little above and another a little below the grade, and the two houses were 100 feet apart, the grade was adjusted between the two houses without any regard to the beauty of the streets or to economy in carrying out the system of improvements" He stated that his own houses on F Street had suffered damages to the extent of $7,000 or $8,000 owing to the change of grade—they now had twenty-one steps leading up to them and were the second highest in the neighborhood. He had no doubt that the property assessments would be collected. The city in ten years time would be the most beautiful capital in the world—at least insofar as its streets were concerned—provided that Congress matched the amount spent by the citizens of Washington—four and a half or five millions, he thought, would suffice. He denied that any members of the Board had a financial interest in the improvements, as was alleged in the memorial to Congress. Of the thousand men whose names appeared in the petition 436 paid no tax whatsoever, and the total property taxes paid by the remainder amounted to only four per cent of the entire amount. Referring to the other charges made by the memorialists, he claimed that the Board had had nothing to do with the advertising of the special election, which had been given out by the Governor through his Secretary.

Shepherd had a brief skirmish with John H. Crane, who had asked him the value of the property which he owned. Irritated by the question, which he had answered on a previous occasion, he replied tersely, "I am worth enough not to leave my window open"—an obvious reference to the charges of bribery which had been made against Crane at the time he had been dismissed from his post of sewer inspector by Mayor Bowen in 1869. This remark threw the committee room into an uproar, which rose again when Shepherd was questioned by his enemy and business rival, Captain Albert Grant. Producing a sheaf of figures, Grant asked Shepherd to read his computation of the cost of improvements, which, according to his estimates, was in the vicinity of $26,000,000. He replied, "I do not think that Grant was any more capable of making an estimate than an inmate of Dr. Nichols' institution across the river" (an obvious reference to St. Elizabeth's Hospital). He defended the amount spent on the improvement of the 7th Street Road, for which the original estimate of $25,000 had been revised upward to $165,000. The road, which was the principal highway to Baltimore, ran past his farm, and opponents had been quick to charge that this fact was the principal cause of the large amount devoted to its repair. Shepherd pointed out the value of the road as an artery of trade and the means of transporting Maryland farm produce to the capital. He himself preferred to use the 14th Street approach when visiting his property.[12]

Francis P. Blair, whose home at Silver Spring lay on the 7th Street Road, spoke of the execrable condition of its former surface. He eloquently endorsed the activities of the Board.

"They do honor to the genius and taste of those who designed them to fill up the outline that nature seems to have destined for the site of the capital of our country. The city and its surrounding district will then become one vast amphitheatre, moving by grades from the Potomac to the hills five miles beyond its Northern boundary and 500 feet above the tides. The first terrace arises from the circle of Boundary Street, making that beautiful coronet of wooded heights that crowns the brow and looks down upon the city and the expanse of the river as far as Mount Vernon and Fort Washington."

Anticipating by many years the plans of the National Capital Park and Planning Commission, he spoke of a drive connecting the chain of forts and of a "Grand Park" east of 7th Street. "That enclosed by the military road westward on Rock Creek and smaller tributaries constitutes a park of itself, all wild and picturesque in a most charming woodland scenery. It is filled with precipitous rocky heights, with rapid currents, the rich hillsides rising at successive points covered with lofty trees, with an undergrowth of laurel, redbud and dogwood, all beautiful in their seasons with flowers, the little brooks running from dells opening at intervals, dressed with floral ornaments springing from woodland which would have induced all lovers of parks who have penetrated this wilderness of tangled forest and mazes of streamlets to assign superiority to this region in sight of our capital and pronounce it destined to become the most charming environ of that sort ever presented to a crowded city." In Mr. Blair's opinion the cost of all improvements would be in the vicinity of $30,000,000, but he felt that the increase in the value of the city property and corresponding growth of wealth was justification for this expenditure.[13]

George W. Riggs was called on April 20 to testify regarding the city debt. In his opinion the indebtedness of the District had increased faster than the capacity of the population to absorb it, and taxes in Washington were higher in proportion to the value of property than in any other American city. He declared himself to be in complete favor of a commission form of government for the District and personally wished neither a vote nor a representative in Congress. The majority of voters in the District, he declared, were incapable of self-government. Congress should, in his opinion, place a specific limit upon the amount of money which the present government could borrow. The Territorial government, he said, was too expensive and he should like the District governed the cheapest way, by Congress. He favored a "pay as you go" system; individuals could do work cheaper than a municipal government. He accused no one of fraud, going only so far as to remark, "I think that in the hurry to do work the money was spent rather imprudently."[14]

On May 14th the Investigating Committee issued its report, which, as had been confidently expected, sustained the actions of the Board of Public Works. It admitted that "the Board did make contracts for some improvements not specified in the plan presented to the Legislature and for some of the improvements they expended more than the estimate of the work." "However the Committee are satisfied that the Legislature did not intend to limit the authority of the Board in making improvements to a strict and literal following of the exact plan presented. It had been somewhat hurriedly prepared, and it seemed to be understood that to some extent it was incomplete and the Legislature only intended that the Plan should be the general guide as to the kind and character of the improvements to be made with the money appropriated . . . The appropriations were very loosely made, and it does appear that the Legislature intended to confer the power on the Board to expend money where they deemed expedient. Whether they acted wisely or not, it cannot be said that the Board violated the law in making contracts and improvements which the Legislature had left to their judgment and discretion."

"The Committee," the Report continued, "say that while in all these improvements they find great cause of commendation for the energy and liberality and generous desire to improve and beautify the National Capital on the part of all Departments of the District Government, they also find the ordinary and usual errors attendant upon the establishment of a new system of government. There was inexperience on the part of many; there was the lack of careful and cool legislation. In the anxiety to redeem the city from the charge of being behind in its new streets and public institutions other cities in the country, the authorities had become somewhat intoxicated with the spirit of improvement.

"The Committee are disposed to think that more work of improvement was undertaken at once than was wise, though the delays caused by the injunction and the suspension of work by the unusually early winter makes it impossible to say whether all the work begun could have been completed if these drawbacks had not existed. The Committee are also prepared to believe that all the District authorities at the outset were not sufficiently mindful of the small extent of their official jurisdiction and the slender constituency upon which all the public burdens were to rest, and that therefore sufficient care was not taken to have rigid economy prevail in every department and no unnecessary drafts made upon their small treasury."

The Report concluded by clearing all the individual members of the Board of charges of personal profit from the improvements, and by patting them on the back. "The Governor and members of the Board are, on the whole, to be commended for the zeal, energy and wisdom with which they have started the District upon a new career of improvement and prosperity; and the District itself is entitled to fair and generous appropriations from Congress in some manner corresponding to the valuation of property owned by the United States."[15]

Robert B. Roosevelt and John M. Crebs, both Democrats, signed a minority report. The expenses incurred by the Board over the original estimates were particularly stressed: for example, the 7th Street Road, which had already cost $95,000 and would require an additional $70,000 to complete, making a total expenditure of $165,000 as against $25,000 according to the Board's first figures. The grading of the "West End" for which an original appropriation of $91,000 had been requested, would when complete cost more than $200,000 in excess of this figure. The expenses of the District government, the report pointed out, were more than the contingent expenses of any state of the Union, and the special election was both unjustified and needlessly costly. The minority report concluded with a resolution to make all offices in the District government elective except that of Governor. Members of the Board of Public Works should be required to give their bond and security for the faithful performance of their duties, and they should be placed directly under legislative control. The Board should be prohibited from making payments from the District treasury; such payments should in future be made by warrants and an exact quarterly statement of all such expenditures should be made to the District Treasurer, giving the name of the person to whom payment was made and for what specific purpose. The tone of the report was not hostile, and though its recommendations were never even seriously considered by the leaders of the District government, the suggestions which it embodied would have well merited some earnest thought. Had they been put into practice, the entire future of the Territorial administration would have been vastly different.[16]

Two weeks after the publication of the Report, Mr. Corcoran, who had been absent for several months in Europe, returned in the company of his daughter, Mrs. Eustis, and three grandchildren. A delegation from Washington, including Richard Wallach, Dr. John Blake and W. B. Todd, met him at his hotel in New York. The former mayor offered a welcoming speech, saying that he and his friends had come to express in person "the admiration of those virtues which have made a fellow citizen so conspicuous, and their admiration for that active benevolence which, having made the meridian of your life resplendent, will continue to spread its lustre on your lengthened days and cause them ever to hold you in grateful remembrance." The aged millionaire, now 74, whose eyesight was failing rapidly, sat back on the sofa, overcome with emotion, his head leaning on his hands. A short time previously his last public charity—the

Louise Home established as a "haven and resting place for elderly ladies of gentle birth who by adversity are obliged to find some help for a decent and accustomed support"—had been opened at 15th Street and Massachusetts Avenue at the cost of $200,000.[17]

The Washington delegation, however, was less concerned with Mr. Corcoran's charities than with maintaining his support in their struggle against the Board of Public Works. Its members recalled his invitation by Governor Cooke and Shepherd to a public banquet the previous year, and they were desperately anxious that he should not desert them at this crucial stage. Time was to show that despite his years and infirmities the old gentleman would yet play an important part in the history of the District government.

Chapter 7

"Our Little Monarchy"

At the conclusion of the House Investigation in the Spring of 1872 Shepherd had every reason for confidence. He had been personally vindicated and the actions of the Board of Public Works had generally been approved. Within a few months the presidential elections would be held, and there was every likelihood that Grant would be re-elected. With another four years of Republican administration to look forward to, during which time he could always rely upon the active support of the President, the outcries of the "old fogies" could be disregarded. As the special elections had showed the previous November, the great majority of Washington citizens was solidly behind him.

Though Shepherd had little time to attend to his gasfitting business, his own affairs were prospering. He had extended the scope of his real estate interests and was putting up more houses for public sale. In 1872 his new home at the Northeast corner of Connecticut Avenue and K Street was completed, and he moved in with his young wife and already large family. The blue-stone mansion was in the most modern style. It boasted a mansard roof, a huge porte-cochère and bay windows looking over Farragut Square. Its vast drawing-room with mirrors and blue satin curtains was designed for large-scale entertaining. The "breakfast room" was carpeted in deep red velvet and illuminated by elegant crystal chandeliers. The house contained an art gallery, and in the basement was a billiard room and Shepherd's private offices. During the summer the family would move out to "Bleak House," six miles out on the 7th Street Road. The 300-acre farm had its own fishpond, barns and stables, ponies for the children to ride, a large orchard with woodland running back as far as Rock Creek. His was indeed a happy family, and there was nothing lacking to make the life of his children an idyllic one.

Yet a man of a less confident and buoyant nature than Shepherd's could have detected a few clouds in the bright firmament. The Investigating Committee, though it had exonerated the Board of the principal charges brought against it by the memorialists, had nevertheless administered some definite rebukes for its lack of economy. Congress had also shortly before the publication of the Report set a limit of $10,000,000 upon the amount which the District government could borrow—including in this figure the old Corporation debts of Washington, Georgetown and the County. Since all but $500,000 of the $4,000,000 loan had already been spent, there was left only a margin of $1,000,000 for further borrowings.[1] Even among the ranks of the District Republicans there was growing concern regarding the plans of the Board. In July, meetings were held at which protests against the "dictatorship" of the District government were made by N. G. Ordway, F. A. Boswell and J. W. LeBarnes as well as by prominent Negroes, Dr. J. L. N. Bowen, E. S. Atkinson and Dr. C. B. Purvis. John Gray, the colored member of the Legislative Council, proposed a scheme to protect the small property owners against the confiscation of their property through the heavy special assessments for improvements levied by the Board. Under this scheme the time limit for payment would have been extended and certificates bearing ten per cent interest would be placed on public sale. J. J. Coombes, one of the counsel for the memorialists who had previously helped to draw up the Territorial Bill of 1870, endorsed Gray's plan in a speech on August 18.

But the improvements continued at an ever-increasing speed:

> It was a daily occurrence for citizens to leave their houses as usual in the morning and when they returned in the

evening the sidewalks and curbs which not infrequently had been but recently laid down at their own expense all torn up and carted away . . . The established grades of the streets were changed, some filled up and others cut down, leaving houses perched up on banks twenty feet above the street, while others were covered nearly to the roof. Not infrequently buildings had their foundations so injured that they were in danger of falling and then the owners were notified that they must render them safe within thirty days or they would be pulled down at their expense.[2]

The contractors displayed remarkable callousness towards the feelings of the property owners, as a reporter from the *Patriot* discovered in a conversation with one of the foremen:[3]

Reporter: Why is it that the streets are torn up during the entire length of the contract and then left exposed before they are again touched by the workmen?

Contractor: Well, we get a contract, and as long as we don't violate it the Board does not care how we perform the work.

Reporter: But doesn't the Board know and don't you know that such a system interferes with the health and convenience of citizens?

Contractor: What have I to do with the citizens? I took this contract to make money. Mr. Shepherd told me to do my work as I pleased under the contract and not mind the grumbling of obstructionists. He had to stand the same thing, and he could show them he could defy and beat them.

Reporter: You say you had to do this to make money. Why so?

Contractor: Well, suppose I have the contract for a street to grade and pave. I have horses and carts which are idle, and costing me a large sum every day without any return. I take those horses and carts and tear up the pavement and cart it away, and then let it lay until I can get hold of the material for grading and gravelling. I may perhaps get another contract before the job is finished and thus the horses will be employed and not eating their heads off. And again, I want to keep ahead of my workmen.

Reporter: But don't you think a contractor could do as well by keeping a short distance ahead of his workmen, thus finishing one street at a time and affording no obstruction to travel?

Contractor: Certainly, but he would not make so much money, as I have said before.

Another cause of public dissatisfaction with the Board was due to its supposed favoritism. When Massachusetts Avenue was graded, a deep cut was made between Thomas and Scott Circles, leaving the houses of Senator Edmunds of Vermont and Senator Bayard of Delaware high up on the edge of a great gulf. The Senators estimated that their properties had been damaged to the extent of $2,500 and $3,000 respectively, but settled by accepting a receipted tax bill for $400 on account of the special assessments. Other citizens without political influence, however, were not so fortunate, and the newspapers were daily filled with announcements of the sale of property for the assessment values. Though the tax rate had not been increased, the assessed valuations of District property had gone up from $68,650,000 in 1871 to $74,969,000 in 1872, not all of which was accounted for by new construction. The increased assessments caused considerable resentment, particularly in the Southeast section of the city, residents from which sent a delegation to protest to the Board. The rumors of collusion between Shepherd and the "Real Estate Pool" headed by Kilbourn and Latta were widespread; opponents of the Board stated outright that when it became known that a certain area was to be improved Shepherd and his friends at once secured all available lots in the neighborhood. Property in the vicinity of Connecticut Avenue doubled and quadrupled in value, while in the Eastern part of the city which was the last to be improved, property stood still or actually depreciated.

At the end of August the Board was again faced with an injunction—this time from the Washington and Georgetown Railroad, which operated horse-car service between the two cities. The Board had torn up the tracks, claiming that they had not been laid with stone pavement as had been specified, but only with wood. The counsel for the Railroad maintained that the cost of paving the area inside the tracks with stone as requested by the Board would amount to an additional expense of $100,000. Judge Humphreys in the Equity Court granted the injunction against the Board, stating that it lacked the legislative powers to interfere in the matter.

A few days later Shepherd pulled off his most sensational coup. The Northern Liberties Market at 7th and K Streets North West had long been an eyesore. Rows of filthy stalls and sheds sprawled in the heart of the city, making impossible any real improvement of the area. The Board had sent, two weeks previously, a notice to the market men requesting them to move to temporary structures which had been erected on a site at 7th and O Streets which had been purchased a short time before from Mr. Corcoran. They took no notice of the request, however, preparing to file an injunction.

Shepherd, hearing of their intentions, took the precaution of inviting to dinner at his house in the country the only member of the District Supreme Court who had not left the city on vacation, Justice Olin. At eight o'clock on the evening of September 3, while the market men were arranging their stores in preparation for the weekly market the following day, a gang of workmen in the employ of the Board suddenly appeared and began to demolish the stalls over their heads. John Widmeyer, a well-known butcher, and Millard Bates, the young son of a former Justice, who was out with his terrier dog chasing the rats and mice from the demolished stalls, were both killed by the collapse of rubble. Thieves promptly appeared on the scene, and many merchants lost the greater part of their possessions. At the inquest which followed, Coroner Patterson castigated the Board for not having given public notice of the market removal. A cortège half a mile long followed Widmeyer's coffin at his funeral, and the feeling against Shepherd became so intense that on his return home from the Washington Club he was reported to have asked for police protection.[4]

This episode brought to a head the long-smouldering hatred of Shepherd on the part of the Washington Democrats. On August 14, the *Patriot* at the suggestion of William Merrick had printed a particularly violent diatribe against the Board of Public Works, accusing it of sending 900 Negroes to vote in the North Carolina elections. "The District . . . has been robbed by a Ring of rogues who, having sown the wind, shall reap the whirlwind," stated the editorial.

> After oppressing our people with a low and hated despotism, which has no parallel outside of South Carolina, either for disgusting vulgarity or plundering propensity, it now seeks to introduce these atrocious practices into other states and to determine their political character by an exploitation of the desperate hirelings who have ruled at our local elections under the training of the Board of Public Works.

Shepherd was stung into writing a reply to the charges, claiming that the story was an unqualified lie and asking that the statements be retracted. No such retraction was printed, but Shepherd received instead a letter from Louis Bagger, the assistant Editor, stating that "the controversy had assumed a form that makes it desirable that this discussion be brought to a close," and suggesting that the two parties meet in Baltimore at the Eutaw House "where the subject may be considered more at ease." Believing the letter to be a challenge to a duel, a common practice among French journalists when the question of "honor" was at stake, Shepherd sent a copy of the letter to the trustees of the *Patriot* and took no further action. The fiery Dane waited for him in vain at the Eutaw House, having, according to one newspaper account, borrowed the clothes of the proprietor's daughter to ensure his disguise.[5]

The 1872 Presidential campaign was by this time in full swing. Grant's re-election was opposed by Horace Greeley, editor of the *New York Tribune,* who had been nominated by a group of so-called "Liberal Republicans," composed of newspaper editors and men at odds with the Administration. Greeley had also been endorsed by the Democrats who, realizing the weakness of their own organization, considered that they might have a better chance of winning on a Fusion ticket. Though Greeley had been previously an ardent Abolitionist, he had led a peace movement in 1864 and after the War stood bail for Jefferson Davis. Some of the colored men in Washington, who were perplexed how to vote, addressed themselves to Charles Sumner, upon whose advice they had greatly depended in the past. On July 29, Sumner replied in a long letter, referred to by Benjamin Butler as his "Epistle to the Ethiopians."[6] Sumner had for the past year violently opposed Grant's program to annex San Domingo to the United States, and his letter constituted his final break with the Administration. He pointed out that Grant had voted for the Democrats in 1856, while Greeley had upheld the Republican Party, that Greeley had consistently been in favor of Negro suffrage, and that for these reasons and on account of his superior moral character, he "was the surest trust of the colored people." The Administration, alarmed at the possibility of defections from the Republican ranks in the South, attempted to rally the Negro vote by sending down two of the most able colored orators, Frederick Douglass and John M. Langston, to stump the Southern states for Grant.

The annual elections in the District, which began in September, reflected the issues of the national campaign. On September 30, Delegate Chipman addressed a meeting at the Columbian Law School and spent much of his speech on Greeley's opposition to the improvement of the District. Under Grant, he pointed out, the national capital had received appropriations for the past fiscal year amounting to $2,730,507 more than had been received in the past, and there was reason to expect even larger appropriations in the year to come. Greeley, on the other hand, had supported a proposal to remove the capital to the West in 1871, and had even considered that New York would be a more fitting location than Washington. If he were to be elected, the District could not expect to receive any large appropriations from the Federal Government.

A few of the local Republicans, however, decided to join the Greeley ranks. Sayles J. Bowen, who had been a delegate to the Cincinnati Convention the preceding April which had nominated Greeley, led the movement, and a few colored men followed Sumner's advice to support the Liberal Republican candidate. George Hatton and J. W. Green both endorsed the Greeley platform at a meeting of the ultra-Conservative Jackson Democratic Association. In spite of the national election, however, popular interest in the District election was less than in 1871. Registration of white voters decreased from 17,746 to 13,793 and that of the colored voters from 10,734 to 8,532. The elections held on October 8 resulted in the victory of Chipman over C. H. Hine, a Conservative supported by the Liberal Republicans, by 12,793 votes to 7,155. Among the nineteen Republicans elected to the House of Delegates the two colored men who represented the County districts, Solomon C. Brown and O. S. B. Wall, were again returned. Three other Negroes: Thomas W. Chase, a contractor, J. W. Taliaferro, an employee of the Library of Congress, and Sidney W. Herbert, a doorkeeper, were also elected. The *Chronicle* attributed the falling off of votes to the government clerks, some of whom were under the impression that they would lose the right to vote for President in their home states by participating in the District election. The editor pointed out that such authorities as Daniel Webster and Caleb Cushing had held, however, that in the past clerks who lived in Washington with their families and voted in the District were still qualified to exercise their right of suffrage in state presidential elections.[7]

The national campaign resulted in a sweeping victory for Grant and the Republican Party in November. The Fusion candidate received only 2,834,000 popular votes to Grant's 3,597,000, and in only six states were the Greeley supporters successful. In the new House and Senate the Republicans regained their two-thirds majority lost in 1870. The election results proved how weak the Democratic party machine was, after twelve years of defeat, and how effectively the "bloody shirt" of sectional antagonism could still be used. The Negro vote had been almost solidly for Grant, in spite of Sumner's advice.

On November 11, the *Patriot,* which had staked its hopes on the national election, abandoned the fight. Its valedictory editorial remarked:

> After two years of earnest effort to establish a Democratic journal upon a solid basis at the capital . . . we are pained to confess that the experiment has failed to realize our hopes. In undertaking this responsible work the original founders were aware of the serious difficulties which beset their path and that a permanent success depended mainly upon a change in the National Administration . . . We were defeated, and political disaster brings in its trail material disappointment. Considering the limited population and lack of commerce, the scale upon which the *Patriot* started out was too large and costly for the needs of the city. Moreover, it had to contend with the active hostility of the Administration and the District government.

With the demise of the *Patriot* the opposition press of New York and Baltimore took up the battle. On October 9, the *New York World* delivered a blistering attack upon the District government and Shepherd:

> Not belonging to the privileged class called "gentlemen" in the South . . . he labors under great social disadvantages . . . From a day laborer he has reached the high financial eminence of a millionaire. He lives in luxury, wining and dining Judges, Senators, Representatives and

state officials, and drives one of the finest turn-outs to be seen on the Avenue with liveried footmen and coachmen . . . His entertainments last winter were the most extravagant and expensive ever given in the city.

The paper went on to attack other members of the Board of Public Works. Mullett was excitable and "had no regard for the common man"; Magruder was "an old woman who gives no trouble"; S. P. Brown a real estate dealer with financial delinquencies. The *New York Sun* wrote on November 20:

> This Territorial government of ours is absolutely bankrupt in money, credit and character. They have squandered and stolen the $4,000,000 Loan which the Negroes voted, all the revenue extorted from the special taxes for pretended improvements, two millions of regular receipts from taxation and are $3,000,000 in debt—all within 12 months. There is nothing to show but the sudden wealth of the Ring, gorgeous and vulgar display by its favorites and ostentatious roguery dressed in the loudest and latest style.

The $100,000 which had been voted at a special session of the Legislature for the relief of victims of the Chicago Fire in October had even been misappropriated, the *World* stated. The Relief Committee had succeeded in getting $70,000 in installments after much delay, the remaining $30,000 had to be obtained by the sale of District bonds, kept a dark secret so as not to injure the credit of the Territorial government.

The Conservative Republican weekly, the *Nation,* devoted considerable space on November 21 to the District, under the heading, "A New Experiment in City Government." "It was an absurd fancy," the article stated,

> To create a Territory out of an area with a population less than half that of Brooklyn . . . The system of checks and balances under which the District government operated sounded well on paper; the Board of Public Works, being selected by the President, was too remote from the Legislature to allow the idea of collusion between them. Never-

theless, the debt of $13,000,000 with special assessments of $2-3,000,000 more, gave rise to serious doubts regarding the government's extravagance. The explanation was clearly that taxes in Washington, as in New York, were imposed by those who do not pay them.

"It seems a difficult lesson to learn," concluded the article,

> that city corporations of the present day are simply corporate bodies for the management of certain public property and should be controlled by the responsible and not the irresponsible part of the community. (When to this lesson is added a due appreciation of the fact that we cannot expect any high standard of virtue in public office until society exacts it, and that the blessings of free government do not come from written recipes but from actual performance in the duties of citizenship, we may hope for better things.) In the meantime we may profitably watch how far the feelings and convenience and interests of a city government may be outraged under the official eye of the President and within the legislative hearing of Congress.

On November 10 Justice MacArthur in the District Supreme Court dissolved the injunction which Judge Humphreys had granted in the Court of Equity to property-holders of 7th Street Southwest. Under the judgment of the lower Court the Board had been ordered to put back into the public treasury the amounts received from the taxpayers of the area in special assessments until the case had been settled. When this decision had been handed down in the lower Court the *Patriot* had pointed out that Judge Humphreys' decision had established four important principles:

1. The court of Equity has jurisdiction and can provide a remedy against abuses.
2. The Board of Public Works, as trustees for the public, can be called to account in a Court of Equity.
3. The Board and its contractors under them can be held to answer charges of collusion and other corrupt practices.

4. The so-called office of Treasurer to the Board of Public Works is illegal and the District Treasurer the only recognized guardian of public monies.

The decision of Justice MacArthur dashed once more the hopes of Shepherd's enemies and still further strengthened his determination to brook no further delay in his plans. He had given notice on the 8th to the Alexandria and Washington Railroad to remove its tracks along Maryland Avenue, Southwest, which passed directly across the principal approach to the Capitol and which had been a source of great inconvenience to the public.

> Time and time again the members of Congress and strangers to and from the capital have been compelled to make a detour of half a dozen squares to get past the trains laden with bleating calves, and bellowing steers and grunting porkers which obstructed the Avenue and streets leading from the Avenue to the Baltimore and Ohio Depot.[8]

As the Company paid no attention to the notice, a force of two hundred laborers was dispatched by the Board of Public Works on the night of November 18 to tear out the tracks along the entire course of the proposed improvements. On this occasion, however, the feelings of the public were completely in sympathy with the action of the Board, and the Railroad made no attempt to replace the tracks.

On December 2 the first annual report of the Board of Public Works reviewed the progress which had been made during the preceding year. It endeavored to account for the unexpectedly heavy expense of the improvements by comparing the street areas of Washington with those of other American and European cities. In Washington, it stated, the area of the city occupied by streets and avenues was 54.5 per cent of the total, compared with 35.3 per cent in New York, 26.7 in Boston, 29 in Philadelphia, 25.8 in Paris and 26.4 in Berlin. Summing up the achievements of the past year, the Report claimed that the system of fixed prices was working most satisfactorily, and that it had proved the most economical and efficient means of carrying out public works. "No one investigating the subject honestly and impartially will fail to acknowledge that in no instance has so much been accomplished in so short a period and at a cost so reasonable . . . The Board had to supply the omissions of the past, to meet the demands of the present and to provide, so far as they could anticipate them, for the wants of the future. Perhaps in the opinion of some who have not given the subject thorough attention they have undertaken too much. They fail, however, to see how they could have been justified in attempting less."[9] According to the figures of the Board's treasurer, the balance in its favor stood at $162,252.25, and the amount due from the Federal Government for the work performed adjacent to its property was $1,240,920.92.

In the number of miles of first-class pavement the District was now largely in advance, the Report claimed, of any other American city. The printed map showed the extent of paving which had already been completed: all streets in the vicinity of the White House had been paved in concrete, as well as Connecticut Avenue as far as N Street, and Massachusetts Avenue between 14th Street and Dupont Circle. Wood pavements had been laid down on East Capitol Street and in Georgetown. A new bridge had been built across Rock Creek at P Street, and the wooden bridge on M Street replaced by a sturdy iron structure. The Water Register reported that Tiber Creek had been converted into a sewer 24-30 feet wide, and that Slash Run, a natural water course, had been made into a sewer so large that "a buggy can be driven through it with ease." Washington could now boast of a water supply of 127 gallons annually per capita, compared with 100 in New York, 28 in Paris and 27 in London. Mr. Saunders of the Parking Commission referred to the trees which had been selected to line the avenues, of which the silver maple, linden and elm possessed the "compact stateliness, symmetry of growth and ample supply of expansive foliage" required to adorn the city streets. Adolph Cluss, Architect to the Board, discussed the advantages of the new building code, which provided for more adequate inspection of new buildings.

In President Grant's annual message to Congress on December 3 his reference to the District government was especially favorable:

> Since the establishment of a Territorial government for the District of Columbia the improvement of the condition of the city and surroundings and the increased prosperity of the citizens are observable to the most casual visitor. The nation, being a large owner of property in the city, should bear with the citizens of the District its just share of the expense of these improvements.
>
> I recommend, therefore, an appropriation to reimburse the citizens for the work done by them along and in front of public buildings during the past year and liberal appropriations in order that the improvements and embellishments of the public buildings and grounds may keep pace with the improvements made by the Territorial authorities.[10]

On December 20 the House issued a second report on the District government which had been made after a brief investigation in which the Territorial authorities were again commended.[11] Satisfied that all was in good order, Congress passed on January 8 an appropriation of $1,250,000 in part payment of the improvements made by the Board of Public Works adjoining the property of the Federal government. The size of this appropriation exceeded any single sum which the District had received at any time for such a purpose. The members of the Board could at least feel that Congress was beginning to accept the theory that the Federal government should make a proportionate contribution to the finances of the national capital. The appropriation also reflected the loyalty of the new Congress, in which the Republicans had regained their two-thirds majority, towards President Grant, who had personally associated himself with Cooke and Shepherd in their undertakings.

Kilbourn and Latta a few days later published their annual account of property transfers during the previous year in the

District. Seven hundred and one brick and 615 frame buildings had been erected during 1872 and the valuations of real estate had gone up by $8,209,250.

> A large portion of the real property which changed hands during the past year [the report stated] was purchased by new residents, persons of wealth attracted here from all sections of the Union by the comprehensive plans of improvements by which Washington was being redeemed from the accumulated filth of long years of stupidity and slothfulness and began to assume some of the essential features of a modern civilization.[12]

The memorialists, powerless in the legislature and in Congress and without a single daily paper in the District to support them, endeavored to maintain the battle by means of pamphlets. John H. Crane issued two broadsides accusing Shepherd of turning the improvements to his personal advantage[13], and J. J. Coombes published his "Address on District Affairs" delivered before the November elections.

Francis Colburn Adams, a local hack writer, published still another pamphlet entitled "Our Little Monarchy—Who Runs it and What it Costs." "I propose to prove," the author stated, "that we have here in Washington the worst government the world ever saw . . . It is a selfish, personal and irresponsible government, the highest object of which . . . is to steal from the rich and oppress the poor." The author expatiated on the high salaries of the Territorial officers, the printing bills, and the cost of renovating the offices of the Board of Public Works and the Legislature. "For cheap pomp and circumstance our Territorial government, so called, could beat Haiti." The Board had a "Grand Bureau of Contracts" headed by a colonel and a "Grand Bureau of Picks and Shovels" with a major as chief; the "Bureau of Gas Pipes and Water Closets" was in charge of another colonel, while General Balloch headed the "Bureau of Streets and Highways." J. T. Johnson, the colored barber and oyster-monger at the Capitol, had been made Treasurer to the

Board of Public Works. Adams aired the charges that the West End improvements had benefitted only Shepherd's own houses and accused him of acquiring the "skating-rink" property by sending gangs of laborers to begin working in its vicinity and subsequently purchasing it for one-third of its value. As for the Legislative Council:

> Though monarchical in spirit, it bears no resemblance to the House of Lords. I say this because one of its members invariably spells "Jesus" with a small 'j' and another signs his name with an "X". We call this a Territorial government. It is nothing of the kind. It is simply an old-fashioned British colonial government, with the very worst features of that kind of government retained . . . And yet President Grant looks on with indifference, smokes his cigar and caresses his dogs. The people have looked to him in vain for redress; they must suffer on to the end.

Robert B. Roosevelt, the Democratic congressman from New York who had signed the Minority Report of the House Investigating Committee in 1872, had become the chief spokesman for the opposition in Congress. On May 17, 1872, he attacked the figures given by the Board of Public Works for improvements done adjoining Federal property, claiming that the measurements of the Board Surveyor, which had been passed by General Babcock, were fraudulent, and that the Federal government was being grossly overcharged. The administrative expenses of the District, he claimed, were out of all proportion to so small an area. The salaries paid to executive officers, according to his figures, were twice those of the state of Massachusetts, and even greater than those in New York. The District's bill for printing and advertising was as great as that of New York and three times that of Illinois. Roosevelt claimed that since the publication of the Report of the Investigating Committee many residents had come to him privately, "Republicans as well as Democrats, not whites alone, but very often Negroes, especially men of no great wealth who see the certainty of the property they have accumulated passing out of their hands into the hands of this grasping Board of Public Works."[14] Roosevelt, who had been one of the leaders of the Citizens Committee in New York City, which had ousted the infamous "Boss" Tweed from City Hall, was plainly convinced that Shepherd was a similar type of individual, and that he and his friends were making huge profits out of the improvements in the District.

During the debate on the reorganization of the colored schools in the District on January 24, 1873, Roosevelt again attacked the District government. On February 11, shortly before the adjournment of Congress, he made his last and bitterest onslaught on the Board, whose operations he compared to Milton's description of Satan and his followers. "At one time they are large enough to fill half of heaven, and the next time they shrink so they can crowd on the dry part, the terra firma of Hell. When they want to get as much as possible from us, they present their operations in one way; when they want to extract a little more from the people, they put them in a very different one."[15] The total cost of improvement in the District would amount, he estimated, to between $19,000,000 and $20,000,000, more than twice the amount stated by the Board, and he claimed that residents of the District would be saddled with this huge debt.[16]

Roosevelt's statements in Congress and his interviews published in the *Patriot* roused the supporters of the District government to vitriolic abuse. The correspondent of the *Star* could find only the lowest motive for the New York representative's antagonism: it was due to his disappointment at the insignificant position given by the Board of Public Works to one of his constituents. Delegate Chipman, replying to Roosevelt's attacks on the floor of the House, remarked:

> He will long be remembered at the nation's capital as having achieved the doubtful distinction of friend and counselor to the most uncanny lot of chronic grumblers, fogies and characterless people that ever hung on the skirts of enterprise or laid in wait to retard the progress of a community.

Later at the close of the session, when the memorialists had presented Mr. Roosevelt with a gold-headed cane for his efforts "to secure honest government in the District of Columbia," the *Star* was spiteful enough to remark:

> The citizens of Washington feel that Roosevelt richly deserves a caning for his efforts to defeat District appropriations, but it certainly never entered their heads to give him a cane . . . It is pretty evident that Mr. Roosevelt bought and paid for the cane himself, paid for the inscription on it and paid for the notice in the New York papers, all of which was the handsome and proper thing for a man of his wealth.[17]

On March 3 Congress made still another large appropriation—this time of $2,000,000 for its share of the District improvements. The total for the year was now three and a quarter million dollars, and the Board of Public Works had been handsomely reimbursed for its outlays. The generosity of Congress had, however, unexpected consequences. Many of the hard-pressed property owners delayed the payment of their special assessments in the hope that still further appropriations would be made by the Federal government to the District treasury. Moreover, the large contributions made by Congress increased the stake of the entire nation in the District of Columbia. From now on the taxpayers of the United States were to consider the District budget and administration as no mere local question, but one which directly involved their contributions in taxes to the Federal government.

By 1873 the Territorial administration was beginning to feel the pinch and to explore every possible means of increasing its revenue. The cost was now clearly greater than the highest estimates of the Board, but Shepherd still hoped that by some miracle the budget could be balanced. The burden upon the smaller property owners was becoming so great that on February 21 General Chipman had introduced a Bill in the House providing for an extension of payment of special assessments in four

Vol. XVIII.—No. 916.] NEW YORK, SATURDAY, JULY 18, 1874. [WITH A SUPPLEMENT. PRICE TEN CENTS

"Don't let us have any more of this nonsense. It is a good trait to stand by one's friends; but—"

Ex-Governor Shepherd's Row

Grant Row, Capitol Hill

Hon. Joseph H. Rainey, S. C.

Residence of Gen. Grant on I Street between 1st and 2nd Sts., N. W.

Old "National Intelligencer" Building. Corner of 7th & D Sts., Washington, D.C.

President U. S. Grant and family group at New Jersey summer resort.

Col. Orville E. Babcock, C. E

Dick Harrington

Gen. Oliver O. Howard

Col. C. M. Alexander

Major A. C. Richards,
Supt. of Police

Hon. Henry C. Cooke,
Governor,
District of Columbia

Hon. William W. Corcoran

Rev. Byron Sunderland

Hon. William B. Allison,
Iowa

Hardy Studio, Washington, D. C.

Alexander R. Shepherd

National Archives

Washington and Alexandria Railroad Station, 1872

Seven Negro Congressmen represented the South in the 41st and 42nd Congresses. Currier and Ives drawing made in 1872 shows (from l.) Sen. Revels, Representatives Benjamin Turner of Alabama, Robert C. De Large of South Carolina, Josiah T. Walls of Florida, Jefferson Long of Georgia, Joseph Rainey and R. Brown Elliot of S. C.

Drawn by our special artist, Albert Berghaus.

The First Cabinet Meeting under the administration of Andrew Johnson, at the Treasury Buildings, April 16, 1865.

Negroes in Washington.

Washington, D. C.—An incident of the Carnival; "speeding," before the tilt, on the second day of the fete—scene on Pennsylvania Avenue, looking from Seventh Street toward the Capitol.—

(Sketched by A. W. M'Callum)

Significant election scene at Washington, June 3, 1867.

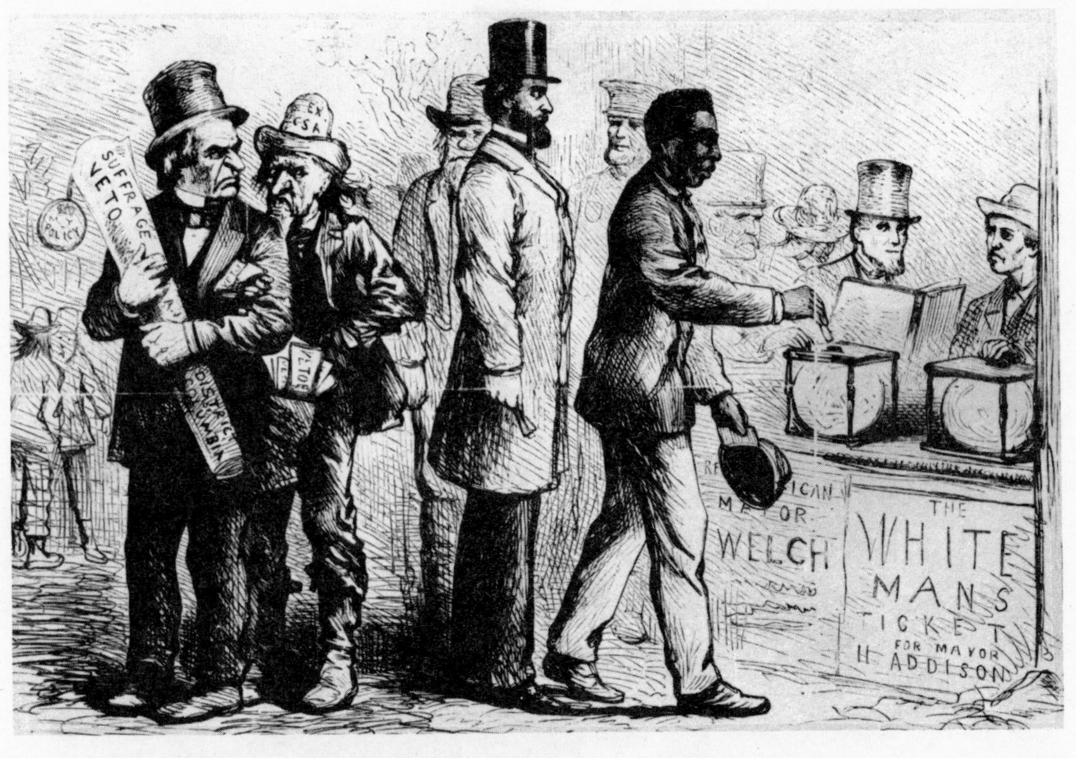

The Georgetown election–The Negro at the Ballot-Box.

annual installments at ten per cent interest—almost the identical proposal which John Gray had made the previous summer in the Legislative Council. The delegate pointed out that the credit of the District was not involved under the Bill, since the assessment certificates were to form the sole security for the new bonds to be issued, and that the funded debt of the District, now perilously close to the limit established by Congress, would not be further increased.

To satisfy the growing list of claims for property damage the Board asked all those who had claims to submit them within ten days before the new Legislature convened.

Since the Legislature had passed in August 1871 an Act providing that no special assessments could be levied on private property until the improvements had been actually completed, the Board now found itself in dire need of funds. To provide the necessary money the Board was authorized by the Legislature to issue "Certificates of Indebtedness" bearing seven and three-quarters per cent interest for work done on behalf of property owners. The idea was a novel one, but it had been endorsed by such legal authorities as Caleb Cushing and Walter S. Cox, who considered that:

> This is a legal and unobjectionable method of obviating inconveniences which will result to individuals and to the public if either the work is left unpaid for or private property holders compelled to pay their assessments as a whole and on such short time as to make their burden oppressive.[18]

Meanwhile the opposition from the newspapers outside the District was continuing. The *New York Tribune* published in April a series of articles on the Board of Public Works, declaring it to be bankrupt. Shepherd was stated to have cancelled about $2,000,000 worth of contracts for further improvements. An interview by "Edmund M. Smith" with W. W. Corcoran was published in which the aged banker stated the pressing need for an unbiased newspaper in Washington. Shepherd was moved to reply at length. He stated that the money appropriated by the

Federal government had been for work still to be completed. He admitted that there had been some difficulties in collecting the special assessments, since by law they could not be charged to the property owners until the actual work had been completed. He complained that the Federal government had during the past 70 years appropriated only $12,000,000 for street improvements, while the citizens of Washington had spent over $15,000,000 over the same period. The streets, moreover, had been laid out in proportions which would have ruined Chicago or New York if either city had attempted to pave, drain and light them.

The financial strain and newspaper attacks were beginning to tell at last upon the Shepherd household. "There was a tone in Mama's voice," wrote Grace Merchant, his daughter, in her diary,

> I had never heard before. Was she angry? I had never heard her angry. Was she crying? I had never heard her cry! . . . "They are persecuting you, Alex," said my Mama's voice, after Papa had read something from the morning paper propped up on his glass of cream. "It is a cruel slander." "It is all politics, darling," said Papa. "They're hitting at the dear old General through me. They must have a Republican Boss Tweed for campaign purposes." Persecution? Slander? In Sunday School . . . I had heard such words with nice words before them—these words: "Blessed are they that are persecuted." So it was all right. Papa was blessed. Dear Papa, so big and so gentle and laughing with us, dear Papa, who smelt so fresh and bay-rummy when we kissed his smooth cheek good-morning.[19]

When the new Legislature convened on April 28 Governor Cooke devoted the greater part of his message to the financial condition of the District. Part of the present difficulties, in his opinion, had been caused by the fact that Mayor Emery had failed to levy the taxes of the Corporation of Washington from January to June, 1871. The existing method of collecting taxes was also cumbrous and expensive. He gave the figures for the expenditure of the District from June 1, 1871 to December 31, 1872 at $9,913,716.64. The Board of Public Works had audited accounts up to $9,970,621.55; cash payments of $8,199,813.35 had been made, while its outstanding indebtedness amounted to $1,570,806.20. A few days later the Governor wrote to the *New York Tribune* endorsing the Report of the Board.

In May, Shepherd called upon the District Auditor to find that all available sources of revenue had been exhausted. He next visited William A. Cook, the Corporation Counsel, at his Mount Pleasant home, in the hope of finding some new method of circumventing the restrictions which had been placed by Congress and the Legislature upon increasing the funded debt of the District. Mr. Cook, who had once been minister of the gospel, prayed for guidance, and as a result of his inspiration the Sewer Tax was devised. The urban area was to be divided into five districts and special taxes levied upon property holders which were to bring in an additional $2,000,000 to the coffers of the Board of Public Works. The tax rates varied from five mills per $100 valuation in the high-lying northwestern areas of the city to 27 mills in the low-lying and swampy eastern areas.

In order to substantiate the claim that the Sewer Tax was not subject to the provisions of the Organic Act, opinions were sought from such legal authorities as A. G. Riddle and Caleb Cushing, who stated that in their view such a tax would not contravene the existing restrictions on the District debt.[20] Their sanction did not, however, satisfy the increasingly burdened taxpayers of the District, especially those of the northeastern sections of the city, some of whom found that the sewer tax on unimproved property, added to existing land taxes and assessments, exceeded its market value.

On May 15 in the Legislature Shepherd called for a stricter interpretation of the provision exempting from taxation the property of churches and other institutions. On June 2 in the House of Delegates Mr. McKnight brought forward a Bill calling for a second $4,000,000 loan at six per cent interest to be amortized over a 30-year period. On June 20 a new tax bill was passed by that body raising the property tax in Washington and Georgetown to $2.00, the maximum amount allowed under the Organic Act, and increasing the county taxes to $1.50. On May 22, 1873, S. P. Brown was replaced as a member of the Board of Public Works by Henry A. Willard. Founder of Willard's Hotel, and a brother of C. C. Willard, the proprietor of the Ebbitt House, he was one of the most influential and popular business men in Washington. The appointment of Willard was an excellent choice to improve the public relations of the Board and to pacify the merchants and other malcontents. He had also the task of mollifying Senator Edmunds of Vermont, of which state he was a native, who threatened to introduce a bill to remove the capital; not only had his own residence been injured by the grading of Massachusetts Avenue, but a sow had entered his garden gate and burrowed through his yard. As a result stringent laws were passed by the Legislature prohibiting cattle and other animals from roving the streets of Washington.

The continued attacks on Shepherd in the New York press were met by unsuccessful attempts at reprisals. On June 27 Charles A. Dana, the editor of the *New York Sun* and the most violent critic of the Board was arrested in New York on a charge of libel, after he had published a statement that Shepherd had perjured himself in the 1872 Investigation by declaring that he had sold out his interest in the Metropolitan Paving Company. It was not possible, however, to extradite Dana to Washington for trial, and the matter was dropped. A warrant for libel against the editor of the *New York Tribune,* was issued on April 12, 1873, but since Whitelaw Reid prudently kept away from the capital, no action could be taken against him.[21]

The troubled question of the District school question was also discussed in 1873 both in Congress and in the local Legislature. Charles Sumner had introduced in the second session of the 42nd Congress his perennial bill to abolish color distinctions in the public schools of Washington and Georgetown, but had found little congressional support. By this time Sumner, who had violently attacked the policy of the Grant administration on the issue of annexing San Domingo, and who had supported Greeley in the 1872 election, had lost his influence upon the leaders of the Republican Party, and had been removed as Chairman of the Senate Foreign Relations Committee. Measures introduced by him were consistently passed over. Senator Ferry of Connecticut, a Republican, had introduced an amendment to Sumner's school bill by which integration of the District schools would have been made subject to a referendum of voters in Washington and Georgetown, but even this controversial measure was not debated on the floor of the Senate, and Sumner's bill died a natural death when Congress adjourned.

On March 23, 1873, Congress had transferred authority over the colored schools in the District from the Department of the Interior to the District authorities, and new trustees had been appointed. The President of the Board of Trustees, Henry L. Johnson, was a man of moderate views, who had formerly served as butler to Secretary of the Treasury Richardson. Because of his opposition to an integrated school system, Johnson soon found himself at odds with the *New National Era* and with other influential leaders of the Negro community in Washington. Thomas W. Chase, one of the colored members of the Legislature, unsuccessfully introduced an amendment to the Bill creating a District Normal School which would have opened it to all students regardless of color on the grounds that the normal school was outside of the District school system.

Chase's amendment became a subject of great controversy among the colored population. It was assailed by John H. Brooks, the recently-appointed member of the Legislative Council, who condemned it in the columns of the *Evening Star* as being "too foolish a point to reply to." Two days later Henry L. Johnson was attacked as he was entering the house of Register John F. Cook on 16th Street. His assailant was a colored journalist, Keith Smith, whose weekly column appeared in the *Sunday Gazette* under the name of "Cordelia."[22] On July 1st a large meeting of colored citizens was held under the chairmanship of John T. Johnson, treasurer of the Board of Public Works, to discuss the school situation. Henry Piper read a message from Charles Sumner regretting the rejection of the Chase amendment. A resolution in favor of mixed schools was passed, repudiating Brooks and Henry L. Johnson, and declaring in favor of a single school system with a common school board. A committee consisting of the most prominent colored men of the District: Dr. C. B. Purvis, John T. Johnson, Dr. William Augusta, James T. Wormley, Alfred Jones, Dr. J. L. N. Bowen, Councilman John Gray and Delegates Henry Piper, O. S. B. Wall, Solomon Brown and Thomas W. Chase, was named to call upon the Governor. On July 17 the committee called on him and complained that Henry L. Johnson had not acted in an impartial manner and that his conduct as President of the Colored School Board had been obnoxious. They cited the case of Richard Greener, who had been brought down from Philadelphia to head the new Preparatory High School, and who had been dismissed at the end of the year in spite of his remarkable achievements in a short period.[23] The Governor listened attentively to the committee, but stated that he did not think they were agreed on the matter, and no action was taken.

Governor Cooke left for the summer capital at Long Branch at the end of July for an urgent conference with President Grant. The ostensible purpose of his visit was the President's approval of the new Sewer Tax. However, far more serious worries beset the Governor. Apart from his concern over the finances of the District he had also to consider his own association with Jay Cooke & Company, whom he represented in the capital.

By the summer of 1873 the situation of his firm had become desperate. The Northern Pacific Railroad, which Jay Cooke had been engaged in building from Duluth, Minnesota to Tacoma, Washington, had been unsuccessful in its efforts to sell bonds in a market already glutted with railroad securities, and for months construction had been halted. The Credit Mobilier investigation earlier in the year had made any subvention by Congress an impossibility. Jay Cooke found himself in the situation of having to put into the railroad more and more of his banking capital; by the summer of 1873 the Northern Pacific's debt to Jay Cooke & Co. had risen to $1,775,000.[24]

The head of the House of Cooke had become increasingly apprehensive of the position of his brother in regard to the equally perilous finances of the District. He had written on February 19 to Henry:

> I am in continual fear in regard to this whole matter of the District and of your connection with these people. They will line their pockets and the odium will fall on you. I wish you could get out of the whole thing at once, if possible. On the 4th of March you can very readily retire and let the President put someone else in your place. Why don't you do this? You will have more peace and more leisure. You have had all the glory that can come from it and can give the best of excuses—that you are overwhelmed with other business . . . I hate to say anything about it, but we must husband our resources, and it will not answer to have a single dollar locked up in anything that is not available.

When Henry Cooke wrote back that he was not ready to resign and that he accepted the position of Governor at his brother's suggestion, Jay Cooke replied:

> Not one of your partners, my dear brother, dreamed of your taking such a position in the Board of Public Works as has been forced upon you. They simply looked upon the governorship as redounding to the honor of the firm (more in Europe than in this country) and as a temporary availing of such a position, to favorably affect our House abroad. We did not dream of your time being occupied in negotiating loans and in financing for an immense set of public works or in mixing with money matters in any shape whatsoever. All that has occurred is entirely contrary to our thought . . . I rely entirely on your promises to resign the position as soon as the Legislature meets and you can send in your accounts. You can do it now with honor and credit. Your health requires it, your partners have a right to request it; and you

> must, my dear brother, have instant relief from the cares and anxieties which beset you.[25]

A diplomatic post to some quiet European capital such as Brussels or The Hague would, Jay considered, "add lustre to the House of Cooke." Hamilton Fish, however, would not have welcomed such a proposal: in 1871 he had written in his diary when Henry had been appointed District Governor that this was "a good escape from a number of embarrassments and some peril."

The *Star,* which reflected closely the views of the District administration, reprinted on July 29 portions of a dispatch from the correspondent of the *New York Tribune* from Long Branch. Before the end of the year, the dispatch had stated, there would be a change in the District administration and it also predicted the abolition of the Board of Public Works and the possible setting up of a commission form of government. The *Star,* commenting editorially on this proposal, remarked:

> So far as this District is concerned the present form of government, despite some cumbrous and unnecessarily expensive features, has had a mission and fitness for carrying out the great work of improvement . . . task accomplished, the future work of controlling here is greatly simplified and can be done at a minimum of expense and a small number of officials. But whatever may be the future form of government for the District, there can be no doubt, we believe, that the present government will be heartily glad to be relieved of their position at the earliest possible moment. They are not office-seekers or drones, but capable business men, who have at the sacrifice of money and health, given their time, brains and energies to the thankless task of pulling this city out of the Slough of Despond.

On September 13 the critical state of Jay Cooke & Co. at last compelled the Governor to hand in his resignation, stating that "the combined demands from my private business and my public duties have become so exacting that I am no longer able to meet them both." He still believed, however, that the imminent disaster of the bank could be averted and accepted an invitation to a testimonial dinner to be given in his honor at the Willard Hotel on the 18th at which General Sherman was to be the principal speaker.

Grant without hesitation nominated Shepherd to succeed him and the Senate, in spite of the criticism of the Board, confirmed him by a substantial majority. The appointment touched off an explosion of abuse from the anti-administration press outside the District. Cooke's relations with the newspapers had always been excellent, and the friendly feelings of many editors to a former member of the profession had in the past deterred personal criticism. In the case of Shepherd it was a very different situation. Fourteen newspapers, including the *New York Sun, Tribune, World,* and *Herald,* the *Boston Advertiser* and the *Cincinnati Gazette,* blasted away at the man whom they considered already exposed and discredited. The *New York Sun* called Shepherd "ignorant, vulgar, venal and low-bred." The *Herald* commented:

> Since the appointment has been formally announced the indignation of the people of the District is very great. No one is censured but the President and this question is asked on every side, "Is it his contempt for public opinion, his ignorance of the sentiment of the people, or is it his stolid indifference that nerves him to such an action?" At a time when the Washington "Ring" was the subject of so much scandalous rumors, Shepherd's nomination was an especially bitter pill for those who had hoped that the new Governor would be a man who would clean up the tangle of District affairs.

Shepherd's inauguration took place on September 16 at 9:30 A.M. in Cooke's Georgetown mansion, Justice MacArthur administering the oath. The following morning members of both houses of the District Legislature called on the new Governor to express their congratulations. William Stickney, the President of the Council, said in his speech that Shepherd's efforts in the past had been eminently successful and that if he could continue in the same vein "he will deserve the thanks not only of Washington but of all Americans." The Governor in reply admitted that the improvements had been expensive but "in a shorter time than most people believed the District would be relieved of this debt by action of the General government." He urged all members of the Legislature to defend the integrity of the District and to build up confidence.[26]

The following evening President Grant arrived at "Ogontz," Jay Cooke's palatial 380-acre estate north of Philadelphia, to place his youngest son Jesse at a private school in the Chelten Hills. "Ogontz," where Grant and his family had been previously entertained on numerous occasions, was the showplace of the United States. The house had cost a million dollars to build and was named after an old Sandusky Indian chieftain whose portrait stood in the main doorway. The house had fifty-two rooms, a conservatory which opened into an Italian garden, a music room and an amusement room with a miniature stage. Here at breakfast on the morning of the 18th, while Grant was chatting with his host, a telegram was handed to Jay Cooke over his private telegraph wire. Fahnestock, his New York partner, who had been violently opposed to Cooke's continued subsidy of the Northern Pacific Railroad, had forced his hand by closing the doors of the New York office. Not a word or gesture escaped Cooke's lips at breakfast, but as soon as the President and his party had left he gave orders that the Philadelphia and Washington branches of the firm should do likewise.

The closing of the massive doors of the First National Bank on 15th Street caused a sensation in the capital. For the first few hours business all over the city was at a standstill—a murder trial in process was interrupted so that the judge and jury could buy a paper with the latest news. There was an immediate run on the other Washington banks to withdraw securities, especially gold and greenbacks; the savings banks, however, which required depositors to give sixty days' notice, were unaffected.

At the Freedmen's Bank a few doors away from the First National the run was particularly heavy, since it was common knowledge that the Bank was closely tied to the Cooke interests. A long line of colored men and women formed at the door, many of them old men and women who had come to town from the country areas. Some carried battered trunks and checkbooks wrapped up in brown paper or concealed in their hats and bosoms. One old colored man with a black hat crowded down over his eyes that looked as if a hen had hatched in it, having in his hands two umbrellas, a fishpole and a blanket wrapped up around his tattered coat, shouted at the top of his voice upon recognizing a female acquaintance, "Fore God, Susan, this chile has walked all de way from Pohick to git that 75 cents. Ain't gwin' to lose anything, shuah, honey." The *Star* reporter on the scene found that the unfailing sense of humor of the colored people relieved the tragedy which they believed had befallen them.[27]

Shepherd, through his friendship with Secretary of the Treasury Richardson, arranged that any local bank depositing in the New York Sub-Treasury could obtain cash from Washington headquarters after telegraphic communication. This would enable banks to convert their collateral security into gold and greenbacks as a reserve against further runs.

The panic, however, continued. On the 24th the Freedmen's Bank gave its depositors sixty days' notice; on the 26th a private bank, Fant's, suspended its operations. The First National Bank published its balance sheet, showing resources amounting to $2,687,541.76 against liabilities of $2,612,233.34 and an indebtedness to the District Government of only $7,698.25. On the 28th the Washington bankers met together to discuss the plan which had been put into operation in New York to meet the emergency. A Clearing House Association was formed with a controlling committee of six members into whose hands banks would be allowed to deposit securities. The Committee would determine their value—bonds were to be accepted at par and promissory notes at fifty per cent of their value. Against this collateral, banks could issue certificates and certify checks which could then be received at their full value by other banks in the association for payment of notes or other claims maturing before November 1. A few days later these certificates were issued in ten-, twenty- and fifty-dollar denominations.[28]

No. ....

CERTIFICATE

issued by the Associate Banks of the District of Columbia

This certifies that .... Bank has credit with this Committee for $........... secured by collateral in the hands of said Committee in conformity with the regulations adopted by the Associate Banks of the District of Columbia, and is good in the hands of bona-fide bearer on representation to any one of said banks.

Lewis Johnson & Company
Freedmen's Savings-Trust Co.
National Metropolitan Bank
Second National Bank
National Savings Bank
German-American Savings Bank

Countersigned by ....
Treasurer of controlling Committee

On October 12 Washington was visited by ex-President Andrew Johnson, who had not set foot in the capital since 1869, in the company of his son, Robert. He confirmed that he had $73,000 on deposit at the First National Bank at a small rate of interest. President Grant, he said, had overdrawn his account there. He reiterated his old plea for the resumption of specie payment and blamed the Administration for having become involved with Wall Street and for buying its own bonds. Serenaded at the National Hotel on the 24th, the former President made a short address to his admirers. The country, he said, was much closer to dictatorship than people were aware, and he favored a single six-year presidential term. The citizens were being plundered to serve special interests; already Americans were involved in more debt per capita than any other people under the globe.

The October elections for the Fourth District Legislature were held in an apathetic atmosphere. The only unusual feature of the election was the presence of a large number of candidates endorsed by the newly-formed Temperance Party, which elected its candidates, Charles Peck in the Second District and W. R. Hunt in the 18th. The Temperance candidates were bitterly opposed by the German-language daily, the *Washingtoner Journal,* which organized an active campaign against them, claiming after the election that the German vote had been responsible for defeating 'Temperenzlers' in the 13th and 14th Districts.[29] Many Germans in Washington owned breweries, bars and beer gardens, and would have been put out of business by Prohibition laws. The *National Republican* had endeavored to muster faithful party members to the polls, but in spite of excellent weather the total number of votes cast was only 14,569. Only two Democrats were elected, of whom Dickson in the 12th District was not an opponent of the Board of Public Works. "The fact is," the *Star* stated in its editorial,

> that the advantages of the improvements so far finished are so great that they compel recognition and consequently the opponents of the District government and its work of beautifying the city have been forced to give up the contest at the polls against the progressive spirit of the age and its representatives, except in one or two of the old fogey districts, where the advocates of mud and cobblestone streets, surface drainage through filthy gutters and hogs for scavengers still hold their ground.

The *Georgetown Courier* considered it significant that six candidates were elected who were not endorsed by the Republican Central Committee and that only two colored men, instead of five as in the previous year, had been returned to the House of Delegates.[30] The new members were Joseph Brooks, a farmer, who had defeated Frederick Douglass, Jr., in the First District, and Albert N. Underwood, a clerk in the office of the District Comptroller, who had been successful in the Sixth.

On November 1 the Comptroller issued his report on the finances of the District, showing that the bonded debt stood at $9,902,251. In order to protect the credit of the former city

Corporations, the report stated, the District government had paid off their old debts by an application of a large portion of the current revenues. The financial crisis had prevented the negotiation of bonds authorized for the financing of the old debt, and as a result the District had fallen behind on its current obligations.

The memorialists were marking time and putting up passive resistance by refusing to pay their special assessments. In October property belonging to Columbus Alexander, William B. Todd and Sayles J. Bowen was advertised for public sale. Until Congress convened in December, they realized that no further action could be taken and in the meanwhile continued to prepare material for a new memorial to Congress based upon fresh evidence of the activities of the Board.

Shepherd, aware that the storm was to break again over his head, took the opportunity to make several changes in the personnel of the District government. Although worried by the turn of events, the Governor was fortified by the continued loyalty of the President, who, even though Shepherd was the most abused man in Washington, was willing to stand up for him and even share in the abuse. General Eaton recalled a conversation with Grant about this time in which the President remarked that he made it a point of calling on Governor Shepherd: "If the maid was slow in answering the door he would not be ashamed to be seen standing on the Governor's doorstep."[31] The changes in the Board of Public Works made in November reflected, however, the desire of the Governor to conciliate public opinion. Dr. J. B. Blake of the National Metropolitan Bank, a Conservative, was appointed in place of Adolph Cluss, and Richard Harrington, a young lawyer from Delaware, took over the position of District Attorney from the much-abused William A. Cook. Lewis Clephane was made Collector of Taxes and several minor officials were dismissed, savings which the *Star* estimated would save the District $50,000 a year in salaries.

On December 1 the Board issued its second annual report, listing its achievements of the past two and a half years. The

District now had 58.5 miles of wooden pavement, 28.5 of concrete and 93 of cobble, macadam, gravel and Belgian block. Two hundred and eight miles of sidewalk had been laid, and 123 miles of sewers. There were 3,000 gas lamps in the city. More than 60,000 trees had been planted by the Parking Commission. Washington was now the best-lit and best-paved city in the United States. The cost of the improvements, the report claimed, had been less per capita than in any large American city, though the rate of taxation on real estate was still lower than in any of the four largest cities with the exception of Boston. Personal property was not taxed, and the funded debt per capita was less than that of New York, Brooklyn, Boston, Jersey City and Rochester. The Board's treasurer regretted that "recent financial troubles" had prevented the sale of the Sewer Certificates negotiated in New York by former Governor Cooke. The Federal Government, he stated, should immediately settle its indebtedness to the District in order that the certificates could be validated and the "faithful contractors" paid. Magruder's accounts still showed a balance in favor of the Board: receipts between 1871 and 1873 had amounted to $14,789,692.85 and payments had been made amounting to $13,386,455.67.

In his message to Congress the third of December President Grant did not fail to put in his usual good word for the District Government:

> Under the very efficient management of the Governor and Board of Public Works of this District the city of Washington is rapidly assuming the appearance of a capital of which the nation may be well proud. The work has been done systematically, the plans, grades, locations of sewers, water and gas mains being determined upon before the work was commenced, thus securing permanency when completed. I question whether so much has ever been accomplished before in an American city for the same expenditure. The Government, having large reservations in the city and the nation at large having an interest in their capital, I recommend a liberal policy towards the District of Columbia and that the Government should bear its just share of the ex-

pense of these improvements. Each citizen visiting the capital feels a pride in its growing beauty and that he too is part of the improvements made here.[32]

The President must, however, have been as aware as Governor Shepherd that Congress was in no mood to grant liberal appropriations to the District without again scrutinizing the state of its finances. The crash of 1873, which had been followed by unemployment all over the nation, had committed Congress to a policy of retrenchment. The generous contribution made during the past two years to the District government could no longer be relied on. Moreover, the memorialists had prepared themselves well for the forthcoming struggle. Led by Columbus Alexander, a wealthy patent attorney, who had served as Colonel in the Union Army and was a Republican above reproach, they had acquired some of the best legal talent in the District to argue their cause. The newspapers of New York, Baltimore, Cincinnati and Chicago were behind them, and anxious to use the financial embarrassment of the District as an opportunity to harass the Grant administration.

The campaign opened on January 27, 1874, with the simultaneous publication in the *New York Tribune* and *New York Sun* of letters from the files of the late W. S. Huntington. Huntington had been cashier of the First National Bank and a partner in the notorious Seneca Sandstone Company, which had been accused on many occasions of using political influence to secure government contracts. One of these letters was from H. H. Starkweather, the Connecticut Republican who had headed the 1872 Investigation of District Affairs. In it, Starkweather asked for contributions to his election campaign "which would put me under renewed obligation to you." A letter from Hallett Kilbourn discussed the formation of a "real estate pool" to control paving contracts. A third letter from the head of a Chicago paving company, George Chittenden, dealt with the means of interesting District officials in his patented wooden pavements.

On the same day the memorialists presented their long-awaited petition to Congress. Signed by twenty-five of the leading property-owners in the District, including Columbus Alexander, John van Riswick, S. D. Castleman, John Purdy and W. Rutherford, it pulled out all the stops in its accusations against the District government. Its officers were accused of "extravagance and carelessness in the execution of the public works, favoritism in the awarding of contracts, defrauding the general government through deliberate false measurements, depositing District funds in unsafe banking institutions, building costly roads to their own residences, exceeding the statutory indebtedness of the District, and establishing a confiscatory system of taxation through special assessments, while amassing large fortunes while in office . . . Said officers have in other respects managed the affairs of said District negligently, oppressively and unlawfully . . . as to bring great scandal upon the people of said District and upon themselves."[33]

Chapter 8

The Social Kaleidoscope: 1870-1875

Before the Civil War the private and public architecture of the national capital had reflected the Roman virtues of dignity and austerity so highly esteemed by the founders of the Republic. The classical style almost universally prevailed; of the public buildings only Alexander Renwick's Smithsonian Institution across the Mall stood as an example of the Gothic Revival which had swept across Europe and had already had an influence on the architecture of the United States.

In 1871 A. B. Mullett, a young architect of English birth, had been commissioned by the Treasury to design a new building West of the White House which was to house the State, War and Navy Departments. Four years later Secretary Fish moved his offices from their temporary location at 14th and S Street into the new building. The newspapers of the day were lavish in their praise of the edifice, which was indeed a fitting monument to the spirit of the Grant era. The exterior, with its multiplicity of columns, resembled a wedding cake with features borrowed from a French Renaissance château; the interior, with its endless corridors and swinging doors, suggested alcoholic associations.

The severely plain three-story brick houses of prewar days were making way for a new style of architecture in which bay windows, mansard roofs, crocheted pinnacles and towers and wide verandahs were all the rage. On K Street facing Farragut Square

Adolph Cluss had built three elaborate residences which he, Hallett Kilbourn and Alexander Shepherd later occupied. The cost of the three houses in "Governor Shepherd's Row" exceeded $150,000. Near the P Street Circle recently christened in honor of Admiral Dupont a group of Westerners known popularly as the "Honest Miner's Gang" were putting up imposing mansions in the Nob Hill manner. The vast octagonal castle of Senator Stewart of Nevada on the northwestern corner of the Circle boasted a tower and cupola with the most extensive view to be found in the city. His business associate, Charles J. Hillyer, had invested heavily in property in the same vicinity, and another Westerner, Thomas Sunderland, had built a number of smaller houses for speculation. James G. Blaine, the Speaker of the House, paid $85,000 to erect a red brick mansion at the corner of 20th Street and Massachusetts Avenue, which he occupied for only a few years. The area, hitherto considered "impossible," was still further improved by the new British Legation, which had been built at the corner of N Street and Connecticut Avenue.[1]

Washington could now claim some first-class hostelries. On December 1, 1869, the Arlington Hotel, built by W. W. Corcoran and named after the estate of his good friend, Robert E. Lee, opened its doors for the first time. The new hotel faced the White House on the choicest site in the city. Theophilus Roessle, who had come down from Albany to take over its management, was one of the most experienced hotelkeepers in the United States, and the Arlington immediately established a new record for comfort and hospitality. The hotel had three hundred and twenty-five rooms, an elevator, huge suites up to ten rooms with private baths, and unequalled food and service.[2] Its rates were in proportion. Senator Fenton of New York paid $1,000 a month for a parlor, an office and two bedrooms, and a two-room suite cost Senator Cameron of Pennsylvania $450 a month. A buffet supper for a hundred guests cost Representative "Sunset" Cox of New York $15 per plate.[3] The Arlington management was determined that the hotel should be "exclusive" and to cater to the congressional and diplomatic set, as well as to the foreign visitors and the more opulent business men and lobbyists who were now crowding into the capital.

Much smaller than the Arlington, but frequented by an equally distinguished clientele, was Wormley's Hotel at the southwest corner of 15th and H Street. It had been built in 1871 by Samuel Hooper, the wealthy representative from Massachusetts and leased to James T. Wormley, whose skill in the catering business was already famous. The hotel contained only one hundred fifty rooms, but it had an elevator and private dining rooms, and the food and service were of the highest quality. Vice-President Colfax made it his headquarters in December 1872, and the new ministers from France and Ecuador were also staying there at the time.[4] Wormley's was especially favored by the foreign diplomats, and its private dining rooms were the scene of important political conferences. It was, ironically, at this Negro-owned hotel that the agreement by which the Democratic leaders consented to the election of Rutherford B. Hayes as President provided that Federal troops were withdrawn from the South, was to be made in 1877.[5]

Next door to Wormley's, John Welcker, a Belgian-born restaurateur who had come to Washington during the War, opened a new establishment. His eighty-foot dining room was always filled with celebrities in the political, social and diplomatic world. On his wall hung a framed letter from Charles Dickens, who had been his guest in 1868, stating that his restaurant was the finest in the world. Welcker's prices were only slightly lower than those of Delmonico in New York. A fine dinner cost $10 to $12, breakfast $5 to $8. During the sessions of Congress he would give two dinner parties nightly; twelve was an average party and the cost was upward of $10 per plate.[6]

The former British Legation on "Eye" Street which had been vacated in 1873 was taken over by another enterprising caterer, John Chamberlain. He had already built up an excellent clientele through his restaurant on the Avenue near the Willard Hotel, and his new "Club," as it came to be known, soon became a favorite resort of congressmen, who retired to drink and gamble in the smaller rooms upstairs. On the Avenue, Harvey's still catered to the connoisseur of sea food, and Hancock's to the devotee of canvasback ducks and other "reed birds."

The Metropolitan Club, which had formerly occupied the site of Wormley's Hotel, moved in 1871 to the opposite corner of 15th Street into the mansion formerly occupied by Commodore Morris. This was the oldest club in the city and a stronghold of the Conservative residents of the District. In 1872 the Washington Club opened at 1409 New York Avenue. Its membership was open to both political groups and its officers included men of such divergent viewpoints as former Mayor James G. Berret, Henry D. Cooke, Alexander Shepherd, Richard T. Merrick and Hallet Kilbourn.

The vast improvements of the Board of Public Works had greatly stimulated the social life of the capital, where only a few years before residents hesitated to venture forth at night. Along the broad avenues, now smoothly paved and well-illuminated, rolled the magnificent carriages of the newly-rich with their fine horses and liveried coachmen. In these days the wealthy society of Washington had little in common with that of the Southern aristocrats who had dominated the city before the War. Industrialists from New York, New England and Pennsylvania, and men who had made their fortunes from the gold and silver mines of the West, now set the social pace. Mark Twain, who had spent a winter in Washington as secretary to Senator Stewart, had painted in *The Gilded Age* an unforgettable picture of these "parvenus"—such as the "Patrique Oreillés," who had come to the capital from Ireland, after a lengthy sojourn in New York and a much shorter period in Paris. No one was particular regarding the sources of their wealth; "indeed," he wrote, "if it had been acquired by conspicuous ingenuity with just a pleasant little spice of illegality, all the better."[7] "Conspicuous consumption" was never as greatly admired and respected in Washington as in the era of President Grant.

To the older generation of Washingtonians, especially to those with Southern antecedents and connections, the new way of life was inexpressibly shocking and vulgar. The "Fulke-Fulkersons" of *The Gilded Age* were careful to avoid as much as possible contact with the "parvenus"; they seldom attended public functions and, by affecting an older style of costume and carriages, they earned the name of "Antiques." Politics, which in their day was the sphere of gentlemen, had now become the exclusive domain of upstarts and grafters. When "Laura Hawkins," endeavoring to sound out the feelings of her "Antique" callers, tentatively suggested to "Mrs. Fulke-Fulkerson" that Long Branch was closer to the capital than Newport as a summer resort, the dowager icily replied, "Nobody goes *there,* Miss Hawkins—at least only persons of no importance. And the President."[8]

But the "Parvenus" could afford to ignore the "Antiques." They were in the saddle and enjoying themselves as they never had before. Receptions were never more elaborate, food more rich nor decorations more magnificent. At the balls which began at midnight and lasted until dawn the mantels of the Washington mansions were covered with moss, tables bedded with violets, vases overflowing with roses, heliotropes, and camellias. The orchestra would be concealed behind a lattice; acacias and scarlet passion flowers encircled the fountain covered with ferns. On the buffet sparkling with gold, silver and crystal sat the bottles of red Bordeaux and Burgundy and the buffet tables were loaded with terrapin and truffle, spiced meat and salads, pastries, elaborate confections and choice fruits. In the room set apart for punches guests could choose between a frozen concoction, champagne punch or claret glowing in a bowl of solid ice.[9]

Then there were the "Germans," where the young people would dance furiously until daybreak, returning at dawn after a champagne breakfast, driven by a drunken coachman who had stayed up shivering all night. Some of the hostesses, aping the new fashions of European society, served buffet suppers at which formal attire and servants were alike dispensed with. These "kettledrums" were particularly favored by the "Grandes dames" and some of the gilded youth, who found the occasion an ideal one at which to make social plans and to dissect their friends.

The "winter picnics," for which the conservatory was stripped of its flowers and the house was decorated with evergreens and to which each guest would bring a hamper containing a different course, was another charming innovation.[10] In the spring and summer months there was moonlight boating on the Potomac, riding parties to Great Falls, picnics in Rock Creek Valley, "a region of great beauty, where the woods abound in lupins and pink azaleas and the great white dogwood boughs stretch away into the darkness of the forest like a press of moonbeams."[11]

The descriptive powers of Washington correspondents had so captured the imagination of the American public that some Republican journalists after the Panic of 1873 and the scandals later revealed considered it advisable to play down the brilliance of social life in the capital. "The rich men of Washington," wrote Gail Hamilton, "are the exception and not the rule. The President and the Cabinet are seldom wealthy men. The officers of the Army and Navy are usually men dependent on their salaries . . . The Judges of the Supreme and other Courts are always of small salaries, but their rank suffers no loss . . . The Senate has perhaps a baker's dozen of rich men and householders but the large majority make no pretensions to wealth and live quietly in the most modest of boarding-houses. And not one out of a hundred of those who reside officially or temporarily in Washington live in such style or comfort as he maintains in his own home in the distant city or country district from which he comes . . . It is idle to imagine such a society as this dominated by wealth or corrupted by extravagance. There are doubtless fraudulent men, pothouse politicians, venal writers, and vulgar, extravagant, ignorant and unprincipled women; for wheresoever the carcass is, there will be eagles gathered together, but the overwhelming preponderance of public sentiment is on the side of good principle, good breeding and good nature. Washington is full of admirable women, as unassailable to temptation, as unbreathed on by scandal, as the dwellers in the uttermost part of the earth."[12]

The domestic virtues were stressed by Madeline Vinton Dahlgren, whose *Etiquette of Social Life in Washington* soon became the official Bible of the new society. "Because we are a Republic, we are not necessarily to be deprived of those amenities which render life agreeable and assist to cultivate good feeling," she wrote. "We should prove to the world that Republican manners are the very acme of elegance in their unaffected simplicity . . . While it is not to be denied that official life constitutes a leading element in Washington society, yet the official, however brilliant it is, is after all so ephemeral that in real solidarity of social importance the resident society must always form an essential feature and be classed as the very élite." Mrs. Dahlgren had persuaded Hans von Bülow, the famous German conductor, to set to music her opening theme: "If order is Heaven's first law, we should not regard as beneath careful attention the proper recognition of rules which tend to avoid confusion in social life."[13]

The wives of the new members of Congress found Mrs. Dahlgren's book an invaluable companion. Coming from remote and sparsely settled communities, many of them had found the formalities and complexities of the Washington social scene bewildering. Every afternoon there would be official receptions between 2 and 5:30. On Mondays the wives of the Supreme Court Justices would be at home to callers; on Tuesdays it was the turn of the wives of the Representatives; Wednesday the Cabinet's; Thursday the Senate's; Friday the Army and Navy; and on Saturday the reception at the White House. Among the scintillating crowds, the elegant toilettes and coiffures, the parures from Tiffany and the gowns from Paris, the Marine Band in its glittering scarlet and gold uniforms under the baton of Professor Scala would always be present to play the martial music and the new waltzes of Johann Strauss which were the rage of America as well as of Europe.

Much indeed of the official life of Washington consisted in the paying and returning of calls. Protocol required that new arrivals to the city should call on persons of social or political prominence within two weeks and that they should leave a card with the appropriate corner turned down. If the visit was returned within the same period, the privilege of continuing the acquaintance was signified; otherwise the matter was not to be pressed further. On every afternoon except that on which they would be at home the wives of Cabinet members and Congressmen would be out in their barouches or landaulets returning these visits, hunting for obscure addresses and trailing their rich garments over three-story stairs. The call would be brief—two minutes or so was the custom—the conversation perfunctory; the only satisfaction which the great lady could obtain was that of checking off still another name in her book, which held perhaps a thousand or more of those whose calls she considered obligated to return. With her social duties and keeping house for her husband, the great lady's life in Washington at this time was not altogether enviable.

Among the Cabinet wives none took their social responsibilities more seriously than Mrs. Hamilton Fish, whose husband was to remain in office through Grant's two presidential terms. An aristocrat like her husband, a descendant of two signers of the Declaration of Independence, she was a pillar of strength to Mrs. Grant, whose social experience was sadly deficient. The Fish mansion on the corner of 15th and "Eye" Streets was the scene of more formal receptions than took place anywhere outside the White House; the Fishes were said to have spent $75,000 a year on entertaining. Each week during the season two formal dinners were held for an average twenty guests and at the Secretary's receptions fifteen hundred persons were often present. Every Wednesday afternoon, assisted by her unmarried daughter Edith, Mrs. Fish was at home to an endless stream of callers. When official Washington was uncertain how to meet a new social problem it waited until Mrs. Fish had taken the first step. Mrs. John A. Logan has recounted how she was taken to visit the pretty young government clerk who had married a man many years her senior (Senator Christiancy of Michigan). The girl was deeply embarrassed by the presence of her distinguished visitors, but the warmth and graciousness of Mrs. Fish soon put her at ease[14] A deeply religious woman, Mrs. Fish still found time for her church work and private charities to which she gave generously.

The Hamilton Fishes were admirably suited to receive the princes and potentates who were beginning for the first time to visit the United States. Washington was not completely strange to European aristocrats; during the War two of the princes of the French House of Orléans, the Comte de Paris and the Duc de Chartres, had come to the capital in the company of their uncle, the Prince de Joinville, to serve as officers in the Union Army. Prince Felix Salm-Salm of Prussia and Count Gurowski of Poland had also spent some time in the city while in the service of the Union. But they were, after all, principally refugees, and could not be given full official honors and recognition by the Department of State.

On January 26, 1870, the Duke of Connaught, Queen Victoria's third eldest son, paid an official visit to Washington. As the first member of a ruling royal house, he was received with much ceremony; the White House banquet in his honor numbered twenty-nine courses, and its cost for a party of thirty persons was $1,500 exclusive of wines. While relations with Great Britain had not yet been restored to their full cordiality, pending the settlement of the *Alabama* claims, Sir Edward Thornton, the British Minister, was one of the best-liked diplomats in the capital, and had done much personally to smooth over the dispute. Tall, with a military carriage, he and his typically English-looking wife, with her blonde hair and fine natural complexion, were considered to be the model European envoys.

In November, 1871, the Grand Duke Alexis of Russia arrived with a large retinue and took over a whole wing of the Arlington Hotel. The Grand Duke himself was a house guest of the Russian Minister, Count Constantine de Catacazy, who received him in the traditional manner with a loaf of black bread and a shaker of salt upon a silver platter. On the following day the Imperial party attended a special levee at the White House and, after a brief sightseeing tour, departed for a railroad tour to the West.

The occasion was memorable in marking the end of Count Catacazy's two-year mission in the capital, which had been the cause of many headaches to the State Department. The Minister had grossly violated his diplomatic status by engaging in public controversy regarding the Perkins claims. The matter concerned the repudiation by the Czar's government of a doubtful munitions contract made during the Crimean War by an American adventurer, Captain Benjamin Perkins. Several prominent Republican politicians—among them, it was rumored, Benjamin Butler, General Banks and two of the President's brothers-in-law, Frederick and Louis Dent—had bought an interest in the claim, which they were urging the Government to press. Catacazy had no scruples in using money and influence at his command to hand out information to the newspapers—including the Washington *National Republican*—which was highly unflattering both to the Administration and to the President personally. Such undiplomatic actions had finally exhausted the patience of Secretary Fish, who retaliated by publishing a letter to the American Minister at St. Petersburg in which the whole background of the affair was exposed and Catacazy's intrigues were castigated. The Russian Government was told in no uncertain terms that its Minister was *persona non grata* and his recall was requested. Though he accompanied the Grand Duke and his entourage on the Western tour, Army and Navy officers were instructed not to salute Catacazy except in the company of His Imperial Highness, and by the time the party had reached St. Louis the formal order for the Minister's recall was received. Official Washington was sorry, nevertheless, to bid farewell to Mme. de Catacazy, a golden-haired beauty many years younger than her husband, whose charms had been warmly appreciated—especially so, it was gossiped, by certain members of the Cabinet.

In March, 1872, Washington welcomed the first Japanese Ambassador to be accredited to the United States government. Japan, which only recently had established diplomatic relations with the West, had sent over as its representative M. Iwakura, accompanied by a large party of notables. The Department of

State had made elaborate arrangements for a reception at the Masonic Temple. The building was completely transformed. A large arch was erected supported by columns draped in pink and white cambric and surmounted by metal urns dripping with ivy. American and Japanese flags were everywhere; from the chandeliers were suspended bird cages with singing canaries. The Ambassador entered in his official Court costume, wearing a purple underskirt and a black tunic, on the arm of Vice-President Colfax, accompanied by Secretary Fish, Speaker Blaine, General Banks and other members of the Cabinet. Since practically none of the Japanese spoke English, young Mr. Rice from Maine, who had accompanied his missionary father to Japan, was the interpreter. At the banquet which followed one hundred twenty-five guests sat down to dinner. The next evening another reception was held at the White House on which occasion the Orientals donned Western evening dress. Some members of the party found difficulty in walking on the polished floor and one of them lost his silk hat. During the performance of *Lucia di Lammermoor* at the National Theatre which some of the delegation attended later, a few attachés fell into profound slumber—whether from the strangeness of the music or exhaustion due to the ceremonies has not been recorded. Mme. Christine Nilsson, the famous prima donna, had great difficulty to keep from giving way to uncontrollable mirth.[15] Washington hosts and hostesses vied with each other in elaborate entertainments for the Japanese visitors; W. S. Huntington, the Washington banker, gave them a dinner at the Arlington costing $50 a plate, and the Hon. James Brooks of New York, leader of the Democratic opposition in the House of Representatives, was their host at a banquet for one hundred twenty-five guests.

On December 18, 1874, King Kalakaua of the Hawaiian Islands paid a personal visit to the national capital. Twenty-five thousand dollars was appropriated by Congress for his entertainment. and he was lodged in a ten-room suite at the Arlington with his retinue. The stout, dark-complexioned monarch with imposing side-whiskers appeared at the White House in full dress evening clothes resplendent with the orders of his realm, while his aides wore the uniform of the Hawaiian Guards. Though still suffering from a cold which he had caught in Omaha en route to the capital, the King was able to pay a visit to the National Theatre to hear the celebrated American prima donna, Clara Louise Kellogg, sing in *Mignon* and to be present at a joint session of Congress. Escorted by Senator Cameron and Rep. Orth of Indiana, respective heads of the Foreign Relations Committees in both Houses, he was welcomed by Speaker Blaine as the first reigning sovereign to set foot on the soil of the United States. Chief Justice Allen, a native of Maine and resident of the Hawaiian kingdom for many years, read a graceful reply on the King's behalf, in which he acknowledged the debt that his country and people owed to American civilization. On the 23rd the King was entertained at a state dinner at the White House at which the entire Cabinet, the British Minister and many other notable guests were present.

While Mrs. Hamilton Fish was the acknowledged leader of official Washington, there was equally little doubt who was the most glamorous hostess of the capital. Ever since Salmon P. Chase had been called to the city by Lincoln to become a member of his Cabinet, his brilliant daughter Kate had charmed and dominated the social scene. She was of medium height, with Titian-colored hair, peach-bloom complexion, a graceful figure, a short nose—inclined to be "pug" as Garfield once said—she wore the most elegant clothes and jewelry Washington had ever seen. The secret of her fascination, however, lay in her intelligence and wit rather than in her looks and wealth. At the large house on 6th and E Streets in which she lived with her father and husband and at the old estate just outside the city, "Edgewood," where she entertained in a lavish style with forty servants, and in the summer at "Canonchet," a vast Gothic edifice with eighty rooms on the shores of Narragansett Bay, Kate Chase lived a life of luxury which was the envy of every woman of America.

Yet underlying the glamor and ostentation of her existence there ran a vein of tragedy unknown to those who read of her in the papers. The man who had made possible this life, William Sprague, her husband, was far inferior to her in intelligence and character. By inheritance a millionaire, he had in his teens succeeded his grandfather as owner of the largest textile mills in New England. During the War he had headed a Rhode Island regiment and on returning home after a distinguished army career had been elected at the age of twenty-eight Governor of his state. In the Senate, to which he was later appointed, Sprague was, however, unpopular. Out of sympathy with the Radical majority, he had even been considered by Gideon Welles as one who would vote for Andrew Johnson's acquittal in the Impeachment Trial. In 1869, when the lobbying by private business interests had begun to become a public scandal, he startled the Senate by a vitriolic attack on "money power," charging that American bankers and industrialists were leading the nation into disaster. Though his speech served to draw attention to a state of corruption unparalleled in American history, Sprague was at heart no real reformer such as Julian, Schurz or Trumbull. He took no part in the Liberal Republican movement in 1872 and voted consistently with his party on Reconstruction and all important issues.

Although four children were born to the Spragues, their married life was miserable. William took out his inferiority complex in drink and in attention to other women. Kate, on her part, had never lacked masculine admirers. Senator Roscoe Conkling of New York—whose wife had no taste for the social life of the capital and had remained at home in Utica—was most often seen in her company. The Senator, six foot three, with a reddish-brown beard and the most elegant clothes of any man in Washington, was the most brilliant orator as well as the Beau Brummel of the Senate. David Barry, a page boy in the Senate, recalled vividly his crisp brown Vandyke, his inevitable morning coat, his letters in mauve ink and handwriting "like that of an ultra-fashionable schoolgirl." To summon pages, he would clap his hands above his head like a Roman emperor, and he would confide a message to the boy on a routine matter as if he were conferring knighthood upon him. Together with Oliver Morton of Indiana and John A. Logan of Illinois he had become known as one of the Administration "Stalwarts" who could be relied upon to back the President through thick and thin. Though Washington society was well aware of his relationship with Kate Sprague, the two were careful to avoid open scandal, and it was not until several years later, after Sprague had publicly threatened Conkling's life at Narraganset Pier, that the final break took place. By that time the Sprague fortune had vanished in the financial crash of 1873; Kate had retired to "Edgewood" after a public auction of her most valuable possessions, and her long reign over Washington society had ended.

Even during her heyday, however, Kate Chase had had her rivals. General Belknap, the genial whiskered Iowan, who had succeeded Rawlins as Secretary of War, had brought to Washington one of the loveliest of wives, a Kentucky belle who had spent some years before the War in Europe. Her brunette good looks, her gay temperament and elaborate receptions in the old house on Lafayette Square which Seward had once occupied, had made her within a few months one of the favorites of Washington society. But the tempo of life was too much for her in spite of her youth, and by the end of 1870 she had died, leaving an infant child. Two years later her sister returned from Paris to marry the General, bringing back one of the most expensive trousseaus ever seen in the capital. "A handsomer or an apparently happier couple never came to Washington in their honeymoon," recalled Ben Perley Poore,[16] "and they were at once recognized among the leaders of society. Her dresses and jewels were among the favorite themes of the industrious lady journalists, who got up marvelous accounts of Washington entertainments, and they were worthy of comment. I remember having seen her one night wearing one of Worth's dresses of alternating stripes of white satin embroidered with ivy leaves and green satin embroidered with golden ears of wheat with a sweeping train of green satin bordered with a heavy embroidered garland of ivy and wheat. A cluster of these in gold and emerald was in her black hair and she wore a full set of large emeralds set in Etruscan gold. The costume was faultless and fitted to adorn the queenlike woman." None of the "industrious lady journalists," however, had been sufficiently curious to inquire into the source of her income and that of her late sister—how it was possible, for example, for the General, whose income from the government was not more than $8,000 a year, to spend $10,000 on a single entertainment. In 1876 the answer was to be given in a scandal which would rock the already tottering Grant Administration to its foundations.

Mrs. Kate Williams, the handsome brunette from Oregon who had married the Attorney-General, was yet another claimant to the social crown. Her lavish entertainments at the mansion on Rhode Island Avenue (the present site of St. Matthew's Cathedral) and her costly gowns were the subject of much excited comment by the Washington columnists. A woman not only of wit but of boundless social ambitions, Mrs. Williams took upon herself to change the protocol of official Washington. She persuaded Mrs. Grant to call together the ladies of the Cabinet and took the occasion to state that the wives of Senators should first call upon the wives of Cabinet members, and that she, as wife of the Attorney-General, would not make the first call. The meeting came to the ears of Mrs. Matthew Carpenter, wife of the Senator from Wisconsin who was one of the most brilliant members of the Upper House, and was not forgotten. In 1873, after the death of Chief Justice Chase, when the President had nominated Williams as his successor, it was Senator Carpenter's opposition which helped to turn the tide of senatorial opinion against his confirmation.

Governor Cooke, who had purchased one of the finest old mansions in Georgetown, entertained more lavishly than the White House. "The atmosphere of the large drawing-rooms was heavily laden with the fragrance of choice exotics and foreign birds sang in the cages which hung in the emerald bloom. The richest Axminster carpets covered the floor; silk, satin and embroidery, ornamented rosewood and ebony; pictures and statuary as profuse as they were costly or extravagant. . . . If refined taste did not prevail," continued *Olivia,* "the effect was covered in Oriental splendor. Two thousand dollars a month was put in the hands of the steward to furnish this small private family with ordinary marketing, and this did not include the wines and staple groceries. Every day the courses were laid as if for a dinner party with preparations for any number of unexpected guests. Fleet horses stood in the stable with coachmen and footmen awaiting call . . . . For an official reception given in mid-winter $1,500 was paid for the single item of roses."[17] The wedding of Henry D. Cooke, Jr., and Anna H. Dodge, the daughter of an old Georgetown family, in June 1873, was attended by President Grant and the majority of Cabinet members. The wedding presents were valued at $30,000, and the Governor presented the couple with a house in Georgetown. After the ceremony a special train was placed at the disposal of the honeymoon couple by the President of the Baltimore and Ohio Railroad, John W. Garrett, for the first stage of their travels.

In contrast with the large-scale entertainments of the Cookes and Fishes were the intimate dinner parties given by Sam Ward, "the King of the Lobby," who had resided in Washington for many years as the agent of Baring Brothers, the important London banking house. A brother of Julia Ward Howe, he had been educated at the University of Tübingen in Germany and was a man of distinction and cultivated tastes. By sympathy a Democrat, he found no difficulty in remaining on excellent terms with prominent men in both parties, who quickly forgot their differences over the Lucullan repasts which he served to them. Sam Ward went to market for his own terrapin and canvasback duck; his tea was imported especially from China, and he personally blended his coffee. The dinners given at his house on Judiciary Square and at Welcker's were acknowledged to be "the climax of civilization." More than any man outside of Congress, Sam Ward knew the intrigues and secrets of Washington politics. In 1879 he published in the *North American Review* an essay revealing the maneuverings of President Buchanan's Cabinet in the hectic days preceding the attack on Fort Sumter; only in recent years has the identity of the author of *The Diary of a Public Man* been revealed.[18]

The lobbyists as a class, male and female, flourished now as never before. The railroad magnates, hungry for public land grants and subsidies, bid against each other for the favors of politicians. Collis P. Huntington, promoter of the Central Pacific, came to Washington with $200,000 in a trunk for "legal expenses" to obtain a Federal charter. General Franchot, his agent, spent $1,000,000 for "general legal expenses" over and above his salary of $30,000. Jay Cooke undertook almost singlehanded to underwrite the expenses of the Republican presidential campaign in 1872. The rewards, however, were commensurate. In 1871 Thomas A. Scott received a 13-million acre grant for the Texas Pacific Railroad, and Jay Cooke obtained a grant of 47 million acres for the Northern Pacific in 1868. By 1870 four Western roads had received as much public land as the combined states of Ohio, Illinois, Indiana, Wisconsin and Michigan.[19] Even Speaker Blaine was heavily involved in the Fort Smith and Little Rock Railroad, shares of which he tried to sell to his fellow members of Congress.

The venality of Congressmen had become a byword. "A Congressional appropriation costs money," said Colonel Sellers in *The Gilded Age*. "A majority of the House Committee . . . costs $40,000. A majority of the Senate Committee . . . say $40,000, a little extra to one or two Committee Chairmen . . . say $10,000 each . . . Then seven male lobbyists at $3,000 each, one female lobbyist at $10,000—a high moral Congressman or Senator here or there—the high moral ones cost more because they give a certain tone to a measure—say ten of these at $3,000 each. Then a lot of small-fry country members who won't vote for anything whatever without pay. Say twenty at $500 apiece . . ."[20]

Mark Twain, who had spent a winter in Washington during the height of the railroad lobbying, humorously cautioned those answering advertisements for room and board never to pretend to be Congressmen; such deception might have unexpected consequences. "If you had been content merely to be a private citizen your trunks would have been sufficient security for your board. Otherwise you would be asked for your rent in advance. If you are curious and inquire into this thing, the landlady will be ill-natured enough to say that the person and property of a Congressman are exempt from arrest or detention and that . . . she had seen several of the people's representatives walk off to their several states and territories carrying the unreceipted board bills in their pockets for keepsakes. And before you have been in Washington for many weeks you will be mean enough to believe her too."[21]

Neither were the manufacturers of New England neglecting their special interests. John L. Hayes was lobbying among the members of Congress seeking for the continuation of the tariff on textiles to protect the mills of the North. The wool interests in the Middle West were endeavoring to increase the tariff on imported cloth, and the steel and iron magnates of Pennsylvania, headed by Representative "Pig Iron" Kelley kept an anxious eye on the importation of steel rails from England; several of the charters granted to railroads specified that the rails laid down must be of American manufacture. The tariff issue was, indeed, beginning to overshadow the "Southern question" as the fundamental concern of the Republican party.

Before the War female lobbyists had been unheard of in Washington, but now they were everywhere. "Laura Hawkins" of *The Gilded Age,* who had come to the capital with her brother, the secretary of the "highly moral" Senator Dilworthy, typified this new political influence. Victorian convention, however, required them to be particularly discreet; while dark scandals were hinted at, they lived for the most part in boarding-houses of unquestionable respectability and kept their affairs closely to themselves.

Women were coming more and more into the limelight during the 70's as a political force. The granting of suffrage to the Negroes had intensified their desire for "equal rights," and there were not a few members of Congress who were sympathetic to their cause. In 1867 a branch of the Equal Rights League had been founded in the District. In 1871 Representative Julian of Indiana had attempted to insert an amendment in the Bill creating a Territorial form of government for the District of Columbia under which the word "male" would have been stricken out of the qualifications for the franchise, as the word "white" only recently had been removed. Elizabeth Cady Stanton appeared before the Senate Judiciary Committee to testify while the Bill was being discussed. In 1871 a national convention of women advocating suffrage was held in Washington, and a memorial was sent to the House Judiciary Committee requesting the right of women to vote on the basis of the 14th and 15th Amendments, by Victoria Woodhull, one of the Convention delegates. At the hearing she scandalized many Congressmen by appearing in a business suit of dark blue cloth with a skimpy skirt and a dark blue jacket finished off with mannish coat tails, wearing a severely plain hat with steeple crown and clipped hair.

The activities of Mrs. Woodhull and her sister, Tennessee Claflin, were indeed a source of considerable embarrassment to some of the advocates of the Cause. Mrs. Woodhull was the operator of a brokerage business on Wall Street—financed by Commodore Vanderbilt—and the sheet which she and her sister edited, *Woodhull's and Claflin's Weekly,* had ardently espoused not only women's rights to the suffrage but also to "Social Freedom." Victoria later proclaimed herself a candidate for the Presidency in 1872; when a scandal involving her marital relations was revealed, she retorted that "men did not regard in politics the domestic life of their nominees." Recognizing the potential strength of the suffrage movement, the Republican party considered it expedient to insert in the 1872 election platform a plank expressing "gratification that wider avenues of employment have been granted to women" and declaring that "her demands for additional rights should be treated with respectful consideration."

The women who had been fortunate enough in finding "wider avenues of employment" in Washington outside the ranks of the lobbyists were, however, few in number. The newspaper correspondents such as Emily Edson Briggs, whose *Olivia Letters* were widely read, Gail Hamilton and Mary Clemmer Ames, were all known and respected. Other female writers were placed in a different category. Jane Swisshelm, the ardent propagandist for the Union cause who had lived in Washington for many years, had driven the pro-slavery Governor of Minnesota into a sanitorium through her violent newspaper articles. Now dressed in bloomers and an ardent women's suffrage advocate, she had become one of the city's recognized eccentrics. Dr. Mary Walker, a former Army surgeon, went around the Washington streets in a man's frock coat and trousers, much to the scandal of the respectable ladies and the delight of small children. Dr. Walker, in addition to being a suffragette, was also a devotee of spiritualism and the author of two novels.

Most of the women in search of legitimate employment found the openings few and the salaries pitifully small. The female employees of the Bureau of Printing and Engraving who had been brought in by Secretary Chase during the War to trim the new paper currency received only $50 a month. Since they were obliged to pay $30 for room and board the margin for subsistence was indeed a small one, and officials of the Bureau were found guilty on more than one instance of using their position for taking advantage of their employees. Other girls working for newspapers received as little as $6 weekly. "It would be an odd circumstance," said Colonel Mulberry Sellers in *The Gilded Age,* "to see a girl get employment at $3 or $4 a week in one of the great public cribs without any political grandee to back her, but merely because she was worthy and competent and a good citizen of a 'free country' that 'treats all persons alike.' "[22]

The acknowledged "ladies of the town" who had multiplied in such a remarkable manner during the War, were still finding their occupation a profitable one. In the alleys of the Northern Liberties, on the "Island" in Southwest Washington, and especially in "Murder Bay" on the South side of the Avenue, the lowest kinds of dives catered to the sensation-seekers of all classes and races. On September 13, 1871, the *Patriot* gave an interesting account of a meeting to redeem their inmates under the arresting headlines: THE GREAT EVIL. HOW SHALL IT BE DEALT WITH AND HOW SHALL ITS VOTARIES BE REDEEMED? Describing the meeting organized by Mrs. H. C. Spencer, a prominent advocate of prohibition and women's rights, its reporter noted "occupying prominent positions were several keepers of well-known bagnios who had marshalled their girls and marched them out to attend the meeting. These were elegantly attired. Next to them sat ladies who, under other circumstances, would have felt contaminated by the close contact. 'Soiled doves' who were not known as such by the public, but who were recognized as the mistresses of 'gay young men' (and of old men too) occupied seats near the pure and virtuous. Preachers and profligates elbowed each other and gamblers and libertines met on a common level with pious young men who attend church regularly and are active workers as members of the YMCA. The philanthropic ladies who take the lead in this movement seem to treat it as an occasion not only to develop their peculiarities but as a fitting one for the display of their toilettes. Mrs. Spencer . . . presented herself on the stage in a starched white marseilles dress with a blue overskirt, the arrangement of which permitted a view of her kid slippers and of the delicate attractions which they encased."

Mrs. Spencer was successful in reclaiming from the toils of vice at least one notorious publican, "Reddy" Welch, who closed his den in "Murder Bay" and accompanied her to the platform on subsequent occasions. But the tone of the Washington press continued to be mildly amused—the reclamation of prostitutes, women's suffrage and temperance reform were causes to which "no real lady" would devote herself.

Most insistent in their activities were the temperance workers, who had been active in the District for many years. In Congress Senator Pomeroy of Kansas had been an ardent temperance advocate, and a Congressional Temperance Society had recommended that the House adopt a resolution instructing the District Committee to draw up a Bill under which the sale of intoxicating spirits would be prohibited. In the 1873 election campaign for the House of Delegates, when the opponents of the Board of Public Works were concentrating their attacks through Congress rather than the polls, a separate party had been formed and two delegates were elected on the temperance ticket.

The moralists could point with a warning finger at the passing of two picturesque figures from the Washington scene. The King of Patent Medicine, Dr. Helmbold, who had dazzled the spectators of the 1871 carnival with his magnificent display of horsemanship, had become bankrupt. In August of 1871 he had tried unsuccessfully to commit suicide at Long Branch when the extent of his reverses had become plain to him; later he fled the country to Europe, leaving large unpaid bills to the newspapers of Boston and New York. He had managed, evidently, to recoup his fortunes sufficiently to send to the *Star* in July 1873 a notice of a magnificent party given at his apartment in Paris; by October, he was writing to the *New York Herald* complaining of Jay Cooke and Henry Clews being called "Buchu bankers"; he had, said Dr. Helmbold, "a name to protect"! Such was the man, gossips smugly told one another, who had been the crony of President Grant.

In 1873, "Beau" Hickman, a ghost of his former elegant self and of a past generation, died in complete destitution in a small house on Maryland Avenue. Washington was shocked to learn that his body had been mutilated by corpse-snatchers; his remains were later gathered together and a public subscription was taken for their reinterment in the Congressional Cemetery. It was a particularly tragic form of irony that the body of a man who had at one time worn the most elegant clothes in Washington should be treated in so gruesome a fashion.

The reformers could at least take satisfaction that the lowest form of entertainment in the city, the notorious "Canterburies," had finally disappeared. The Metropolitan Police, under the strict direction of Major Richards, and no longer faced with the problem of keeping in order thousands of soldiers, had at last been able to wipe out all such forms of questionable entertainment.

Some of the more prudish theatregoers were nevertheless shocked at the musical extravaganza, *The Black Crook,* which made its appearance at the National Theatre in 1872. This production, the first attempt at musical comedy in the United States, displayed a multitude of feminine charms in a manner considered at the time to be extremely daring. It was, however, a great success in Washington and remained on the boards for a run of many weeks.

The National Theatre, under the direction of J. G. Savile, brought to the capital the best available talent from New York. In 1870 the bills featured George Jordan and Miss Bateman in *Mary Warner,* Mark Maretzek, the Italian Opera Company, and America's favorite Shakespearean actor, E. L. Davenport. The following year the visiting celebrities included Chanfrau, Charles Fechter, Lester Wallack and Dion Boucicault. In May, 1872, the celebrated Austrian actress, Janauschek, played the title part in Schiller's *Mary Stuart,* a performance which the critics agreed had never been surpassed in Washington's theatrical history. Galt's, the jewelers, displayed in their windows at the time some of the jewelry given to the great tragedienne by her admirers, the Czar of Russia, the Emperor Napoleon III of France and the King of Holland. On January 28, 1873, the National Theatre was destroyed by a fire of mysterious origin—the third in its history—and it did not reopen until December 1 of the same year. At the opening President Grant, Governor Shepherd and Kate Chase Sprague were among the box-holders to hear the incomparable American singer, Clara Louise Kellogg, in a performance of *Mignon.*

The Corcoran Gallery opened its doors to the newspaper correspondents on January 17, 1873, and to the public two days later. The cost of the building, designed by Renwick, had been a million dollars, and its endowment fund yielded an income of $60,000. During the War years when Mr. Corcoran had been in Europe he had purchased a large quantity of paintings and sculpture, and these, together with his earlier acquisitions, formed one of the largest private collections yet assembled in the United States. Prominently featured was *The Greek Slave* by Hiram Powers, which stood in an octagonal room, the walls of which were covered with maroon cashmere. There were many bronzes of animals by Barye, *Dead Caesar* by the noted French artist, Gérome, a copy of a head of Napoleon I by Canova, paintings by Murillo, Corot, Vernet, the German artists Raphael Mengs, Ary Scheffer, Emanuel Lenthe and Schreyer, Majolica vases, Roman utensils from Hildesheim, and paintings by Gilbert Stuart, Thomas Cole, Eastman Johnson and many other esteemed contemporary Americans.[23] Perhaps the most popular of all the pictures in the Corcoran Gallery was the giant Niagara landscape by Church. "It is to me the gem of the collection," wrote Jane W. Gemmill, in her recollections of Washington. "To look upon this painting when the sun is shining overhead is the next best thing to standing beside the mighty cataract. The mist is there, the beautiful rainbow, the vast volume of vivid green water, the boiling and rushing rapids, the distant trees in their autumn foliage—everything but the strange solemn roar—what a great pity the artist could not transfer that also to the canvas! I have heard that $12,000 was the price paid for it, and I am sure that the sum is moderate, considering the pleasure that 12,000 have had in looking at it, many of whom will never have an opportunity of beholding the reality."[24]

While by contemporary European standards the Corcoran collection could hardly be considered an important one, few American galleries of the period could boast of anything superior. Owners of great works of art in the '70's preferred for the greater part to show them only to their intimate circle of friends. The Corcoran Gallery, open to the public on weekdays between 10 and 4, kept out the impecunious by an admittance charge of 25 cents on alternate days, when the copyists could work undisturbed.

Washington possessed, however, an attraction which was of perpetual interest—and always free of charge. The sessions of Congress continued to provide as before the capital's most reliable form of entertainment. Though Grant's eight-year term of office failed to produce as dramatic a performance as the Impeachment Trial of Andrew Johnson, it provided at least in the Credit Mobilier investigation, the Belknap trial and the District investigations sufficient scandalous revelations for the curious. The Administration's Southern policy and the President's San Domingo scheme could also be counted upon to stimulate oratorical fireworks. An announcement in the press or a well-circulated rumor that Sumner, Conkling, Thurman, Hendricks or Morton were to be given the floor of the Senate would result in a rush of dozens of spectators to Capitol Hill. Conscious of their roles as principal actors in the great arena of American politics, the elder statesmen rehearsed their speeches, polished their classical quotations, and let flow their rhetoric for the benefit of their nation-wide audience.

Chapter 9

The Day of Reckoning

The 43rd Congress to which the memorial of the District taxpayers had been addressed was in a sober mood, not only as a result of the financial crash of the previous year, but also on account of the revelations of corruption in high places which had been made in 1873. In January the investigation into the affairs of the railroad holding company, the Credit Mobilier, had shocked the American public by revealing the lengths which Republican congressmen—and even some Democrats—would go in order to make a quick profit at the expense of the government. Shortly before the 42nd Congress had adjourned, the bill proposed by Benjamin F. Butler to increase the salaries of the President, Judiciary and members of Congress—popularly known as the "Salary Grab"—had been passed. Grant's appointment of his own brother-in-law, J. F. Casey, to the lucrative post of Collector of the Port of New Orleans had been condemned as nepotism, and conservative Massachusetts Republicans had been outraged by the President's selection of Butler's protegé, William A. Simmons, for a similar position in Boston. In April the matter of the Sanborn contracts had aroused public indignation. Sanborn, another crony of Butler's, had been given a contract to collect delinquent taxes under which he retained one-half of the proceeds. When it was discovered that Sanborn had been abusing his privilege and that Secretary Richardson had done nothing to intervene, Richardson was forced to resign and the contract was voided by Congress.

The opposition press had seized upon the appointment of Shepherd as Governor in October, 1873, as yet another instance of Grant's blindness and gullibility. Shepherd was well-known to be a member of Grant's "Kitchen Cabinet," along with Butler, Conkling, Morton and other administration "Stalwarts." Since the large District appropriations of the preceding years the financial affairs of the District had become of general interest to the people of the entire nation. Although the Republican leaders in Congress were reluctant to examine for a second time the finances of the District, they could not have avoided this action without giving the appearance of being themselves implicated. That was a risk which, in an election year, they could ill afford to take.

Shepherd, who had long anticipated the action of the memorialists, had been quick to reply to their charges. In a long letter to congressional leaders published on January 30 he retorted that the report of the Board of Public Works published the preceding month represented a true statement of the District finances. He appended a list which showed that many of the men who had signed the memorial had paid little or nothing on their special assessments, and that the straits in which the District were now placed were in part due to their delinquency.[1] The *National Republican* commented the following day: "Mr. Corcoran is a fair specimen of that class of people who have been injuring the credit of the District, accusing men who have made Washington in some measure worthy of its position in the Union of fraud and corruption . . . Demanding the punishment of others for alleged violations of law, he should certainly first place himself in the position of being a law-abiding citizen."

On the same day on which the Governor's letter was published, a masked ball took place at his residence on Connecticut Avenue, the most elaborate entertainment yet held there. Shepherd and his wife were dressed in dominoes and the guests in a motley array. The ball was to be the first in a series of official receptions which the Governor had planned for the winter season, and to which he intended to invite members of the Cabinet and leading members of Congress. Now that District affairs were again to be scrutinized by Congress, its goodwill was more than ever necessary to the Territorial authorities.

On February 2 Jeremiah Wilson of Indiana, a Republican who had headed the Credit Mobilier Investigation in 1873, introduced a motion to appoint a joint committee to examine the conduct of District affairs, and this motion was carried three days later. Three members were chosen from the Senate—William B. Allison of Iowa and George S. Boutwell of Massachusetts, both Republicans, and Allan G. Thurman of Ohio, a Democrat. The House named to the Committee Lyman K. Bass of New York, Jay Hubbell of Michigan, and Jeremiah Wilson of Indiana, Republicans, and H. J. Jowett of Ohio and Robert Hamilton of New Jersey, Democrats. Boutwell, who had succeeded to the Senate upon the election of Henry Wilson to the Vice-Presidency, agreed to head the Joint Committee.

The Committee met for the first time on February 16, and asked the Territorial government to clarify certain points in order that they might determine the financial status of the District. The Governor was asked to furnish complete information regarding the amount of indebtedness incurred before the Territorial administration and up to the present, the current methods of raising taxes, the disbursements made by the District government since February 21, 1871, the contracts which had been entered into, the contributions for improvements made by the Federal Government, and the obligations due to officers and employees of the District.

On March 1 the Governor's reply was received. Dr. William Tindall, his secretary, carried the answer proper in a huge portfolio tied with red tape. The District Auditor, J. C. Lay, and F. H. Johnson, of the Contract Department, followed with a guard of seven laborers bearing eleven boxes about two feet square containing 10,537 vouchers and measurements. The work had consumed the time of 31 clerks for three whole weeks.

Shepherd's answer to the Committee Chairman, Senator Boutwell, was courteous and cooperative, and he made a good impression by his promptness in furnishing the desired information. His figures showed that the assessed value of property in the District had increased by $17,000,000 since the inauguration of the Territorial government. Up to the end of February the receipts of the Board of Public Works had been $15,256,231 and its expenditures $14,603,052. He estimated the present assets of the Board at $3,765,297 and its liabilities at $4,552,958. Shepherd blamed the deficiency on the fact that the Federal government had still not contributed its proper share of the District budget in proportion to the property which it owned, and also to the delinquent payment of special assessments by private property owners.[2]

On March 5 the Joint Committee began to take testimony. The proceedings were given great prominence in the Washington newspapers, the *National Republican* issuing a two-page special supplement during the entire course of the investigation. The first item on the agenda was the charge of the wealthy memorialists who had offered to advance two months' salary to the white teachers in Georgetown. The District Comptroller, George E. Baker, testified that the amounts due to teachers over a three-year period totaled $371,322.52. Though steps had been taken to tax private schools and other property hitherto exempt, Lewis Clephane, the Collector of Taxes, who testified the following day, pointed out that payments were so far in arrears that the teachers were inevitably affected. On the 1871-72 tax levy $62,388.51 was still due, and $229,412.89 on the 1872-73 assessment. Of the current taxes due on June 30, 1874, $1,126,-311.84 was still to be collected. Thirty-one per cent of the children in the public schools were those of government employees, most of whom did not pay taxes to the District. Moreover, when the Territorial government had taken over from the Corporation in 1871, the Washington school fund was $173,000 in arrears, since Mayor Emery had not collected taxes for the first six months of the year. This charge was denied by Merrick, counsel for the memorialists, who claimed that the school fund showed a balance of $42,548 at the time of the change of government, and William Syphax, the former treasurer of the colored school trustees, supported him by stating that he had handed over a check amounting to more than $2,700 to the new authorities after having paid all outstanding accounts. Later, however, under cross-examination by Harrington, the District Attorney, he admitted having received a certificate that the Corporation owed the money to the colored school fund, but not the actual cash. On the 9th to meet the emergency the House District Committee agreed to report a bill advancing $97,000 for the arrears of the teachers' salaries, to be deducted from future District appropriations. In order to be certain that the sum would not be used for other purposes by the District government the bill was passed with a clause stating that the disbursement be made by the United States Commissioners of Education.

On March 11 the memorialists, who had been permitted to examine the official records of the District government, produced more detailed charges of malfeasance to the Investigating Committee. They claimed that a "Ring" which included former Governor Cooke, Hallett Kilbourn, William S. Huntington, Samuel P. Brown, the contractor John O. Evans, Lewis Clephane, and others had entered into a conspiracy to secure the contracts of the District government, and that the Board of Public Works had shown favoritism to several of the contractors by permitting them to raise their prices during the course of the work. The $10,000,000 debt limit set by Congress after the investigation of 1872 had been exceeded by the issue of assessment certificates and by the sewer tax, both measures which they asserted were illegal. The Board was also accused of carelessness in the allocation of contracts and permitting false measurements to be made by contractors in the work performed by them on behalf of the Federal government.

The death of Charles Sumner on March 12 and the subsequent recess of Congress interrupted the sessions of the Investigating Committee until March 17. In the interim Boutwell, who had been suffering from poor health, resigned as Chairman, and Senator Stewart of Neveda was nominated to succeed him. The proposal of Senator Carpenter that Stewart should head the Committee was violently attacked by the opposition newspapers, the *New York Tribune* accusing the Senator of having been involved in real estate speculation in the Dupont Circle area, and claiming that the grade of Massachusetts Avenue as far as Thomas Circle had been cut down solely to give an uninterrupted view to his residence. Stewart denied the charges, stating that he had sold his property to Sunderland and Hillyer in December, 1872, for $18,000 which he needed for his mining operations, that he had no connection with the Board of Public Works and knew nothing of their plans. Nevertheless, when the Committee reconvened, the nomination of Stewart as Chairman was rejected and Senator Allison of Iowa appointed in his place. Allison, though an Administration supporter, was noted for his extreme caution and fair-mindedness, and consequently the Investigating Committee would be free of the "white-washing" charges which had been levelled at the House Report of 1872 under the chairmanship of H. H. Starkweather.

The Committee settled down to a prolonged session for the hearing of testimony. Congress appropriated on March 19 the sum of $10,000 towards the cost of the investigation and ten days later the hearings were moved to a smaller room at the rear of the Ladies Gallery of the Senate. The *Star* bitterly complained of the poor acoustic qualities of the room and of its shabbiness: "the outer space is supplied with old-fashioned hair settees for witnesses and for the benefit of the loafers who are daily on hand." The memorialists were now asked to produce written charges against the members of the District government accused of conspiracy, with the proof of their complicity and a list of specific questions which they should be required to answer.

Harrington on the 20th took up the first charge of the memorialists against the District government. He stated that Evans, the largest contractor, who had been paid almost a million dollars for his services, had been able to pave the streets for $3.20 a yard instead of $3.50 per yard, which had been the cost of the Scharf payment favored by Corcoran and Riggs. He conceded that some of the estimates received were below the actual cost to the District, but that the Act of the Legislative Assembly in July, 1871, had allowed for such deviations "as full as may be practicable and consistent with the public interest," and that the 1872 Investigation had substantiated this interpretation of the law. He admitted that thirty cents general increase had been given to contractors in order to get the work completed. Merrick, in rebuttal, pointed out that the original proposal of the Board did not call for wood or other expensive paving, and that road beds of stone had been considered sufficient at the time.

On the 21st the Committee received a request from Columbus Alexander in his capacity as leader of the memorialists. He asked that a competent and disinterested engineer be appointed to examine the work performed by the Board of Public Works, and that the Board be asked to furnish a list of all materials purchased and their source. He further requested that their journals be open for inspection and that a list of bond issues made by the District government be given together with a note of all District securities pledged as collateral. The cost of improvements made adjacent to churches and other tax-exempt institutions was also demanded as well as the amounts which had been received from the Sewerage tax in order that the sums paid by the citizens of the District and the Federal government might be clearly distinguished.

James M. Latta, the partner of Hallett Kilbourn, testified on the 23rd that the District Government had been in no way involved in any of his real estate speculations. When questioned by Senator Thurman on the extent of his dealings with Senator Stewart, he refused to answer, on the ground that he should not be asked to violate the confidence of a client. He agreed, however, to produce the deed books of his firm. The *New York Sun* estimated on the 27th that the amount of money invested by Stewart in Washington real estate was $361,490.

Sayles J. Bowen appeared before the Committee on the 25th.[3] "With a smile, child-like and bland, he sat a quiet looker-on until he was summoned as a witness." After the abuse which he had undergone only four years previously it was doubtless a pleasure to be present at the humiliation of his enemies. Bowen could not state exactly which streets had been graded during his administration, but established an important point against Shepherd's administration of the Board of Public Works. Only one price, he stated, had been paid to contractors for hauling and dumping of earth, and dumping was to be done at no extra charge wherever specified by the ward commissioners. Contractors had been selected by him on the basis of an adequate bond and personal responsibility in their payment of employees; he did not know of a single instance where contractors appropriated surplus earth for their own uses. His personal difficulties with the Board resulted from the removal of a brick footway next to his house on K Street at the time the street was parked. He had refused to pay the expense of having the footway relaid, and consequently a certificate of indebtedness had been issued against him.[4]

On the following day Col. Theodore Samo, an engineer in Babcock's Department of Public Grounds and Buildings, was called to answer the charge that improper measurements had been made by the Board for work done on behalf of the Federal government. He admitted that mistakes had been made at Dupont Circle and Rawlins Square[5] but claimed that the amounts involved had been grossly exaggerated. The *New York Tribune* had on February 16 published a report that the Board had charged $19,442 and Babcock allowed $29,824 for work which at the fixed Board prices should only have cost $8,898.50. Since the date of the letter the paper stated that $14,000 had been refunded to the Government by the Board.

The contractors now appeared at the investigation. Peter McNamara divulged that he had paid over $1,000 to Joseph Carroll of the House of Delegates and George F. Gulick of the Legislative Council to obtain the contract to macadamize Pennsylvania Avenue Northeast from 1st to 8th Street. He had refused a further request from Carroll for $1,000 and had later reported the matter to Shepherd, who threatened to deprive him of further contracts if bribery were again attempted. However, in a later effort to obtain a contract he had put $150 in an envelope and sent it to Barney, the Chief Assistant Engineer of the Board with a note, "Mr. McNamara lends to Mr. Barney $150 for 60 days." Barney reported the attempted bribe to Shepherd, who again called in McNamara, though he did not make good his previous threat.

The case of Samuel Strong which came up on the 31st was of particular interest, since it involved the Corporation Counsel of the District, William S. Cook, who had also acted as Strong's attorney.[6] The contractor was accused of making twice as large an excavation as was necessary in the construction of a sewer on R Street and attempting to bribe the inspector. Sawyer, the District official involved, testified that after he had refused the bribe in the form of a certificate, Strong and his friends had conspired to get him drunk, and that when he woke up he found in his pocket $115 worth of Board certificates. He was later told by Strong that the papers in question had already been sent to the Board and that he could not see them; when he reported the matter to his superiors he was complimented on his efficiency and later dismissed on the ground of insufficient work. Resuming the witness stand on April 2, Strong testified that he had lent $125 to A. K. Browne, a member of the House of Delegates, and that Adolphus Hall, one of the colored members of the Council, had been a timekeeper in his employ. William A. Cook, he contended, had been acting for him in a legal capacity for several years, and he denied hotly the accusation of having bribed him. When he was requested, however, to produce his check book, the stubs were found to be missing.

Cook, who took the stand on April 6, had long been a target of abuse in the District. The *New York Sun* correspondent described him as "a wizened little creature with a face that makes you think of Mr. Quick of that celebrated firm of Quick,

Gammon and Snap." A former minister, he had served in the Pennsylvania Legislature as a Democrat; in 1865 he had come to practice law in Washington and had served in the General Land Office. Cook admitted having acted as Strong's lawyer since 1870 in suits against the Federal government. He estimated that his services had been worth $5,000 to the contractor, though he had only received "a few hundred." It was true that Strong had sent him a check for $3,000, but, since it had been made out jointly to him and A. K. Browne he had not cashed it.[7]

Up to now, the Board had managed to maintain its position relatively unscathed. On April 8, Mr. Quincy, a member of the Chicago firm of de Golyer and McClelland, appeared to give the most damaging testimony so far against its officers. Shepherd, he said, had at the pressure of Representative Farwell from Illinois ordered that the contract for the de Golyer wooden pavement be finished, even though it had been demonstrated by experience in Chicago that such pavement would last for only one year. The contract, moreover, had been so remunerative that one of the firm's executives, George Chittenden, had been given a lobbying fee of $72,000 to secure it; $15,000 had been allotted to Col. R. C. Parsons, now a member of the House from Ohio for the same purchase; and $10,000 to the Rev. Colvin Brown, a former United States Consul in Hamburg, Germany. Out of the sum paid to Parsons $5,000 was later given to James A. Garfield as "legal advice." Chittenden, testifying on the 17th, admitted having paid over the $72,000 to Col. A. B. Kirtland to help secure the contract and mentioned his meetings with Chipman, Governor Cooke and Huntington.[8]

Public opinion in Washington was now openly turning against the Board, and for the first time in more than a year the local press was becoming critical of its activities. On the 19th, Forney's *Sunday Chronicle* printed an outspoken plea for Congress to assume charge of District affairs: "We are in trouble and unless relieved by the powers that are in all fairness responsible for it, there is no hope for us . . . Let us get rid of half of the unnecessary machinery of our present government, which, as far as being a representative body of the interests of the District, is a fraud and an expense large enough to run many of the single states in the Union." If the Investigation, it said, resulted in closer relations with Congress, it would have the strongest support from the people of the District. Donn Piatt on the 12th had written in the *Capital:* "The Legislature of this now distracted District is to assemble before long and it is the fit precursor of dog-days, cholera morbus and the mosquitoes. As a morbid excresence on the body politic it has no equal except that of the South Carolina amalgamation. Its very existence is a disgrace to the power that can wipe it out tomorrow by an almost unanimous vote, and the sooner our affairs are managed under the agency of Congress the better." The *Georgetown Courier,* commenting on April 25 of prospective changes in the District government, put itself on record as favoring the abolition of the Legislative Assembly in favor of "a single intelligent directing body under the supervision of Congress; but by all means let the man for the position be our trusted and proved incorruptible Governor Shepherd."

When the Legislature convened on the 27th the Governor sent a message to both Houses suggesting that "a proper respect for the authority of Congress would indicate the propriety of deferring action while those subject are under its special consideration. I therefore recommend that the Legislative Assembly adjourn or postpone the transaction of business until Congress shall have made a final disposition of the matter in question." F. A. Boswell, appointed head of a special committee of both Houses to consider adjournment, replied on the 29th that since the Investigation was directed not at the District government but at the Board of Public Works, the Legislature should continue in session. The business transacted, however, was negligible, since the District was without available funds for further improvements.

On the morning of April 24 the Washington newspapers reported an attempt to break into the safe of District Attorney Harrington; three men were being held for their part in the crime. Few details were given of the robbery, though some of the editors such as Donn Piatt were of the opinion that the memorialists were implicated. The affair, coming at such a crucial point in the District Investigation, immediately attracted the attention of the Joint Committee. In view, however, of the fact that important figures in both the local and national administrations were involved, the Committee decided to hold its hearings and examination of witnesses in closed session.

On the 30th Christy, one of the counsel for the memorialists, returned from New York with the missing witness, Col. A. B. Kirtland. Ever since his name had been mentioned in the Investigation he had been searched for in New York, Detroit and Chicago to answer the subpoena issued by the Sergeant-at-Arms of the Senate. The opposition press reported that Kirtland had come to Washington on the 16th and had registered at the Washington Hotel and Ebbitt House under various names, but that he had been dissuaded from testifying by the attorneys for Chittenden and by the counsel of the District government, Mattingly. Kirtland had accordingly quietly slipped out of the town, taking a train from Alexandria to Richmond and a freight boat from Norfolk to New York. The "mystery witness" appeared as "apparently on the sunny side of forty; has dark hair sprinkled with grey, and wears his whiskers à la muttonchop. He has a pleasing countenance which is lit up by dreamy eyes. He wears a suit of black not gaudy in cut or finish and had no visible ornaments in the way of jewelry about his person. His appearance would indicate that he is not given to fast horses or women."[9]

Kirtland was disarmingly frank in his first remarks to the Committee. "Mr. Chairman," he said, "I have come without counsel at all. I put myself in your hands. I have no statement to make and no grievances to make—nothing to complain of. I shall be frank and brief."

Senator Allison replied: "Colonel Kirtland, you tell the Committee now that you have nothing to conceal. That being so, I want you without any reservations to tell us what you did—

what negotiations you made, what transactions you had with any person whatsoever relating to this contract."

KIRTLAND: I told you I had no statement to make, Mr. Chairman. I am under oath.

ALLISON: Well, then give it . . .

KIRTLAND: I told you what I did.

ALLISON: Did you tell us all that you did?

KIRTLAND: Yes, sir.

ALLISON: Do you pretend that $72,000 was given to you to go about the streets here and there and then report to Chittenden every day that things were progressing?

KIRTLAND: I told you you would have to believe me under oath. Don't you believe that?

ALLISON: Not if you stop there, I don't. I tell you frankly.

KIRTLAND: Well, you are obliged to believe me.[10]

Seeing that further direct questioning would be useless, the Committee then proceeded to hear an explanation from Shepherd regarding his relationship to the witness. The Governor explained that his former partner, Colonel W. G. Moore,[11] had been a friend of Kirtland, who had endeavored to make use of his contact in order to secure the paving contract for his firm. The first intimation Shepherd had received of the transaction was through a letter which Henry D. Cooke had received from ex-Senator Doolittle of Wisconsin acting as Chittenden's counsel, which threatened legal proceedings if the de Golyer contract was not reinstated. The letter had mentioned that the contractor had been obliged to give notes in order to obtain the contract. As soon as this information came to Shepherd's attention, he summoned Colonel Moore and dissolved their business partnership.[12]

Kirtland, recalled, became somewhat more explicit. He denied that Moore had done him favors, but stated that he had offered to pay him half of his $72,000 commission as "an act of charity, perhaps." He had up till now received about $31,500 in cash and property from the sale of the notes—a house in Chicago, $12,000 in cash and a pair of horses and a carriage. Ten thousand dollars had been credited to his account at Riggs & Company shortly before his arrival in Washington. He had given this money as a down payment on "Harewood," the Corcoran estate in which the Rev. Colvin Brown was also interested, but the deal had fallen through. A letter written by Kirtland to G. H. Wilcox, a member of Congress, was produced by the Committee which he was asked to explain. It contained the sentence, "I am perfecting a scheme that will, I expect, knock the legs from under a certain crowd," and it added that "some one will be sorry if he is obliged to testify."[13] When the letter was read Kirtland, thoroughly uncomfortable by now, refused to clarify his statements on the ground that it would render him liable to criminal prosecution, and he was finally discharged by the Committee. Though Shepherd's straight-forward testimony had made a good impression, the fact that a paving company could afford as large a sum as $96,000 for lobbying expenses clearly indicated that the fixed price schedule of the Board of Public Works had in this instance been more than generous. A further indication of the trend of congressional opinion was revealed on May 4, when Stewart introduced into the Senate a bill calling for a new District government directed by a Board of five Commissioners appointed by the Federal government to take over all powers.

The affairs of the Metropolitan Paving Company, in which Shepherd had been financially interested, were investigated on the following day. Lewis Clephane, the treasurer of the company, admitted that the directors had permitted various persons—among them Crosby S. Noyes and S. H. Kauffmann of the *Star* and William Murtagh of the *National Republican*—to buy stock on a twenty per cent down payment and to receive immediately afterwards a twenty per cent dividend. Shepherd had been represented as a stockholder up to the formation of the Board of Public Works by his brother-in-law, Young, who had subsequently sold out his interest. This whole pattern, which resembled so closely that of the Credit Mobilier, did not reflect well on the integrity of the Washington press. The *New York Tribune* correspondent commented: "Some out of town correspondents were heckled by Washington newspapermen; now it is obvious why."[13]

On the 7th of May, Shepherd was recalled for prolonged questioning. He denied at the outset any complicity in the assignment of contracts and vigorously defended the system of fixed prices which the Board had set up. The contract rates of the District, he said, compared very favorably with the current scale in other large American cities, citing figures in Baltimore, New York, Philadelphia and Boston to prove his contention. Asked to explain the financial embarrassment of the District, he again referred to the large area of the city—500 acres—which was occupied by wide avenues which would not have existed if Washington were not the capital; in other cities commercial property paying taxes to the municipality would have occupied their place. Though the 1873 Legislature had made an abatement of three-quarters of one per cent for advance payment of taxes, money had been worth since the crash of the previous autumn nine per cent a year, and few were in a position to make advance payments. There was, therefore, no method of meeting the current needs of the District government before July, when the 1873-74 tax fell due. "If our taxes had been collected," he asserted, "we would have means enough to pay every dollar that the District owes to school teachers, firemen and all its employees, and if the assessments were in such shape that the money on them could be collected, the Board of Public Works would not be short over one or one and a half millions." Again producing figures, he showed that the taxation rate in the District was not as excessive as his opponents had claimed compared to those of other American cities. The property tax of $2.00 was considerably less than that of New York and Brooklyn ($3.22 and $3.50) and less than St. Louis or Jersey City ($2.15 and $2.10). Moreover, while the District now possessed over 75 miles of paved streets, St. Louis could only claim 50 and Chicago 45, and both these cities had populations of over 400,000. The District now had 133 miles of water mains and 140 miles of sewers, a far higher ratio in proportion to the population than any city in the United States. About $15,000,000 had been expended by the Territorial government since 1871 and $18,000,000 worth of certificates had been granted by the Board, but the bonded debt of the District had not been exceeded. The Sewer Bill, concerning which there had been so much controversy, had been checked by such legal experts as W. S. Cox and Caleb Cushing, who had found that it did not contravene the provisions of the Organic Act; no favors had been granted to the members of the Legislature to insure its passage. He defended the unequal features of the tax by stating that the amount of work in the Eastern part of the city had been much greater; property owners in this area should therefore be willing to pay a higher rate for the improvement of their land, much of which was still under water through lack of drainage. As regards the January interest on the District debt, not a dollar of Sewer bonds had been borrowed; the money had been taken instead from the Sinking Fund for the amortization of the Corporation debts.

Shepherd admitted that the improvements had caused much damage to private property; out of the $1,300,000 which had been claimed in damages the Board had already awarded $463,541.07 as compensation. It was true that the assessments on the houses of Senators Edmunds and Bayard on Massachusetts Avenue had been taken as paid in compensation for the damages which they had sustained, and that the house of Justice Wylie on Thomas Circle had been moved by the Board free of charge. He made no apologies for having placed first-class pavement in front of public buildings, saying that it would have been a disgrace to the country to place cobblestones around them. He had generally been in favor of concrete pavements, except in cases where the residents had specified wooden ones, and had in these instances acceded to their requests. He considered that the Federal Government had in its appropriations of 1873 recognized the principle of its responsibility for the maintenance of the principal avenues of the city of Washington.[14]

Mr. Corcoran testified on May 19 regarding the offer of James Harlan, the editor of the *Chronicle,* to which he had referred in his letter a few months before to the *Baltimore Sun.* Harlan, to whose paper the District government was indebted for a printing bill which he had been unable to collect, had devised an ingenious scheme for obtaining the money. He had already paid about $7,000 worth of partnership taxes for Riggs & Co., and had been handed back the proceeds as an offset against the *Chronicle* account. Corcoran had been tempted to do likewise and thus secure a ten per cent rebate on his special assessments plus the legal six per cent discount for payment of his tax in advance, but on second thought he had decided against the proposal.[15]

On the same day Shellabarger summed up the case of the memorialists, stressing the legal issues involved, and Merrick followed him with an eloquent plea on behalf of the citizens of the District whose rights, he said, had been so grossly violated. It was the intention of the Committee, which had now listened to testimony for more than two months, to close the proceedings on Saturday, May 23. Enough evidence had been disclosed to show great laxity in the conduct of the Board of Public Works—even though actual corruption on the part of its officers had not been established. However, on May 20 the Investigating Committee was startled to hear testimony from the German-born Engineer of the Board of Public Works, Adolph Cluss, which appeared to confirm the most extravagant charges of personal dishonesty which Shepherd's enemies had made against him.

Closely questioned by Representative Jeremiah Wilson of Indiana, Cluss appeared on the witness stand at 10 in the morning and remained to testify until 4:30 with only a brief intermission. He admitted he had found evidence of faulty measurements in the work performed for the Federal government by the Board, and testified that he had transferred Forsyth, the guilty surveyor in the employ of the District government, whom he considered had been working for the contractors. He said that Shepherd was aware of the faulty measurements, but that he still continued to make use of them in billing the Federal government for their share of the improvements. When Evans, Gleason and other contractors wished to have their work assessed, they sent for Oertly, Cluss's assistant, and vouchers were made out without his approval. He spoke of Shepherd's autocratic methods of conducting the business of the Board; during the time he had been a member from October 1872 there had been but eight meetings, the longest of which had lasted an hour and a half. He had decided to testify because he was not willing that his reputation as an engineer should be ruined on account of the false measurements which Shepherd had required him to make.[16]

The testimony of Cluss was the sensation of the entire Investigation. In Washington it became the sole topic of conversation. The opposition press was jubilant. "If anything were needed," wrote the correspondent of the *New York Tribune,* "to prove that the Board of Public Works is rotten with fraud, and corruption, it was supplied to-day by the evidence of Mr. Adolph Cluss." The *Sun* correspondent wrote on the 22nd, "It is admitted on every hand that the Ring is not only hopelessly gone but that the Boss and other members of the wicked combination will be proceeded against criminally and sent to the pen." The Washington press supporting Shepherd was startled and nonplussed. Donn Piatt in the *Capital* considered that Wilson's line of questioning revealed his prejudice against the District Government, and the *National Republican* believed that the witness had been suborned. The *Star* was even forced to admit that Cluss's testimony was extremely damaging to Shepherd. To the Governor the defection of his long-time friend and personal architect, the man who had designed his home and was his neighbor, was a bitter blow. It was not long, however, before he recovered, and Cluss was made to feel the full impact of his revenge.

When the counsel for the District, Mattingly, was permitted to examine the witness, he had as his consultant Jeremiah S. Black, and no opportunity was lost to entangle the Engineer of the Board in his own statements. Cluss was a man of excitable temperament, and his imperfect mastery of the English language led him into errors of which Mattingly took full advantage. Many of the fraudulent measurements which Cluss had denounced bore his own signature, though he claimed that they were merely certified during the routine of business. Such apparent carelessness, however, did not sit well on a man who had accused other members of the Board of fraud, and when the District counsel resumed cross-examination on the 23rd, Cluss was forced into a confession of his own shortcomings.

"As the cross-examination went on, momentarily compelling from the witness a point-blank contradiction of his previous testimony, his attitude and bearing was truly humiliating. His pallid face, his parched lips and tongue that refused to obey the helm when he essayed to speak and his trembling knees all told of his confusion and discomfort. Finally he asked permission to take a seat."[17] "It is hard to read that cross-examination without emotion," wrote Donn Piatt, "but torturing as its perusal is, it bears no relation whatever to the ghastly horrid spectacle exhibited when it was taken. None but a heart of stone could have remained unmoved."[18] During the entire three hours of the cross-examination, Jeremiah Wilson, who had originally induced Cluss to speak, never lifted a finger to help him out of his agony. The sympathetic correspondent of the *New York Tribune* commented that Cluss had blamed the corrupt system rather than the individual members of the Board; whereas the defense had tried to throw on him the onus of responsibility for the irregularities. While he had undoubtedly been guilty of signing the vouchers for the work which the Board had performed for the Federal Government, the work had not yet been paid for. The production of those papers in Court, while embarrassing to the witness, did not detract from the truth of his original statement.

On the 25th President Grant at Shepherd's suggestion sent to the Senate a message removing Cluss as Engineer to the Board and nominating to replace him Lt. Richard L. Hoxie of the U. S. Engineer Corps. The nomination was acted upon favorably and promptly. Cluss was certainly a convenient scapegoat, but it was clear that his dismissal would not be sufficient to compensate for all the irregularities of the Board. Magruder, its treasurer, summoned on the 25th, was found to have kept his books in an exceedingly unsatisfactory manner and no stubs could be found for the many checks which he had issued. Out of the $15,000,000 worth of certificates for work performed by contractors for the Board he could trace only $3,500,000. The Board's secretary, Charles S. Johnson, admitted the following day that although 149 meetings were recorded in the minutes there had been only 14 at which other members had been present besides Shepherd. He stated that on one occasion Oertly, Cluss's assistant, had ordered $25,000 to be paid to a contractor for work which Shepherd had only ordered to be measured the following day. Another engineer, Barney, testified that he had been asked many times to make measurements by Shepherd personally, but that he had referred the matter to Cluss on each occasion. Cluss, brought back briefly to the witness stand, reiterated his charges in a calmer mood, and the testimony of the Committee was then brought to a close. The investigation had lasted for three months and twenty-two days and had cost, the *Star* estimated, $5,000. The report which it was to publish, covering three volumes of 1,000 pages each, was one of the longest ever undertaken by any congressional committee.

Grant's hasty action in dismissing Cluss had been taken in New York, where he had accompanied his daughter Nellie on the first lap of her European honeymoon. The opposition papers lost no time in attacking him for his decision. On the 26th the *Tribune* editorially accused him of violating the law of July 15, 1870, under which all U. S. Army officers were declared ineligible for public office unless they immediately resigned their commissions, and it also censured the President for acting before the publication of the Committee's report. "President Grant has done nothing in his administration," the same paper commented on June 2, "so thoroughly indicative of a purpose to be absolute in his possession and exercise of power and to regard nothing but personal motives and the suggestion of his own caprice in appointments and removals . . . This is personal government of the most irresponsible and unscrupulous sort." The *Sun* on May 27 asked editorially, "If President Grant wished to identify himself more completely with the Washington Ring, could he find any other way to do it so effectively as by promptly punishing Adolph Cluss for giving his evidence against their robberies? The plunderers are continued in power and enjoy his fullest confidence; but those who expose them are visited with his swift indignation."

Whatever the outcome of the deliberations of the Investigating Committee, it was becoming clear beyond any possible doubt that the Territorial government could not continue in its present form. The only question was which alternative administration should be adopted. On June 1 William Lawrence, a Republican member from Ohio, introduced a bill abolishing all of the offices in the District government in favor of a Council of 48 elected members. On the following day the House of Delegates sent a petition to Congress requesting that the Upper House be made elective and that the Board of Public Works and the Board of Health be abolished. Provision should be made for the biennial election of a Collector of Taxes, Comptroller and Register. The District debt should be limited to $13,000,000 and the Federal Government should undertake to pay one-third of the annual budget. The suggestions were put in the form of a Bill later introduced by Delegate Chipman in the House.

On June 5 the Committee on the Judiciary published its report on the relationship between the government of the District and that of the United States, with special reference to the question of municipal expenditure. Congress had for decades evaded a frank discussion of this problem, and in view of the imminent reorganization of the District government, the report was of particular importance. "In a strict legal sense there can be no such thing as local government within the District," stated the report "for there can be no government within the District independent of that of the Federal government, and whatever local authority there may be now existing or which may hereafter be set up within the District, it can only be regarded legally as an agency of the Federal Government, and whatever authority this local government may exercise, it must be regarded as the act of the United States through their delegated representatives." On the question of taxation the Report indicated that at last Congress had determined to accept its responsibility for the national capital. "There is something revolting to a proper sense of justice in the idea that the United States should hold free from taxation more than half of the area of the capital city, should require to be maintained a city upon an unusually expensive scale from which the ordinary revenues derived from commerce and manufacture are excluded; that in such a case the burden of maintaining the expenses for the capital should fall upon the resident population."

Governor Shepherd could at least take some encouragement from this Report, which substantiated the arguments which he had repeatedly made for larger Federal appropriations for the maintenance of the National Capital. The Report gave every reason to hope that in the new form of government for the District which the Investigating Committee would recommend provision would be made for the assumption by the Federal government of a substantial portion of the District budget.

During the period between adjournment of the Investigating Committee and the publication of its report all kinds of rumors and gossip were discussed in the opposition press regarding Shepherd and the District government. The Congress would shortly be adjourning. There would be elections in the fall, and the affairs of the District were temporarily the current Administration scandal. The *Tribune* correspondent reported that the popular feeling in Washington against the "Ring" was now so intense that Senator Allison was said to have remarked that the

Committee did not dare to put out another "whitewashing report," and that even the commission plan currently favored would permit Grant to nominate Shepherd as one of the commissioners whom the Senate would probably confirm. The same correspondent later stated that if the investigation had been continued more frauds would have been uncovered; the *Sun* stated editorially that it was a disgrace that Babcock had never been called to testify, since he had been Shepherd's colleague and fellow-conspirator, and blamed Allison for permitting him to "shelter behind the throne." It was said that Senator Stewart had been in constant conference with Shepherd, Kilbourn and Evans and that he had been sent by them to the memorialists with terms of compromise.

On June 9 the future pattern of the District government was outlined in the Bill recommended by the Investigating Committee and foreshadowing their report. The text of the bill was published on the same day as a letter from Governor Shepherd to Senator Allison which contained his own suggestions for the reorganization of the District administration. His suggestions were: (1) that the District government be simplified; (2) that provision be made for funding the debt of the Territory and that of the Board of Public Works, the interest and principal being guaranteed by the Federal government; (3) the appointment of an auditing commission to examine the unsettled accounts of the Board of Public Works.[19] The meekness of Shepherd's letter, which was an interesting contrast in tone to his letters of a few months before, seemed to indicate that either a compromise had been reached with the memorialists or that he was determined to put on the best possible front and to take his defeat with good grace.

The *Tribune* correspondent gloated: "The officers of the Board of Public Works stand before the country irretrievably disgraced. The air of Washington resounds with premonitions of ruin . . . There is a general packing of carpet bags and settling of accounts and in a few days we may expect to see an extensive hegira of all contractors and other prominent statesmen very much like the flight of gentlemen with dyed mustachioes and diamond stud pins which took place in New York in 1871 [after the exposure of the Tweed Ring]." The *Tribune* correspondent, pursuing the comparison further, remarked, "Tweed lived in princely luxury but never got recognition from gentlefolk that money cannot purchase. Shepherd thirsted for the smile of society. The Governor was a civil and smiling gentleman who spread a bounteous table and knew everybody, and while half Washington society denounced him as a rogue, the other half courted his civilities. It is not worth while, perhaps, to inquire whether Shepherd was dishonest himself or was merely the cause of dishonesty in others . . . Surely there can be no reasonable compassion over his fall. Tweed only united a band of predestinate and irredeemable vagabonds for an attack on the City Treasury . . . but his Washington imitators have gone far in the corruption of decent society and the destruction of the whole moral tone of the capital."[20]

The bill reported by the Investigating Committee followed the general plan of simplifying and rendering less costly the administration of the District. The Legislative Assembly and the Board of Public Works were to be abolished as well as the offices of Secretary of the District and Delegate to Congress. Three Commissioners, to be appointed by the President at a salary of $2,500 a year, were to carry out the administration of the District and an Army engineer was to be named to take charge of the public works program. The First and Second Controllers of the United States Treasury were to examine and audit the floating debt of the District and investigate claims of damage to private property. Sinking Fund commissioners were to establish a 50-year fund for the District debt at 3.65%.[21] The Bill provided that for the following year a tax rate of $3.00 should be established for real property in Washington, $2.50 for Georgetown, and $2.00 for the County; one-quarter of the proceeds of this tax should be paid to the Federal government as interest on the old Corporation debts and to reimburse advances which it had made to the District teachers. The Bill furthermore proposed a twenty per cent cut in the salaries of all employees of the District government.

Coming after more than seven years of municipal crises and financial difficulties the Bill, even though it did away completely with representative government, seemed to many citizens the solution of an otherwise impossible situation. The *Star* remarked editorially that the Bill showed haste in its preparation but believed that in the main it would be acceptable. The *Chronicle* and *National Republican* attacked the abolition of suffrage and the low interest rate on the proposed District bonds. The *Chronicle* blamed the memorialists for having retarded the appropriations of Congress which they considered would have solved the financial crisis and for having increased the tax rate of the District. The Bill was, it considered, harsh, onerous and undemocratic.

On June 10 the *New York Tribune, Sun* and *World* devoted their pages to an account of the District Safe Robbery which had been secretly investigated during the past two months by the Joint Committee. While the conclusions of the Committee were indefinite, the evidence disclosed was of a more sensational nature than anyone anticipated. The safe cracker, Michael Hayes, a professional from New York who had been apprehended at the scene of the crime, had testified that he had robbed the safe to secure the account books of J. O. Evans, one of the leading members of the "Ring" and that Columbus Alexander had offered to pay him $1,000 if he could place the books in his hands. The anxiety of Alexander to secure the books was due to his dissatisfaction with those which Evans had produced during the investigation and which contained no information regarding his real estate transactions. However, there was no evidence to show that Alexander had suggested or paid for the robbery; his character was such that any attempt of this nature would have been unthinkable. The *Sun* correspondent suggested that it was more likely that District Attorney Harrington had attempted to frame him by placing the ledgers in his safe and conniving with Hayes to have him crack it open in order to incriminate the enemies of the "Ring." According to current gossip the papers had been prepared in the office of Attorney-General Williams and one of the cracksmen who had escaped had been accompanied to the railroad station by Secretary of the Navy Robeson and ex-Secretary of the Treasury Richardson![22] The Washington Club had been kept open all night on April 23, and Shepherd, Cooke, Mattingly, Stanton, Evans and the other "Ring" members were on hand to await news from Harrington. Since the name of Colonel Whitely, the head of the United States Secret Service, had also been mentioned in connection with the robbery, the Investigating Committee recommended that the affair be jointly examined by the Treasury Department, of which the Secret Service was a unit, and by the Department of Justice.

On June 16 the long-awaited Report of the Investigating Committee was published. The document was remarkable for its clarity and in its moderation of tone. Senator Thurman had prepared the section dealing with the legal issues involved, Bass, the financial situation, and Wilson, the part dealing with the Auditing Commission. The actual text had been written by Senator Allison and reflected his caution and objectivity. The responsibility for the financial condition of the District was placed squarely upon the Board of Public Works, which it stated had "contracted and expended $18,872,565.76, or more than twelve millions in excess of estimated costs." The argument of the counsel of the Board that authority had been given by appropriations from Congress and the Legislative Assembly to incur these obligations was summarily dismissed. "Good faith," the Report declared, "required that so large a burden as has been imposed should in some manner have received advance Legislative sanction" even if there was no need to have furnished detailed plans and estimated costs to the Legislature. The provision of the Organic Act that the District debt should not exceed five per cent of the total property valuation had been disregarded, and the Legislative Assembly had not been consulted in regard to further increasing liabilities. "Your Committee are of the opinion that the present embarrassments of the District and the serious complications which now environ its finances and affairs are primarily chargeable to the attempt partly made by the authorities placed over it to inaugurate a comprehensive and costly system of improvements to be completed in a brief space of time which ought to have required for its completion several years."[23] "While your Committee join in the general expression of gratification of beholding the improved condition of the national capital, the embellishments and adornments everywhere visible, they cannot but condemn the methods by which this sudden and rapid transition was secured."

Proceeding to the discussion of methods employed by the Board of Public Works, the Report condemned the system of fixed prices which it had established. "This opened a way for favoritism in the letting of contracts and for a system of brokerage in contracts which was demoralizing in its results, bringing into the list of contractors a class of people unaccustomed to perform the work required, and enabling legitimate contractors to pay large prices in order to secure contracts." This, stated the Committee, was the cause of nearly all the irregularities which the investigation had disclosed. "Any system which would enable an adventurer to come from a distant city . . . and binding his principals the contractors to pay $97,000 for a contract of 200,000 yards of pavement after an effort of five months to secure it, the gross amount to be raised being only $700,000, in its nature must be vicious and ought to be condemned." The Report also listed the cases where contracts had been given to other parties by the Board and later sold to legitimate contractors and it did not omit mention of the faulty inspections and measurements which its engineers had performed.

While Shepherd personally escaped criticism, the autocratic administration of the Board was not spared. "The Vice-President," it stated, "ultimately came to be, practically, the Board of Public Works and exercised the powers of the Board almost as absolutely as though no one else were associated with him. The Treasurer has kept no cash account and the checks he has issued do not correspond with the several amounts reported by him to have been paid, so that there is, as he himself concedes, no means of ascertaining his accounts other than by examining his books and papers in detail." "The auditor has kept no books by which the certificates of indebtedness which he had issued could be checked; the only way his books can be verified is by comparing them with the many thousand vouchers on file at his office."[34]

The devices to raise additional funds which had been sanctioned by the Legislative Assembly were discussed—in particular, the authorization of the Legislature to create $2,000,000 of "certificates of indebtedness" upon the property adjacent to the improvements and the special Sewerage Tax. "The Committee comprehend the distinction sought to be drawn between a debt created by the issuance of a certificate and a charge upon specific property in payment for work done and an actual obligation signed by the Board itself or some authorized officer thereof. Such certificates, however, create a burden which might be reduplicated as to violate the spirit, if not the letter of the limitation fixed by Act of Congress."[25]

The Report stated that the amount of the total District debt could not be accurately ascertained in view of the large floating debt in excess of appropriations which it estimated at $11,013,756.89 over the funded District debt of $9,902,251.18. Assets, chiefly in the form of uncollected taxes, amounted to only $6,726,260, it estimated. Of the floating debt $8,305,886.59 could be funded at the option of the District's creditors. For the coming financial year the budget would amount to $4,606,166.17; even after increased taxes there would be a deficiency of $1,405,166.17. The Committee recommended that no less than $1,000,000 be appropriated by Congress in order to pay the interest on District bonds which fell due on July 1 and to pay salaries to employees of the Board and the District government.

Regarding the change of administration which had been foreshadowed in the Bill previously reported, the Committee stated that they did not intend by abolishing the Legislative Assembly "that there should not be some representative body in the District, but that the one now existing is not such a one as is contemplated by the Constitution or as the wants of the District require, and inasmuch as the next assembly will be elected before the next session of Congress they think it unnecessary to incur the expense of electing a Legislative Assembly which, if not abolished now, would be abolished at the next session." The Delegate, however, should be permitted to retain his seat in Congress in order that the District should have voice in the discussion of the form of the future District government. The Committee recommended the appointment of a commission form in the interim "under limited and restrained powers," since sufficient time for the creation of a new system of local government was lacking. Such a system, they urged, should be drawn up by a Committee composed of two members of each House on a nonpartisan basis "so that whatever system of government may be established, it will not be subject to the shiftings and changings of party politics." The same Committee, it recommended, should settle and determine the proportion of expenses which should be borne by the District and the United States respectively.

"Your Committee have unanimously arrived at the conclusion," the Report summed up, "that the existing form of government in the District is a failure, that it is too cumbrous and too expensive; that the powers and relations of the several departments are so ill-defined that limitations intended by Congress to apply to the whole government are construed to limit but one of its departments; that it is wanting in sufficient safeguards against maladministration and the creation of indebtedness; that the system of taxation it allows opens a door to great inequality and injustice and is wholly insufficient to secure the prompt collection of taxes, and that no remedy short of its abolition and the substitution of a simple, more restricted and economical government will suffice. Your Committee have therefore reported a Bill for temporary government until Congress shall have time to mature and adopt a permanent form."

The moderate language used in the Report pleased the *Star,* which considered it a "calm, temperate document." Hallett Kilbourn, one of the most publicized members of the "Ring," stated in an interview with the *Chronicle* that he was in favor of the Commission form of government, though he objected to the increased tax rate, and that "to report without qualification that the government which carried out improvements is a failure and not to commend its genius and energy is a sign of absence of manliness."[26] Donn Piatt stated that what the Committee failed to investigate was the source "from which the imbecility, extravagance and fraud originated—the White House . . . The system, not the man, oppresses us. It is not Grant, but the President. This coarse, dull soldier is less to be feared than an adroit unscrupulous politician who would cover his tracks while strengthening his usurpations and abuse."[27] The new York opposition press commented that "two of the worst rascals, Forsyth, the surveyor whose measurements had proved to be faulty, and William A. Cook, the Corporation Counsel, were not molested." *The Nation* complained, "the tone of the Report was so mild that it has given a suspicious amount of satisfaction to the friends and organs of Mr. Shepherd. The latter are industriously disseminating the theory that the memorialists are discomfited . . . the adverse opinions on his policy and doings being only the mild admonitions of a loving parent, and finally that the District government is abolished not because there was anything serious to condemn in its administration but because it was cumbrous and expensive in form. All of which shows very clearly that the same man would like to continue at the helm of affairs under the new name and organization."[28] In his own reminiscences Shepherd remarked "That the object fought for by Governor Shepherd and his party had been obtained was well appreciated and expressed by Hon. James G. Blaine, who, in congratulating him at the close of the Investigation, remarked . . . 'Shepherd, you have landed this heretofore unfortunate waif, the District, in the lap of its unnatural mother, the United

States government, with its mouth at both teats. If it does not get its fill, it will not be for lack of suction power.' "[29]

On June 18 the House passed the Bill recommended by the Joint Investigating Committee, raising the salary of the Commissioners to $5,000, abolishing the office of Secretary of the District and exempting District teachers and employees of the Fire Department from the twenty per cent salary cut originally proposed. The Bill passed the Senate without amendment the following day.

On Capitol Hill, reported the correspondent of the *New York Sun,* the "Ring" gathered around the offices of Secretary of the Senate Gorham "in the hope that they could salvage something of their reputations and patronage."[30] They were hoping that the President would name Shepherd to the Commission and that the Committee appointed to audit the accounts of the District would be made appointive in order to cover up the traces of their fraud and to raise the rate of interest of the 3.65 bonds to four per cent or five per cent in gold. In his message to Congress on June 20 Grant suggested that the bonds be made to bear a higher rate of interest so that they might not be sold at less than par and result in injury to the credit of the District. However, according to the *Tribune,* the Investigation Committee members who called on him after he had delivered the message, "revealed that a Ring syndicate had bought about $3,000,000 worth of District securities and had a personal profit at stake . . . They also pointed out that those to whom the District owed money did not have to take payment in bonds but could wait until the District had sufficient money to pay its obligations." Grant signed the Bill accordingly without further objections.

On June 22 the Legislative Assembly met for the last time and voted to adjourn *sine die.* With an enthusiasm for souvenirs unusual in a legislative body, "some of the members of the House of Delegates seem to have carried away almost everything portable about the Chamber—desks, chairs, clocks, watercoolers, mirrors, inkstands, and even the second-hand toothbrushes. One member in his solicitude to preserve some memento of this last representative body and bulwark of the people in the District, took away a large feather duster, and, not to be ostentatious about it, he concealed the same under his person with considerable ingenuity by passing the handle down a trouser leg and buttoning the feather end securely about his vest."[31] Dr. Tindall recalled Henry Beverly, the old colored watchman, rushing up to him and shouting, "They're a stealin' the Chamber." The Speaker of the House and the Governor's brother, Arthur Shepherd, gave orders immediately that nothing further be removed and that all purloined articles be returned. Mr. Urell brought back five of the members' chairs, Matthew Trimble two chairs, a desk and the chair of the Speaker. Later the furniture was carted away to the dealer who had originally supplied it, and the "Feather Duster" legislature took its immortal place in Washington history.

Meanwhile the appointment of the District Commissioners was being considered at the White House. The *Sun's* correspondent reported that the President, on the advice of Attorney-General Williams, wished to postpone the nominations until Congress was no longer in session, but that he had been dissuaded by the visit of two members of the Senate Judiciary Committee, who had called on him saying that this would be an unwise procedure and advising him against the nomination of Shepherd. The *Tribune* reported on June 23 that had the House felt that Shepherd would have been nominated it would have stricken out the $1,300,000 deficiency appropriation for the District out of the Sundry Civil Appropriations Bill. Nevertheless, Grant, acting according to his lifelong principle of personal loyalty, proceeded to name Shepherd for the post, together with William Dennison, the former Governor of Ohio who had served as Postmaster General under Lincoln and Johnson, and Henry T. Blow, a former member of the House from Missouri.

The appointment of Shepherd as Governor the previous autumn had been attacked by the opposition press but his nomination after the exposures of the Investigating Committee was too much for even the friends of the Administration. Nast published in *Harper's Weekly* his one and only caricature against Grant, showing the figure of America telling the President that "Friendship can go so far but . . . ." The editor of the *Tribune* wrote, "General Grant deliberately insults the country, Congress and his own party by trying to put this stained and condemned politician once more in charge of the government of the District. We can afford to smile at the fractiousness of spoiled children, but a fractious President is no laughing matter. No President has ever before made so disgraceful an exhibition of vulgar petulance. The dignity of the Executive is lowered by it."

News of the appointment spread all over Washington like wildfire. At 2:30 p.m. the Senate went into session. Its corridors were crowded. Shepherd was in the office of Secretary Gorham conferring with Chipman, and Senator Jones of Nevada carried the news of the proceedings there from the Senate floor. Strong speeches were made against the nomination by Sherman, Edmunds, Logan, Oglesby, Allison and Thurman. Sargent of California, who supported Shepherd, wished to talk until the four o'clock adjournment. However, Speaker Blaine in the House had ruled to keep that body in session in order that the two Houses would end their 43rd Session concurrently. This motion, carried unanimously, was sent to the Senate by its Clerk, McPherson, and Sargent was removed from the floor. An amendment was called to extend the session until 9 p.m.; Sargent capitulated and the vote was called. Only six Senators voted for confirmation of Shepherd, most of them Southern Republicans, and 36 against. Grant, informed of the result, "was terribly enraged and expressed his opinion of the Senate in terms more forcible than complimentary."[32]

Whatever celebrations may have been planned by Shepherd's followers were cancelled—the cancellation included the salute of 100 guns and the Marine Band which his enemies alleged were prepared to celebrate his triumph. "The joy of the people is unbounded," wrote the *Sun* correspondent. "There has not been such rejoicing in the national capital since the surrender of Richmond was announced." Crosby S. Noyes, faithful to the end, wrote in the *Star:* "Governor Shepherd can afford to wait for his vindication. The great work he has accomplished for his native city cannot be undone. It will stand forever associated with his name, and neither envious detraction nor political chicanery can harm him here where he is best known, or do aught but increase the sympathy and regard felt for him by his fellow citizens."[33] Donn Piatt in the *Capital* went still further in his defense: "After the Corcorans, Riggses and Alexanders have been damned into utter oblivion, Shepherd's name will survive, linked with our national capital, and men will say what Washington dreamed of Shepherd made possible—the Father of his Country projected what this brave man has accomplished."[34]

Chapter 10

The Negro Millennium

During the Reconstruction period the colored people of Washington were able briefly to enjoy some of those advantages and privileges for which they and their Radical friends had so long struggled. They also were fortunate in possessing the collaboration of those members of their race who had been sent to Congress as representatives of the reconstructed Southern states. The leaders of the Republican Party, well aware that only the solid support of the colored voters of the South had regained the two-thirds majority of their party in Congress and therefore anxious to preserve their loyalty, treated the colored representatives with a healthy respect.

The largest contingent of Negro congressmen had come from South Carolina, which had been under Republican control since the new state constitution of 1869. The white "Scalawag" members who had been returned to the 41st Congress had reflected little credit on either their state or their party. One of them, B. F. Whittemore, had resigned after his sale of West Point cadetships was revealed. Another "Scalawag," C. C. Bowen, the representative for the Charleston district, was jailed for bigamy after a long and sensational trial in the District courts. Convicted by a mixed jury, Bowen was freed after serving two weeks in prison; he was not, however, renominated for his congressional seat.

Bowen's successor in the 42nd Congress was Robert C. De Large, a 28-year-old colored man. "Olivia," in one of her weekly letters, described him as having "very little resemblance to the African race. His mother was a Haitian, and he inherits a rich olive skin. In stature he is rather below the medium size, and his exceeding grace of manner might be imitated to the advantage of more experienced Congressmen."[1] During the War De Large had been impressed into the Confederate Army to work on building fortifications; later he had become a clerk in the Freedmen's Bureau, entered politics and took part in the South Carolina constitutional convention. He was elected to the Legislature, where he had served as Chairman of the Committee on Ways and Means, before being sent to Washington.

Three other colored men represented South Carolina in the 42nd Congress. Joseph H. Rainey was a native of Georgetown, where he had worked as a barber. His scanty formal education had been improved by travel in the West Indies. Rainey was forty years of age, a mulatto with a complexion more Asiatic than African. "In size he has attained sufficient height for exceeding grace, and then he has a voice like a flute and the smooth-soft ways of an Oriental," wrote "Olivia."[2] Rainey was popular both among his fellow-Congressmen, who appointed him to the Committee on Indian Affairs and on Freedmen's Affairs, and with his constituents. He served for five consecutive terms in Congress.

Richard H. Cain, his South Carolina colleague, was a man whose appearance and temperament were of a very different nature. "African in looks, eloquence, wit and dramatic power," Marie LeBaron described him.[3] Cain, born in Virginia of free parents, had graduated from Wilberforce University in Ohio and had become a minister in the African Methodist Episcopal Church. Coming to South Carolina after the War, he had become editor of the *Missionary Record* and had quickly risen to political prominence. Starting out as an opponent of Governors Moses and Scott, he eventually made his peace with the state Republican machine. Cain was a violent racial partisan and a powerful speaker, but his alliance with the carpetbagger, Scott, cost him his seat in the 1874 election.

The third South Carolina representative, Robert B. Elliott, was one of the most remarkable men ever to enter the House. Born in Boston of well-to-do parents, he had been sent to England for his education. He had entered High Holborn Academy in London and had later attended Eton College, from which aristocratic institution he graduated in 1859. Seven years later he was living in Charleston, where he worked in the office of the *South Carolina Leader,* the Republican journal edited by Alonzo J. Rapier, a colored man who later became a member of Congress. In his spare time Elliott studied law, and was admitted to the South Carolina Bar, where his remarkable eloquence and educational background soon brought him to prominence. He acquired one of the best law libraries in the state, and was able to read French, German, Spanish and Latin.[4] Elliott later removed to Columbia, the state capital, which returned him to Congress.

Marie Le Baron in her article on Negro congressmen described his appearance: "His lips are full, his nose broad, complexion bright, teeth perfect, and white, in strong contrast with surrounding color. His forehead is high, somewhat sloping, and his head well covered with crisp, close-curled ebony hair. Deep in the chest, broad in the shoulders, shapely in limb, in his neat dress of black he is a distinguished and agreeable figure, and there is no awkward gesture, no obsequious movement to point back to a life of cringing servitude."[5]

On January 5, 1874, Elliott made a memorable speech in the House at the opening of the debate on Sumner's Civil Rights Bill, answering the arguments of the former Vice-President of the Confederacy, Alexander Stephens. Elliott's forceful arguments and his ease of delivery made a powerful impression on his audience; when he sat down the applause was deafening, and so many members rushed forward to shake his hand that they formed a line in the aisle and marched up in a single column.[6]

Georgia had returned to the 41st Congress a colored tailor, Jefferson T. Long, who represented the Macon district. Alabama's Negro representative, Benjamin S. Turner, had formerly been a slave who rose to be Collector of Taxes in Dallas County. Florida had sent to Washington Josiah T. Walls, who had received his education in Philadelphia and settled in Florida after the War to become a farmer. Walls was an excellent speaker and a zealous advocate of the interests of Florida, rising on many occasions to advocate the construction of harbors and canals in that still undeveloped and backward region.

John R. Lynch of Mississippi, elected in 1872 to represent the Natchez District, was the youngest and in many respects the most distinguished of the Negro members. Born in 1847 of free parents, he had risen through his brilliant oratorical gifts to the position of Speaker of the Mississippi State Legislature at the age of 24. He was "of light complexion with bright, quick, black eyes, regular features, curly black hair, aristocratic hands and feet. He was said to speak fluently, with terseness, as if his subject matter were well-weighed, and his speech contained no Negroisms nor provincial accent."[7] Eight days after Lynch took his seat he made his first speech, and he was appointed to the Committee on the Interior Department and later to the Committee on Mines. A firm proponent of civil rights, but less didactic in his views than some of his fellow Negro members, Lynch won the friendship of President Grant, who consulted him frequently on matters relating to the Administration's Southern policy. Lynch was elected to serve two consecutive terms in Congress, delivered the eulogy of Vice-President Henry Wilson after his death in 1873, and later received many honors from his party.

Hiram Revels, who had been named by the Mississippi State Legislature to fill the unexpired Senate term of Jefferson Davis, arrived in Washington on January 30, 1870. Tall, portly, of a benevolent disposition, with a pleasant and well-modulated voice, he made an excellent impression on Congress. John W. Forney entertained him at a dinner attended by the President and all members of the Cabinet a few days after his arrival. On February 22 Henry Wilson presented the credentials of Revels to the Senate, which voted to confirm him 48 to 8. On March 1 Revels delivered his maiden speech on the readmission of Georgia to the Union, a historic occasion, which was of intense interest to the public and press. "Africa's sable representatives, with skins like polished satin," wrote the reporter of the *Philadelphia Press,* "were to be seen not far removed from the colorless blondes of haughty French ancestry . . . Senator Revels did not grow pale under the ordeal, but his Scotch blood burned steadily, and the flame was visible through his bronze cheek."[8] The speech, which supported the Unionists of Georgia, was well received, and even Revels' political opponents were forced to concede his taste and grace of diction. On May 17 he made a second speech, favoring the removal of political disabilities from former Confederate officials. Revels served, however, but one year in the Senate, being unable to come to terms with the state Republican machine, and later transferred his allegiance to the Democrats.

On March 4, 1873, P. B. S. Pinchback, who had served as Lieutenant-Governor and for a short period as Acting Governor of Louisiana, was elected a member of the Senate. His admission was, however, hotly contested by the Democrats of that state, and also by the Republican Warmoth faction. Since he was a nominee of the opposing group of Republicans under Kellogg, whom Grant personally favored, the situation of Pinchback was an extremely delicate one, and his credentials were held up by the Senate Committee on Elections and Privileges for almost three years. Some of the strongest supporters of the Administration, such as Carpenter, were opposed to Pinchback's recognition, while the "Stalwarts," led by Conkling, Morton and Logan, supported him. In March, 1876, Pinchback by a vote of 32 to 29 was finally denied his seat on the ground that the Louisiana Returning Board of 1873 had been improperly constituted, although his salary as Senator was paid to him in full. Pinchback, the son of a wealthy planter, had received a good education and was a man of unusual accomplishments. Unlike many Negro members, who died in poverty and obscurity, he continued to receive patronage from the Republican Party, and retired to become a successful racehorse owner and financier.

James G. Blaine, who as Speaker of the House of Representatives during this period, had occasion to know the colored members well, spoke highly in his autobiography of the generosity which they displayed to their former masters. "So far as chivalry, magnanimity, charity, Christian kindness were involved, the colored man appeared to be at an advantage. Perhaps it is not surprising that lingering prejudice and the sudden change of situation should have restrained Southern white man from granting these privileges, but it must always be mentioned to the credit of the colored man that he gave his vote for amnesty to his former master when his demand for delay would have obstructed the passage of the measure." Of the Negro in Congress he said, "If it be viewed simply as an experiment, it was triumphantly successful. The colored men who took seats in both House and Senate did not appear ignorant and helpless. They were as a rule studious, earnest and ambitious men whose public conduct would be honorable to any race."[9]

Yet, in spite of their conduct and their position as members of Congress, the colored representatives were subject in the capital to constant indignities, some petty, others of a more serious nature. When Elliott's wife entered the gallery of the House reserved for the wives of members, the wife of a Radical member from Ohio left in indignation.[10] Mrs. Elliott, whom Marie Le Baron described in the *National Republican* as having "the complexion of the creamy type of Southern magnolia, large brown eyes with the sweetest and brightest expression and manners in the world," henceforward found it more tactful to sit in the regular Ladies Gallery. The *Star* under the heading of "Served Him Right" reported an episode in a Pennsylvania Avenue oyster bar when her husband, who had ordered "a few on the half-shell," was insulted by a drunken government clerk. Elliott finished his meal in silence and then inquired the name of the "belligerent young gentleman." The matter was laid before the head of the Department in which the clerk was working and he was summarily dismissed.[11] Joseph Rainey, in an interview, stated that it was hard to find rooms in Washington and that colored Congressmen were charged more than white men. At Falf's Bar, across the street from the Post Office, he had been obliged to pay fifty cents for a glass of beer, the waiter freely admitting that the extra charge was on account of his color.[12]

In order to obviate such continued discrimination Lewis Douglass, who succeeded his distinguished father on the District Legislative Council, had introduced in 1871 a bill "To regulate the sale of ice-cream and soda water." Under this Act the keepers of restaurants, soda fountains, and saloons were required to mark the prices of their beverages and to serve all "respectable and well-dressed persons without regard to race, color or previous condition of servitude." Failure to do so would come under the category of a misdemeanor, and be subject to a penalty of not less than $20 and not more than $50, and the license of the offending party would be forfeited for one year.

On the evening of the same day a meeting was held at the Congregational Church to endorse the Bill attended by Senator Henry Wilson of Massachusetts, Frederick Douglass and J. W. LeBarnes of the District House of Delegates. A letter was read by Vice-President Colfax which stated, "If orderly, sober citizens of the United States entitled by its Constitution to equality under the law cannot obtain food and lodgings at public hotels like the rest of mankind or even average accommodation on railroad trains after paying first-class fares, we should either acknowledge that the Constitution is a nullity, or should insist on that obedience to it by all and protection under it to all, which are alike the right and duty of the humblest as well as the most influential in the land." Frederick Douglass, answering in his speech the usual charges that the Bill was framed to force "social equality," said that he did not know the meaning of the phrase. "Is it to walk in the same streets with other men? Is it to attend the same public meetings? Is it to ride in the same railway car? Is it to drink at the same fountain as our white friends? If so, then I am in favor of social equality. But if it be understood that the colored men are endeavoring to force their white neighbors to invite them to their drawing-rooms or to force them to marry them, I am against it. It is wrong to confound the common school subject with this idea. The common school is the basis of the democratic system, and without it the United States would be little better than Mexico or San Domingo. It is the basis of our republican institutions, and what the colored people desire is to make our nominal school system a common school system in reality." Mixed schools, he pointed out, had been successfully instituted in Massachusetts, Connecticut, Vermont, Rhode Island and New York.

The Douglass Bill passed the Council by a vote of seven to four on June 11, was approved by the House of Delegates, and on the 20th received the Governor's signature. It was little mentioned in the Washington press, though the *Georgetown Courier* commented, "Of course, such laws as this excite only contempt and they cannot last."[13]

After Grant's re-election in November 1872, R. W. Tompkins, a young clerk in the Freedmen's Bank, entered the fashionable ice-cream parlor run by Frederick Freund and his wife. Tompkins was accompanied by a well-known colored Washington physician, Dr. Augusta.[14] Though both men were "respectable and well-dressed," they were denied service at first, and later, upon their insistence, were each asked to pay in advance two dollars for a plate of ice-cream usually priced at fifteen cents. The case was brought before Judge Snell in the Police Court, who awarded the decision to the plaintiffs and adjudged a $100 fine against the Freunds. The waiter on the premises claimed that the plaintiffs were smoking cigars and had not removed their hats in violation of the rules of the establishment, and that they had used profane and threatening language towards Mrs. Freund. The Judge, however, declared that he "was satisfied that the demand of $2 for a single ice-cream, was a pretext within the meaning of the 3rd section of the Act for refusal to serve complainants." The defendant was unwilling to make a direct and positive refusal to serve to complainants in terms, and as a cover for his real reason, he sought an ostensible reason which he hoped would shield him from the legal consequences of direct and positive action. It was precisely this the law intended to prevent. "Several cases in different forms but involving the same principle, the absolute equality of all men before the law, have been before this Court, and it is hoped that a speedy adjudication of the questions raised by them may be reached by the Supreme Court of the District. It is the duty of the Courts to take judicial notice of the Constitution of the country and the law of the land. This act is in apparent harmony with both. It would seem to be the part of sound philosophy and good sense to accept with liberality and good faith that which has become both history and established law, but if communities or individuals, misled by prejudice or other considerations however tempting, fail to recognize the logic of events, it is quite certain that the logic of events will not fail to recognize them. Rights which have cost a revolution will not stand aside for any pretexts."[15]

The counsel for the defense immediately filed an appeal, and the case was brought the following month before Justice MacArthur of the District Supreme Court. However, it was found by the Court on this occasion that the indictment had been improperly drawn by the counsel for the plaintiffs, and that the nature of the offense as stated "did not come within the scope of the Act." Though William A. Cook, acting on their behalf, offered to alter the language of the complaint, the Court denied his request and the appeal was successful.

In June 1873, John H. Brooks, who had succeeded Lewis Douglass as a member of the Legislative Council, introduced a further bill to strengthen the Act of 1872 which, it was clear, contained a number of loopholes. In this Bill, which became law the same month, restaurant and hotel proprietors were required to print their bill of fare with the prices usually charged; two printed cards were to be posted in the restaurant itself and a further copy filed with the District Register. Failure to post such cards and attempts to charge any customer more than the regular price on any pretext whatsoever, or direct or indirect refusal of service, would render the offending party liable to a fine of $100 and a year's suspension of license.

On September 29, 1873, Messrs. Harvey and Holden, the proprietors of Harvey's Restaurant on the Avenue, were prosecuted by Professor John M. Langston of Howard University and Dr. Charles B. Purvis[16] of Freedmen's Hospital for refusing to wait on them. This was a case of more than ordinary interest, since the only other occupant of the room in which the two men wished to sit was William J. Murtagh, the editor of the *National Republican*. Moreover, both Professor Langston, who was a member of the District Board of Health, and Dr. Purvis testified that they had previously entered the restaurant in the company of white friends. When the case was discussed in Court, Mr. Meyers, the special officer employed at the restaurant, stated the table selected by Langston and Purvis was reserved, and the proprietors backed him up. Richard Merrick, acting for the defendants, tried to make a case out of the refusal of the plaintiffs to receive service at other tables. Purvis, he said, was not so much interested in getting food as in creating animosity. Judge Snell again awarded judgment in favor of the colored men, and ordered that the owners pay a fine of $100 and that the license of the restaurant be taken away for one year under the provisions of the Act. A suit of perjury was brought by Harvey and Holden against Dr. Purvis, but when the Judge stated that, if perjury were manifest, the case would be taken before the grand jury, they entered a plea of *nolle prosequi*.

On May 23, 1873, A. K. Browne, a white Republican member, introduced in the Legislative Council a bill relating to the advance sale of theatre tickets, under the provisions of which theatre proprietors and managers would be denied the right to mark as "Reserved" any sections of the house for which seats had not been sold previous to the time of the performance. The purpose of the bill was obviously designed to prevent the current practice of Washington theatres which, forbidden by the law passed in 1869 under the Corporation to refuse colored people admittance to any part of the house, were evading the spirit of this legislation.

The Browne Bill became law on June 23, and shortly afterwards a case involving the National Theatre came before the Courts, in which the proprietor was indicted for declining to sell tickets for the section usually reserved for white patrons to a group of colored men. Judgment was granted to the plaintiffs by the Police Court and on November 7, 1874 the case came up before Justice Olin in the District Supreme Court. On this occasion Edwin M. Stanton, Jr., appeared for the District and the National Theatre was represented by Merrick. Stanton pleaded that the Legislature had had full power to draw up the Act, and that it did not conflict with the rights of the proprietor to use his own property as he desired. A place of public amusement, argued Stanton, citing a similar ordinance in the city of Cincinnati, was subject to municipal regulation. Merrick argued for the defendants that the practice of reserving seats was a private right of the proprietor, and that, since it did not conflict either with public or with private rights, it was not the proper subject for legislation. Justice Olin found in favor of the defendants, considering that the law was "an unwarrantable infringement of private rights." "If this law can be enforced," he said, "it is made a penal offense for the manager or proprietor to reserve for the use of his friends or patrons a few desirable seats," and he also pointed out that under wording of the law those who purchased even the cheapest tickets could legally occupy any vacant seat in the house unless the manager could persuade him that the seat had been sold prior to the performance.[17] On this occasion it would appear plain that Justice Olin, like his associate MacArthur in 1872, was more concerned in finding loopholes in the law than with the broad principles involved.

On March 2, 1875, President Grant signed the Civil Rights Bill, for which Charles Sumner had labored so many years, and which was a tribute to his memory. Southerners and Democrats in Congress had bitterly contested the Bill, which imposed a $500.00 fine, payable to the party bringing suit, upon owners of restaurants, theatres and hotels which refused to accomodate all persons regardless of color. The Bill did not, however, apply to churches nor to schools. In the South the legislation was held to be an unwarrantable interference with the rights of the individual states, and eight years later, after a number of test cases in the lower courts, this opinion was sustained by the United States Supreme Court. What took place in the intervening period in the District and neighboring states is obscure. According to newspaper reports there were a number of disturbances in Baltimore and Richmond restaurants when Negroes insisted upon being served; in Alexandria, Virginia, the two leading hotels in the city, the Mansion House and City Hotel cancelled their licenses and operated as boarding-houses. There is little evidence to show that in the District Negroes received more or less service than in the preceding years. The *Star* reported a suit brought against Carter Stewart, proprietor of the barber shop in the Willard Hotel and a former Washington alderman, who refused to accomodate a Negro, claiming that he could not do so without damaging his business, which was exclusively for white customers.

The foreign diplomats in Washington, the majority of whom had grown up in countries where slavery was unknown, were sometimes incapable of appreciating the more delicate distinctions of racial etiquette in the United States capital. In October 1869 the Washington correspondent of the *New York Herald* reported an "affaire d'amour" between a certain young gentleman connected with one of the legations and a beautiful young lady of color. Not only were the couple seen together on the streets, but they had on several occasions visited the theatre. When the secret was discovered by other Negroes who smuggled themselves into the theatre to "spot" the girl, "the respectable white ladies who were acquainted with the gentleman were scandalized." The unfortunate hero of the episode who was naive enough to think that political equality and social equality were synonymous, fled to New York, and his superior made an abject apology to the Department of State.[19]

However, in December 1871, a wedding between a similar pair was actually performed in Washington. Paul Gérard, a Frenchman, brother-in-law to the Minister of Portugal, was married to Marie, the niece of the famous restaurateur, James

Wormley. Since the bride was a Presbyterian, the ceremony, which was performed in St. Matthew's Catholic Church, was kept a close secret. The *Star* described the bride as being a "bright mulatto of rather prominent features; large brown eyes, heavy eyebrows and straight hair. She is rather full and of graceful figure." Dr. White in his wedding address uncompromisingly stated, "God has ordained that this great institution which is the foundation of society shall not depend upon the whims of human passion and the vagaries of human opinion."[20]

Whatever were the sympathies of the Republican politicians and the foreign diplomats towards the Negro, they were certainly not shared by the middle and lower classes of the white population of the District. For the most part the opposition to mixed schools came from the humblest classes, whose early training had indoctrinated them with the belief that they would be lowered by association with the colored race. Lacking the means to send their children to private schools, they were bitterly determined to preserve them from such "debasing" contacts. The nature of the Negro population of the early '70's, containing so large a proportion of illiterate ex-"contrabands," encouraged them in their attitude, with which was inevitably associated the dread of intermarriage.

The case of Henry Johnson, a handsome young colored man employed as a foreman of the Abbott Paving Company in 1873, affords an indication of the strength of such sentiments among the lower-middle class. The Negro had successfully courted a young white girl, Kate Bowling, who eloped from her mother's home, and the couple were married by a colored minister. A suit for assault was promptly brought against Johnson by the outraged mother, who claimed that her daughter had been intoxicated and enticed from her home. Though the suit was not successful Mrs. Bowling succeeded in persuading Kate to return home, where she was placed under lock and key. Later, however, the girl managed to escape and rejoined her husband. Mrs. Bowling, stricken, told a reporter that "henceforward she would pray for her daughter's death."[21]

Within the colored race itself, class feeling after the War was particularly strong. Ellis, writing in 1869, remarked, "The colored people proper of the District, by which we mean those who were born in it or have lived in it for many years, are very different from the refugee freedmen. They are as a class intelligent, respectable, and industrious. Nearly all of them have some steady employment at which they work faithfully. They hold themselves aloof from the free men in the camps and villages and justly so. As a class they have the good-will and respect of their white neighbors and are proving themselves worthy of it. Some of them are men of property, and nearly all have a knowledge of reading and writing. They send their children to school and exert themselves in every way to benefit their condition. They feel keenly the discredit which the refugee freedmen have brought upon their race and are exceedingly anxious that they should leave the city."[22]

However, few of the refugees had left, and as a result the social lines of the colored population became drawn as tightly as those of white society. The dominant group was determined that the prestige and good reputation which it had painstakingly established should not be submerged by the uneducated masses. On occasion its efforts to be "exclusive" led to extreme and often ludicrous situations described by John Edward Bruce, a colored satirist.[23] "The 'fust families' [have] all the habits and customs of the day before yesterday hanging about them as tenaciously and persistently as the barnacles upon sea shells. They live in old-fashioned houses way uptown, downtown and crosstown. They dress in the same style that their illustrious ancestors did half a century ago. All the leading whitewashers, coachmen, valets and servants *in ordinaire* were furnished the 'fust families' of the white race from this class half a century ago. Those living in Washington wouldn't be caught dead with an ordinary Negro if they could avoid such a dire calamity. The most of their company consists of antiquated old white people, many of them so near death's door that they can hear the creaking of the hinges. The 'fust families' of Washington keep a servant, two dogs and a tom cat and a rifle that saw service in 1776. They are pensioners, provided that they or their ancestors lived with the 'bloods' of their day and generation. If they do not keep a servant, they are not pensioners. There is more family pride to the square inch in the hide of the 'fust families' than there are fleas in a dog's back. To marry their daughter out of the circle in which they have been accustomed to mingle is decidedly out of the question and contrary to both their religious and social views."

By the '70's some of the colored men of the District had amassed very comfortable fortunes. The 1870 Census listed the real property of James T. Wormley at $75,000 and his personal property at $15,000. John A. Gray, William Syphax and Isaac Johnson (a messenger at the Capitol), were listed as owners of houses worth more than $17,000, and property valuations of many colored laborers exceeded those of white men. The same census listed many houses valued at more than $5,000 in the possession of colored barbers, hackmen and contractors, indicating that thrift and industry were not exclusively confined to members of the white race.

In 1869, George T. Downing, a well-known caterer of Newport, Rhode Island and New York, came to the capital to take charge of the Restaurant of the House of Representatives. He was also a keen politician, and had been a member of the group of colored men who had interviewed Andrew Johnson in 1866 on behalf of Negro suffrage.

Downing was probably the most successful and wealthiest colored man at this time in the United States. At the age of 26 he had opened a catering business on Broadway in New York and in 1846 had moved to Newport, where he became the owner of a hotel for wealthy summer visitors and later built the first block of business houses in the Bellevue Avenue section. His influence had largely been instrumental in securing the abolition of segregation in the Rhode Island schools. Downing was a friend and regular correspondent of Charles Sumner, who thought highly of his political ideas. During the debate on the Civil Rights Bill in 1872 Downing's arguments were quoted extensively by Sumner.[24] When Senator Revels came to Washington in 1870 he was a guest at Downing's house on Capitol Hill.

The House Restaurant under Downing's charge maintained the highest standards. "The bill of fare," remarked Ellis in 1869, "contains every delicacy, and his dishes are served in a style which would not shame Delmonico himself."[25] For the first time colored people were served there, and through Downing's influence they were also admitted to the Senate Gallery. Immediately after Grant's inauguration Downing gave a reception for Senators, judges and representative men to meet the colored intelligentsia, and opened the eyes of many for the first time to the new type of Negro which was emerging in America.

In 1870 Downing's daughter, Cordelia, was married to Mark de Mortie, a member of a real estate firm in Chicago, at his house. President Grant sent a bouquet to the bride, and guests came from New York, Baltimore and Philadelphia; several members of Congress were also present. "The display of rich and costly dresses and jewelry," wrote the *Star* reporter, "was equal to the display at the most fashionable receptions in this city. The bridal presents were arranged in the front parlor; among them were several valuable articles of jewelery, silverplate, etc. The newly married couple are to leave on an extended tour of the West and will return to Newport for the summer."[26]

The acknowledged leader of the colored people in Washington and in the entire nation, Frederick Douglass, was also an international figure. He had lectured with conspicuous success in Europe before the War, he was in correspondence with the great men and women of two continents, his autobiography had run into several editions. Now in his late fifties, with a massive, leonine head, a great shock of hair and a beard tinged with gray, Douglass was a man whose superb command of language matched his impressive appearance. Few lecturers could draw such attentive audiences, and his services were in constant demand. In 1871, after a long residence in Rochester, New York, Douglass had come to Washington to publish a national weekly magazine for Negroes. The *New National Era,* so called after the pre-War Abolitionist journal, the *National Era,* which Dr. Gamaliel Bailey had edited in Washington, was founded to maintain the loyalty of the colored people to the Republican Party. Despite his long friendship and admiration for Charles Sumner, Douglass had remained unswervingly faithful to Grant during both election campaigns. He had been rewarded by a seat in the District Legislative Council in 1871 and subsequently by an appointment to the San Domingo Commission the same year. The Douglasses—his wife, daughter and three sons—at first lived in modest quarters in the vicinity of the Capitol at 316-18 B Street, N.E. In 1878, Douglass, through the remunerative proceeds of his lecture tours, was able to purchase a large mansion in Uniontown across the Anacostia River named "Cedar Hill" which had belonged to the aristocratic Van Hook family. It adjoined Barry Farm, the settlement for colored refugees which had been established in 1867 by the Freedmen's Bureau.

The *New National Era* was edited by J. Sella Martin, the former minister of the 15th Street Presbyterian Church, with Douglass as its corresponding editor. His two sons, Lewis and Charles, were also associated with the paper. Excellently printed and ably edited, the weekly was a credit to the leadership of the Negro race. It devoted much space to political conditions, especially in the South, published occasional literary articles and poems; in local affairs its primary concern was with the school system, and it took a firm stand in favor of integrated schools.

From the outset, however, the *New National Era* was plagued by financial difficulties. Its circulation, since its appeal was primarily to the small élite class of colored readers, was inevitably restricted. Moreover, its editors had unwisely amalgamated with the *Colored Citizen,* a shoestring publication set up by some clerks at the Freedmen's Bank. The understanding had been that these men would put $2,000 of new capital into the enterprise, in return for which they would be given stock in the company, which included printing presses and material worth $10,000. Only $275, however, was received in cash, and $1000 in notes, and accordingly the Douglass brothers did not turn over the company stock. In 1874 at the instigation of one of the sponsors of the *Colored Citizen,* John H. Cook, an injunction was issued by the Courts against the Douglass brothers, and the weekly was closed and placed under the receivership of James T. Wormley. Though the injunction was subsequently dissolved and the paper resumed publication, lack of capital obliged it to cease on October 22.

The focal point of all the business enterprise of the Negro race, the Freedmen's Savings and Trust Company, had located its central offices to Washington in 1867. At first situated at 19th Street and Pennsylvania Avenue, it moved in 1869 into a magnificent new brownstone building which cost $260,000, at the corner of Madison Place across from the Treasury. The interior was handsomely equipped with marble counters, and its woodwork was of black walnut. At this time the Bank had branches in every large city in the South, and money on deposit was over $12,000,000.

Up to 1870 the affairs of the Freedmen's Bank had been conservatively managed by a group of benevolent white men with a sincere concern for the improvement of the Negro race and the stimulation of steady and frugal habits. J. W. Alvord, its President, was a white Congregational minister, but the Vice-President, D. W. Anderson, and the Cashier, W. J. Wilson, were colored. According to the original articles of incorporation, two-thirds of the Bank's deposits were to be invested in United States securities; the remainder was to be placed in an "available fund" to meet current payments of the corporation. The officers were required to put up bonds for their fidelity and good conduct as the Board of Trustees might from time to time require. No provision, however, was made in the original charter for the regular inspection and supervision of the Bank's affairs by agents of the Federal government.

Alvord had become seriously ill in 1868 and had spent much time in a sanitarium. Though retained as Vice-President, he became merely a figurehead and had no important voice in the direction of the Bank's policy.

In 1870 the control of the Bank passed into the hands of the officials of the Freedmen's Bureau: Generals Howard, Balloch, and Eaton. In the same year the charter was amended and officers of the Bank were permitted to invest up to half of the funds on deposit in notes and bonds secured by mortgages or real estate. A finance committee consisting of Henry D. Cooke, Lewis Clephane, William S. Huntington, General O. O. Howard and General Eaton were given authority to re-deposit one-half of the Bank funds in other institutions, invest in securities or loan on call.

From this time on the affairs of the Freedmen's Bank declined steadily. Henry D. Cooke found it convenient to unload on it some of the bad loans which he had made as President of the First National Bank. Much of Freedmen's Bank funds was invested in the Northern Pacific Railroad, and thus the Bank was severely hit by the failure of Jay Cooke & Co. in 1873. At one time Henry loaned his brother money from the Freedmen's Bank at five per cent when the established rate of interest of the Bank was six per cent. The officers all borrowed money from the Bank and encouraged their friends to do the same. Cashiers in all branches of the Bank accepted second mortgages as collateral. When the financial situation of the District became desperately tight in 1873 the Freedmen's Bank accepted the certificates of the Board of Public Works, the market value of which was greatly depreciated. J. W. Vandenburgh, a contractor who had previously served as Washington agent of the Freedmen's Bureau, was granted in 1874 loans amounting to $180,000, of which only $30,000 was repaid. William Stickney, General Eaton's nephew, who became an actuary, was personally responsible for some of the Bank's worst losses. Loans were granted on stock of the Seneca Sandstone Company, the Metropolitan Paving Company, the YMCA and considerably less substantial collateral. Francis Colburne Adams[27] claimed that Shepherd, Kilbourn, Huntington, Kidwell, Clephane and Generals Howard and Eaton were involved in a conspiracy to rob the Bank by exchanging government securities for Seneca Sandstone stock, in which they were all financially interested.

The Bank's depositors were naturally in blissful ignorance of what was going on behind the scenes. The deposits increased from $12,605,781.95 in 1870 to $31,260,499.97 in 1872, and by 1873 had reached approximately $57,000,000. When Frederick Douglass, a Trustee of the Bank who had previously taken little part in its administration, was asked to become President in March 1874, he was highly flattered. He little dreamed that he was merely being used by the directors in a desperate attempt to retain the confidence of the investors before the crash which they knew to be imminent. Douglass had long admired the Bank as a symbol of the industry of the Negro race. "In passing," he wrote in his *Life and Times,* "I often peeped into its spacious windows and looked upon three rows of its gentlemanly and elegantly dressed colored clerks with their pens behind their ears and button-hole bouquets in their coat fronts and felt my eyes enriched. It was a sign I had never expected to see. I felt like the Queen of Sheba when she saw the richness of Solomon that 'the half had not been told me.'" It did not take him long to discover that indeed half had not been told him, and that he had been married to a corpse. "The fine building with its marble counters and black marble finishings was there, and the affable and agile clerks and the discreet and colored cashier, but the LIFE which was the money had gone, and I found that I had been placed there in the hope that 'by some drugs, some charms, some conjuration' or mighty magic I might bring it back."[28]

Immediately upon learning of the Bank's desperate situation Douglass asked that its affairs be investigated by Congress, since the overhead expenses were rapidly consuming what little remained in its coffers. When the Freedmen's Bank finally closed its doors on June 30, 1874, only $400 worth of government bonds were found among its assets. Douglass himself had lost $10,000, with nothing to show for his three-months' term as President except headaches and abuse. The failure of the Bank, in which so many of the hopes of the Negro were centered, was a severe blow, especially to the small investors of the South. The Bank's affairs were placed in the hands of receivers. Nine years later depositors were to receive 62 per cent of their savings.

To the colored men of Washington emancipation and suffrage had by no means brought unlimited economic opportunities. The number of unemployed continued to be large, and it was indeed many years before jobs could be found for the majority of them. Negro workers discovered that as their political power increased they met with more opposition from their white competitors, and especially from organized labor. In 1869 the Bricklayers' Union local in Washington forbade its members to work alongside colored men, and four members were expelled by unanimous decision for having accepted a government job on which colored bricklayers were also employed.[29] Lewis Douglass, who had secured a position the same year in the Government Printing Office, encountered the greatest difficulty in joining the Columbia Typographical Union. Though he had had considerable experience as a compositor in Denver, the Union refused to admit him on the pretext that he had worked in a "rat office" for less than the regular wage scale and was "an improper person for membership." Two years passed before the National Typographical Union could come to a decision in his case, and it was finally decided to admit Douglass and two other Negro compositors "until such a time should come when the numbers of the colored members would be sufficient for them to form their own union."[30]

On January 13, 1868, the first National Convention of Colored Labor met in Washington to discuss the relationship between white and colored organized labor. Douglass was one of the first speakers and Downing also participated in the discussions. The main topic was whether Negroes should be affiliated with the National Labor Union, which had recently been organized, but the individual units of which largely excluded colored membership. The Convention adjourned, however, without coming to a decision on this crucial issue. In April, 1870, a Negro National Labor Meeting was held in Washington with Isaac Meyers of Baltimore as President, George Downing Vice-President and Lewis Douglass Secretary. The new organization made a point of opening its ranks to all races and classes of working men in the hope of forming a broad basis for united labor interests. However, it soon became clear that the time for a united labor front had not yet come, and the Negro Labor Congress soon withdrew from the white Association. The differences between the groups were ideological and political as well as racial. The white workers leaned towards Populism and the Democratic Party; the Negro deprecated class conflict and stood with the Republicans, who had guaranteed his political rights.

In Washington a small group of colored men had begun to practice in the professions. Boyd's Business Directory for 1872 listed seven colored physicians and one dentist. James T. Wormley, son of the hotelkeeper, established his own drug store at the corner of Connecticut Avenue and L Street. John H. Cook and Charles N. Thomas were practising lawyers. Since 1865 Negroes had been admitted in small numbers to clerkships in government departments. Solomon Johnson was appointed to the Treasury Department in 1867, and the youngest son of Frederick Douglass, Charles, was named to the War Department the same year. Negroes found many positions with the District Government, in which they had served for some years previously as members of the Metropolitan Police: one colored policeman was to become nationally famous for having the temerity to arrest President Grant for speeding in his horse and buggy. In 1870 Negroes were admitted for the first time to the District Fire Department.

In their traditional occupation the colored tradesmen were continuing to flourish. John A. Gray, who had assisted in the preparation of the banquet at Grant's second inauguration, had become the proprietor of the Hamilton House at 14th and

E Streets, and another man, Alfred Cook, was the owner of yet another hotel in downtown Washington in the 1400 block of F Street. Wormley's Hotel in its heyday was patronized by leading members of Congress and by foreign diplomats. Although barbershops, which had been for many years run entirely by colored men, were now being invaded by foreigners, Negroes in 1872 still owned and operated more than half of Washington's hairdressing establishments.

For colored women the most remunerative employment was to be found in the District schools. Since the time of Mayor Bowen white and colored teachers in the District received the same rate of pay, and the relatively high salaries and prestige of the teaching profession attracted to Washington outstanding Negro educators from all over the country. The Preparatory School on M Street had as its first three principals Mary Patterson, an Oberlin graduate, Octavius Catto, the distinguished Philadelphia educator, and Richard Greener, the first Negro to graduate from Harvard. Though more than half of the teachers in the colored schools in 1869 were still white, their places were rapidly taken by qualified colored men and women.[31]

The majority of the new élite class of professional Negroes in Washington—doctors, lawyers, teachers and government clerks—were graduates of Howard University. On March 2, 1867, Congress had approved a charter for an institution of higher learning in Washington, which later took the name of its founder, General Oliver Otis Howard, head of the Freedmen's Bureau. The first classes were held the same year in a small building on Georgia Avenue and W Street. A few months later General Howard purchased from the funds of the Freedmen's Bureau a 150-acre farm on a hilltop just outside the limits of Washington City, and later under the authorization of Congress turned the land and buildings over to the University Trustees. In 1870 the new classrooms were completed, and the University was able to boast of one of the handsomest and most beautifully situated campuses in the entire Washington area.

The original sponsors of the University had been New England ministers and soldiers, many of whom had been active Abolitionists before the War. Several members of the faculty, notably Dr. A. T. Augusta and Dr. Charles B. Purvis, had served as officers and surgeons in the Union Army. The first head of the Law Faculty, John M. Langston, was nationally known as an orator and prominent Republican politician.

Although primarily intended to provide for the education of Negroes, Howard University from the beginning excluded no one on account of race from either the faculty or the student body. Many of the first students at the University were white youths, too poor to afford education elsewhere, and women, who at this time were denied higher education in all but a handful of American colleges. In the year 1872 Howard had students from such distant lands as Austria, England, Scotland, Prussia, the West Indies, China and Liberia. Many of the first youths to enter the University were so poor that they brought along with them a pick, shovel or spade to "dig their way through school." Through their efforts the great hill on which the University was situated was levelled and drained, and the first streets were cut through in that section of the county.[32]

The missionary zeal of General Howard, the "Christian soldier," as he was called, was reflected in the discipline of these first students. Reveillé was at 5:30 and chapel was, of course, compulsory. The dress of each student was carefully scrutinized and regulated, and men marched in military formation to classes and chapel. At this time the emphasis of the university authorities was more on character building than on pure scholarship, and several years were to pass before the level of the curriculum offered was on a par with that of white colleges. There were severe restrictions against smoking and chewing of tobacco, drinking and card playing, and even popular music on the campus. James Bland, one of Howard's earliest students, and the composer of "Carry me back to Old Virginia," was not encouraged in his musical ambitions while at college. "Anything that smacked of vaudeville comedians or music halls," wrote Dr. Kelly Miller, "was put under the ban. Even to hum a tune on the campus was frowned upon as showing a lack of concentration."[33]

By 1872 Howard University had expanded its curriculum to include a Normal Department, Night School, Library and Museum, and Agricultural, Medical, Law, Music, Theology, Military and Preparatory departments. It was also helping to support the Miner School, founded before the War for the education of colored girls, which reopened after the War as a school for teachers. The finances of the University, which had benefited by more than $500,000 from the Freedmen's Bureau, suffered severely from its abolition in 1873, and the financial panic of the same year cut off most private sources of income. General Howard himself was indicted on charges of misappropriating the funds of the Bureau, and, though subsequently acquitted, resigned as President in 1874. The University professors were forced to accept a cut of half of their salary, and for more than ten years the future of Howard University was in serious jeopardy.

From its foundation Howard University had been under attack from Southerners and Democrats, who bitterly resented the interest of the Federal Government in sponsoring an institution which, in their opinion, promoted "miscegenation." The Southerners were particularly incensed that the funds of the Freedmen's Bureau, much of which had been derived from the confiscation of Confederate property, should have been applied to this purpose. The very existence of Howard University in the nation's capital was both an outrage to the South and a challenge to the determination and ability of the Negro race. That the University administrators were able to maintain successfully its liberal tradition through subsequent decades of political reaction and Congressional indifference was indeed remarkable. Of all the achievements of the Negroes and their white friends during the Reconstruction in Washington, Howard University was to prove the most outstanding, and that which was to have the most lasting influence upon future generations.

Epilogue

Whatever chagrin he may have felt at the overwhelming rebuff which he had received in the Senate, Shepherd accepted the situation philosophically. In a letter of thanks to the editor of the *Troy Times,* one of the newspapers which had supported him, he wrote: "It is a relief to be a free man once again and have more time to devote to my private business, which has suffered sadly in the past three years. I am worth less by $200,000 than I should have been, had I given the time and energy spent in improving this city to my own business. However, I would not undo it if I could. I have never wronged anybody or any community, have striven to do my duty to God and man, and can to-day look them in the face, conscious of having done the right. It required a sacrifice to be offered up to satisfy the 'independent press.' I demanded that they should point to one act of mine where, directly or indirectly, wrong had been done by me, or that they would put it to a vote of the people here, guaranteeing to carry 8/10ths in my favor. I shall live it down right here, conscious of having done a good job honestly, fearlessly and intelligently, and trusting to time for vindication."[1]

In July 1874, Shepherd filed suits against the *New York Sun* and the *Tribune* for libel, and a similar action against the *Baltimore Sun,* which had been almost as hostile to the District government as the New York press. The New York courts denied a subpoena against Charles A. Dana of the *Sun,* who prudently kept away from the capital. In January 1875, Whitelaw

Reid of the *Tribune* who had come to Washington to testify in connection with the Pacific Mail subsidies, was served with a warrant by the District Marshal while staying at the Arlington Hotel. Reverdy Johnson immediately took a train from Baltimore to offer his legal services, which, however, were not required. The following day George F. Hoar offered a resolution in the House to appoint a committee to inquire whether the privileges of Congress had been violated by the serving of papers upon a witness while he was under its subpoena, and Shepherd was obliged to drop the suit.[2]

The temporary commission, to which former Congressman John H. Ketcham of New York had been appointed by Grant in Shepherd's place, met first at the Arlington Hotel and later moved to the former offices of the Governor on Pennsylvania Avenue. The clerical staff of the District government was cut down almost immediately from 371 to 133. Before the commissioners had been at their desks for more than a few days claims for damages caused by the city improvements started to pour in; by July 20, 3,000 claims amounting to $2,000,000 had been received.[3]

On July 10 the report of the Solicitor of the Treasury on the Safe Burglary appeared. Bluford Wilson completely exonerated Columbus Alexander from any complicity in the theft, but refused to make any direct charges against Harrington and members of the District government. The report was equally guarded in its references to Colonel Hiram C. Whitley, the Chief of the United States Secret Service, who had been named during the course of the testimony as having been implicated in the affair. The opposition newspapers also noted that no reference was made to General Babcock, who they felt certain was also involved. His own reputation, they pointed out, was as much at stake as that of the Board of Public Works, on account of the faulty measurements which had been made of the work performed by the District for the Federal government. Babcock's close relations with Whitley were well known, and the suspicion that the Safe Burglary was a deliberate attempt to incriminate

Alexander and the memorialists by Harrington and his friends continued to gain wide currency.

The Administration would have been happy to let the matter of the Safe Burglary rest, but the opposition would have claimed the government unwilling to face the truth, and would have used the case as further political propaganda. Moreover, the Treasury Department was now headed by Benjamin Bristow, a very different man from his two immediate predecessors, who was determined to root out corruption from the Republican party. Bluford Wilson and A. G. Riddle, who had been appointed special assistant to the new Attorney-General, Edwards Pierrepoint, continued their investigations through the summer of 1874. At every turn, however, they found their efforts blocked by false information spread by the ringleaders of the conspiracy in order to cover their tracks. Michael Hayes, a former detective in the Secret Service, who had reached Alexander with regard to the Evans papers and had endeavored to drag his name into the affair, was released from custody through the efforts of Harrington. Benton, one of the burglars, was let out on bail, and Riddle was not able to re-arrest him, even though armed with authority of the Attorney-General. Hayes's assistant, Zirruth, was placed on board a ship bound for Europe by Whitley's assistant, Nettleship, but removed as he was about to sail and sent to Washington to await the trial. Nettleship himself took refuge in the office of his friend, the District Attorney of Newark, who discharged him upon payment of $1000 bail, which was later forfeited. One of the key witnesses, Colby, the clerk of the Joint Select Committee, was conveniently sent to China as United States consul. In September, after a visit to Boston and New York by Riddle for the purpose of examining witnesses, the government entered indictments on a charge of conspiracy against Harrington, Whitley, Hayes, Zirruth, Nettleship and other Secret Service employees.

When the trial began on October 20, 1874, before Justice Humphreys in the Criminal Court, only eight members of the jury had been sworn in. The counsel for the defense had found innumerable objections to the jurymen, even though the officers appointed to impanel them—James T. Wormley, Sayles J. Bowen and George W. Phillips, Chief Deputy Marshal of the District—had all been loyal Republicans. When the jury—of whom five were Negroes—was finally selected on the 21st, Whitley's counsel promptly entered a plea for abatement, questioning the legality of the jury on the grounds that three of its members did not pay taxes to the District. Harrington, even though he had as District Attorney tried many persons using a similar type of jury, also chose to file the same plea.[4]

Owing to the absence of more than half of the defendants, only three were brought to trial: Whitley, Harrington and A. B. Williams, a Washington attorney who had acted as intermediary between Harrington, Whitley and Nettleship, and who had been present at the scene of the burglary. On October 23, Riddle opened the case for the prosecution in a speech acknowledged to be one of the most brilliant ever heard in a Washington court room. He undertook to make clear the connection between the men on trial and their common motive for wishing to involve Columbus Alexander while the District Investigation was proceeding. After several more witnesses had been heard, Harrington rose to make his own defense in a stirring address to the jury, in which he completely denied any part in framing the conspiracy, claiming that he had too much at stake to risk his reputation in any such attempt. Whitley boldly denied the testimony of Hayes and Zirruth, maintaining that they were taking out their spite against him as Chief of the Secret Service for having dismissed them.

After the defense had concluded, Riddle without notes summed up the final arguments for the government prosecution in a speech which took two hours and a half to deliver. The jury was out 45 hours. When it returned the foreman announced that Williams had been acquitted and that no agreement had been reached in the cases of Harrington and Whitley. Four members of the jury had disagreed as to Harrington's guilt and Whitley escaped conviction by the margin of three votes. The Negro jurors, with only one exception, had voted to convict both men. Attorney-General Bristow promptly ordered another trial, but before a fresh jury could be impanelled, the District Supreme Court on December 5 announced that it had granted the plea for abatement entered by the defense counsel in October. A short time previously the Supreme Court had upheld a similar plea on the grounds that the Grand Jury had been improperly constituted, and the Court's decision was now held to be applicable to the Safe Burglary case. Davidge, Harrington's counsel, asked leave to withdraw his plea and to submit to a new trial, but a letter was read in Court from the Attorney-General stating that the government did not intend to proceed further at that time.[5]

During the course of the following two years three separate attempts were made in Congress by the Democrats to reopen the case, but the Republicans were still powerful enough to defeat a House resolution, which would have required a two-thirds majority. Not until the 44th Congress assembled in 1876 was a new investigation ordered. In the meantime Riddle, whose zeal and eloquence had proved embarrassing to the Administration, had been dismissed, along with his assistant, Charles A. Hill, but Bristow, still Secretary of the Treasury, retained the services of his Solicitor, Bluford Wilson. As a prominent candidate for the Republican presidential nomination, Bristow had been tireless in his efforts to cleanse the Republican party from the corruption of which the Democrats had made such effective propaganda in 1874. When the second Safe Burglary trial opened in April 1876, Whitley and Nettleship had been persuaded to turn state's evidence and to disclose without fear of retribution the details of the conspiracy. They were again indicted along with Harrington, Babcock and Sommerville, an attorney who had acted as go-between of Bliss, the other burglar who was now serving time in Vermont. Babcock and Sommerville were able to get bail, and the case postponed until September.

When the District Criminal Court met on September 20 for the second Safe Burglary Trial the presidential campaign was in full swing, and the case received comparatively little attention in the national press. Harrington had gone into hiding, but Whitley, Babcock, Nettleship, Williams and Sommerville were present. William A. Cook was Babcock's counsel, and A. G. Riddle was once more called into the prosecution by the government. On this occasion Whitley and Nettleship freely admitted details of the conspiracy, stating that the plot had been engineered to protect the interests of the District government by Harrington. Babcock, who had been worried by his implication and that of Col. Samo in the faulty measurements of the District Surveyor, was also in the plot. When called to the stand, however, Babcock flatly denied the charges. Columbus Alexander, testifying on the 23rd, recounted again the incidents on the night of the safe robbery. Shepherd and Dr. J. B. Blake both testified on Babcock's behalf, and Major Richards gave details regarding the burglary, of which he had been a spectator.

Even before the Judge's instructions to the jury had been given, it was evident to some of the newspaper correspondents that the defendents would again escape. The *New York Herald* reporter had written at the opening of the trial that Whitley's testimony lacked conviction, and that he was under pressure from the Republican party leaders, who feared the possible repercussions of the trial on the national elections.[6] When Babcock, Williams and Sommerville were acquitted on October 13 there was little surprise at the verdict. Harrington came out of hiding and offered himself up for a new trial, but the government showed little alacrity to prosecute him. Thus the Safe Burglary affair ended, as far as the Courts were concerned, but even those who had hitherto supported the late District administration began to wonder whether they might not after all have been mistaken, and the memorialists received additional vindication.

When the commission form of government had been inaugurated in 1874, it had generally been looked upon as a temporary expedient, since the Joint Committee's report had been published too close to the end of the session for Congress to devise a new permanent form of local administration for the District.

The Commissioners were at first considered as receivers in bankruptcy, and as a means of curtailing the extravagance of the Territorial authorities. It was not long, however, before the commission form of government began to receive the support of the local property owners and press. Donn Piatt wrote in the *Capital* on September 6: "We are now possessed of the best form of government under the Constitution that can be given to the District of Columbia." Crosby S. Noyes, who had endorsed the commission administration the preceding June, wrote an editorial in the *Star* on November 9, 1874, which might have been taken from the columns of its late rival, the *Patriot*:

> Frankly we may say that we know of no city where the taxpayers and bona-fide citizens are so hopelessly swamped by the illiterate and untaxed as in Washington . . . . From the nature of the case, the seat of government will always be over-run by a floating population of non-taxpayers. To say nothing of the large number of government employees who are generally non-taxpayers. We have always a good sprinkling of office-seekers, originally from the States, but stranded here so hopelessly, apparently, that they consider themselves qualified voters of Washington, though paying no taxes. Then we have an immense "contraband" army brought upon us by war, and who have been kept afloat here by our local politicians for voting purposes . . . . Under these exceptional circumstances it is not very strange that the taxpayers should not hanker to any great extent for the right of suffrage . . . . They doubt if it is worthwhile going through so much to get so little. As Congress has "supreme legislative power over the District," they prefer, as at present advised, that Congress should exercise that power.

Two weeks later the *Star* reported the circulation of a petition to Congress signed by prominent businessmen favoring the continuation of local government in the District under the Commissioners. The memorial contained the signatures of men who had in the past been bitter political enemies: S. P Brown (former member of the Board of Public Works), ex-Mayor Emery, William B. Todd (one of the most violent opponents of the Territorial government), William Stickney (the former President of the Legislative Council), D. C. Forney of the *Sunday Chronicle* and W. W. Moore of the Jackson Democratic Association, an ultra-Conservative. The *National Republican,* on the other hand, in an interview with leading citizens published on November 20, found considerable divergence of opinion among them as to the best permanent form of organization for the District. Shepherd went on record as favoring an appointed chief executive and a legislature half appointed and half elected; he was also in favor of abolishing the Board of Health and the Police Commissioners. Henry Willard, another former member of the Board of Public Works, supported Shepherd's opinion, and was also anxious to maintain a Delegate in Congress to represent the District. Dr. J. B. Blake considered that the right of suffrage should be restricted to those who had paid taxes of at least $5.00 per annum. Ex-Mayor Wallach was for returning unconditionally to the old corporation governments of Washington and Georgetown. The *National Republican* asked bluntly in its editorial: "Is the Republican Party to acknowledge that suffrage in the Nation's Capital has been a failure? The Party would be putting a sword in the hands of the enemy to slay itself."[7]

On December 7, 1874, the Joint Committee headed by Senator Justin Morrill of Vermont, which had been preparing a bill for the permanent organization of the District of Columbia, submitted a 200-page report. A Board of three Regents was to be appointed by the President to constitute a department of general government. Under the Regents were to be Bureaus, each with an appointed executive at its head, except for the Board of Education, which was to consist partially of appointed and partially of elected members. All local taxes were to be paid into the Federal Treasury, and all payments and disbursements were to be made by the Treasurer of the United States.

The Morrill Bill was discussed in the Senate on December 17, when its lack of provision for local suffrage was strongly attacked by Senator Morton. "It seems to me," he said, "that when we undertake to disenfranchise 100,000 people we are taking a step backward, and I know what will be said about it . . . that it is intended to get clear of colored suffrage. In this District, where it was first established, it is to be the first stricken down. I understand that there are many people in the District who are willing to be disenfranchised for the purpose of getting clear of the colored vote, who have always been opposed to the colored vote and are to-day . . . If the powers of Congress may be deputed to three Commissioners or Regents . . . it has the powers to depute it to all the people."[8]

Bayard of Delaware replied that, while he had no doubt that Congress had the authority to devise many forms of government for the District, Negro suffrage had proved to be a tragic failure. "When Congress," he declared, "represented in both Houses by an overwhelming majority of the Republican party, sought fit to wipe out the existence of the government which was then in force and which was founded upon this universal suffrage so far as race and color are concerned, they knew it has brought ruin upon this District and a debt which this people cannot pretend to pay . . . . The debt has been created mainly by a Board of Public Works appointed by the President of the United States and confirmed by the Senate in whose selection the people who hold the property of this District had no voice whatever."[9]

When asked by Morton if he considered this a good reason for totally disenfranchising the people of the District and putting them under the control of a like Board, Bayard replied: "I am not saying yet whether I am in favor of disenfranchising this people entirely or not . . . I am endeavoring to state the proposition so that . . . the people of this country shall know the pass to which the Senator and his party have brought the people and affairs of this District."[10] When Senator Allison reminded Bayard that $4,000,000 of the debt created by the Board of Public Works had been submitted to the vote of the people of the

District, who had been in favor of the loan by an overwhelming majority, and that $5,000,000 of the District debt had been incurred by the old Corporations, he answered lamely: "Possibly I am not as familiar with the precise history of the formation of the debt of the District as the Hon. Gentleman from Iowa." Undeterred by this confession of ignorance, the Senator went on in his tirade against the evils of unrestricted Negro suffrage.

Senator Thurman took the view that the Federal government as the largest owner of property in the capital, should directly govern the District. "I will not say," he declared, "that a frame of government might not be constructed allowing of suffrage which would work well. My impression is that the old municipalities did very well . . . There never were any complaints against them until Negro suffrage came." "Negro suffrage in the states and in the District," Thurman maintained, "stood upon a wholly different formation. In those states where slavery had existed the whole population had been assumed to entertain a hostile feeling towards the colored population, and suffrage was placed in their hands for their defense. But that reason entirely fails in the District of Columbia, where you cannot have hostile legislation against them. As long as Congress is friendly to them, they need no such legislation . . . In considering the question, you must consider it precisely as you would the question of conferring it upon a woman or upon an alien or upon anyone else. You must consider it simply in reference to the capacity of the person to exercise the right beneficially to the public and for the good government of the District."[11]

Senator Thurman was astute enough to realize that a frontal attack upon Negro suffrage based upon prejudice of a typically Southern nature was not likely to cut much ice in a Senate where Republicans were still in the majority. Although there had been much publicized corruption following the participation of Negroes in state governments in the South, Conservative Republicans could distinguish the difference between conditions in Louisiana and South Carolina and those in the District of Columbia. Thurman was aware, however, that many Republican

Senators would prefer to avoid if possible the thorny question of creating a suitable form of administration for the District by evading it on a constitutional pretext. After Morton's amendment to elect the commissioners by popular suffrage had been defeated by a tie vote, Democratic Senator Merrimon of North Carolina on February 11 made a long speech carrying forward the Thurman line of argument. Citing an imposing number of constitutional authorities, he endeavored to show that the delegation of Territorial authority to the District had been without the sanction of the Constitution. Though ably answered by Senator Wright of Iowa, who pointed out that the precedent of over seventy years could not be disregarded, Merrimon's point had been well and skilfully made. The Senators were not reassured by the Minority Report on the Morrill Bill by Senator Spencer of Alabama, which had been published on January 11. Spencer was one of the last remaining carpet-baggers in the Senate, and his political reputation was scarcely unblemished.

On February 18, the Senate received a petition in support of the Morrill Bill signed by such leading Washington citizens as Crosby S. Noyes, William Murtagh, Thomas Florence (editor of the *Gazette*), S. P. Brown, W. B. Todd, Moses Kelly, Adolph Cluss, Henry D. Cooke, William Stickney and Richard Harrington. The petitioners made it clear that, while some of the citizens of the District favored the election of officers by popular suffrage, they themselves were all strongly in favor of government by commission and would be satisfied by an amendment providing for the election of a Delegate to Congress. The fact that most of the signers of the memorial were Republicans and that many of them had occupied prominent positions in the late Territorial administration must have made a profound impression upon the senators. Nevertheless, they decided to table the Morrill Bill and thus for another session the question of the ultimate form of District administration remained unsettled.

On February 22, 1875, Norton P. Chipman was able to say a few good words for the late Territorial government. He emphasized the fact that the Board of Public Works had been appointed by the President, and that therefore the Federal government should legally be held liable for the Board's expenditures. He reminded the House that such an eminent authority as Caleb Cushing had held that the Act of March 3, 1873 had repealed the former Act by which the ceiling on District debt had been placed at $10,000,000, and that the Board of Public Works had acted upon this authority. Quoting from the Southard Report of 1835 and the more recent document of the Senate Judiciary Committee on the relations between the District and the Federal Government, he contended that at least half of the cost of running the national capital should be contributed by the nation. Although Congress was now in complete control of the District, he considered it to be the worst governed of all places under its control, and he characterized the course of the Commissioners as having been "vaccilating and spineless."[12] This speech was to be Chipman's swansong; after March 4, 1875, when his term as Delegate expired, the District was to have no further direct representation in Congress.

In spite of the general satisfaction of the citizens of Washington with the retrenchment program of the Commissioners, sufficient complaints had been made of their expenditures for an investigation to be held in February, 1876. It had been charged that the Commissioners had entered into new contracts, and that the issue of 3.65 bonds had been greatly increased. During the course of the Investigation the Commissioners were requested to have all work on contracts suspended. They were asked to give full particulars regarding the old contracts of the Board of Public Works which they had taken over, and whether any new commitments had been entered into.

The Report of the Investigating Committee revealed that the District government had principally been concerned in completing the paving of some of the streets which had been left in an unfinished state after the bankruptcy of the Board, and in replacing much of the wooden pavement, which already had begun to disintegrate under Washington weather conditions. The Report showed that the collection of taxes was proceeding satisfactorily and that the Commissioners were dealing fairly with the claims for property damage. The evidence regarding the excess amount of District bonds was turned over to the Attorney-General, who stated that the Commissioners had been acting in good faith. As a result of the outcry, Congress nevertheless passed a law on March 14, 1876, placing a limit on the issue of 3.65 bonds and making it a penal offense to increase the District debt. The District was required to meet the payment of interest on its funded debt from its own revenues; since this was not yet possible, the money was loaned by the Treasury Department, to which it was later repaid.

The Investigation of 1876 did not lack completely, however, its sensational aspects. Ever since 1871 rumors had been circulating of the activities of the so-called "Real Estate Ring," and it had recently been alleged that members of the same crowd had been speculating in 3.65 bonds, with the connivance of certain Congressmen. As the most prominent member of the "Ring," Hallett Kilbourn was summoned to appear before the House Investigating Committee on March 4, when he was asked to produce the record books of his real estate transactions, the same books which his partner had refused to show in 1874 to the joint investigating committee. On the advice of his counsel, Jeremiah Black, Kilbourn also refused to answer questions of members of the committee regarding the other members of the so-called "Ring." On March 22 he was placed in jail for contempt of Congress under the custody of the Sergeant-at-Arms, John G. Thompson. Kilbourn remained incarcerated for more than six weeks, while elaborate meals were sent to his cell from the Senate caterer and he was visited by many friends bringing him delicacies. At last Justice Cartter of the District Supreme Court granted him the right of habeas corpus, and he was released under $5,000 bail. As soon as he attained his freedom, Kilbourn started proceedings for false arrest against Thompson, the Speaker of the House and members of the Investigating Committee and, after two trials was ultimately awarded the sum of $20,000 in 1884.[13]

In August, 1876, Congress appointed another Joint Select Committee to prepare a new bill to provide for a permanent form of government for the District. On December 27 when the 45th Congress assembled the Bill which emerged from their deliberations was published. Much shorter and simpler than the Morrill Bill, the new measure introduced in the House by Representative Eppa Hunton of Virginia provided for the government of the District by three Commissioners, one to be appointed by the Senate, one by the House, the third by the President. The commissioners were to submit estimates of District expenditures to the United States Treasury, and the Federal Government was required to contribute forty per cent. The Commissioners were also empowered to draft and submit to Congress laws necessary for the operation of the District government. No provision was made in this Bill for elected representatives in the District or for a Delegate to Congress. Hunton, who had served as a Brigadier-General in the Confederate Army, had the usual antipathy of his class to Negro suffrage, as his autobiography published many years later, clearly revealed. These sentiments were also shared by another prominent District committee member, Joseph Blackburn of Kentucky, a former Confederate Colonel, who worked closely with Hunton in preparing the Bill. The Hunton Bill was made the special order of the day for January 4, 1877, but owing to the all-absorbing debate over the contested presidential election, it was not brought before the House as scheduled. The Hayes-Tilden dispute put an end to the discussion of District affairs during the first session of Congress, and it was not until 1878 that the measure was revived.

Meanwhile, in December 1877, a committee of one hundred citizens had presented a memorial to Congress asking that the proposed share of the contribution of the Federal Government should be raised from forty to fifty per cent. The committee included George W. Riggs, Alexander Shepherd, Crosby S. Noyes, Chief Justice David Cartter, John T. Given and many other prominent Washington citizens. The figures used by Shepherd in the 1874 Investigation relating to the area occupied by the streets and avenues in the capital city were used as the basis for the Committee's claims that Congress should provide a larger share of the District budget. This was the first occasion that Shepherd had appeared on a committee with his former political enemies, which lent additional strength to the delegation's arguments. It now appeared clear to members of Congress that the citizens of the District were much less concerned over the question of suffrage than that of the financial participation of the Federal government.

The Bill prepared by the Joint Select Committee was reported to the House on January 20, 1878 by Representative Hendee of Vermont. It was practically identical with the measure which Hunton had introduced at the earlier session, the chief difference being in its acceptance of the 50-50 budget proposal of the Citizens' Committee. On the 29th former Governor Claflin of Massachusetts proposed to the House District Committee an amendment; under his proposal the District would be divided into twelve voting areas, each of which would elect two members of a city council. Such a council would, however, possess purely negative functions, having authority only to veto tax measures proposed by the Commissioners, including their budget estimates. The amendment was accepted by the Committee, but when the Hendee Bill was put to a vote in the House it was defeated the following day.

On February 13th, Representative Blackburn of Kentucky introduced a bill very similar in form to that of his Vermont colleague. It provided for the election of members of the Advisory Council by all male District residents who did not vote elsewhere, paid poll taxes, and had resided in the District at least three years. The measure was discussed at length during the months of March and April, objections being made on both sides of the House to the proposed qualifications for voters and to other aspects of the measure. The Blackburn Bill was defeated on April 15th by a vote of 124 to 94, but it was reintroduced on May 7 after having undergone several changes in the District

Committee. The provision for an elected Council was retained, but the Board of Health, which had been criticized as being too expensive, was abolished, along with the Police Commissioners. On May 25 the amended bill passed by a voice vote.

Meanwhile the Committee of One Hundred had presented its case to the Senate District Committee. On February 3rd a delegation, which included George W. Riggs, Columbus Alexander and W. H. Claggett, a former member of the District Legislative Council, called upon members of the Senate who were considering the Blackburn Bill. Though the delegation's chief concern was the equal participation of the Federal Government in the District budget, Mr. Claggett touched upon the proposal of an advisory council and expressed strong opposition to the revival of suffrage, even in as limited a form as that proposed. On May 25th the Senate rejected the Blackburn Bill and introduced its own measure, which eliminated the advisory council but provided for an elected Delegate. In the conference between the two Houses a compromise was reached under which both Delegate and Council were rejected. As the session drew to a close the District Bill was once more taken up: on June 8, 1878, it passed the House by a vote of 127 to 70 and two days later in the Senate it passed by a voice vote.

The majority of the Republican members of the 45th Congress were doubtless none too happy regarding the outcome of the District government question: the number of those in the House who abstained from voting was significantly large. Presumably, however, others were glad to have this troublesome matter settled, after so many years of dispute. The attitude of the wealthier citizens of the District had clearly indicated that they were more concerned with securing financial assistance from Congress than in electing their own municipal government. And, indeed, few of the less prosperous, even the Negroes, had petitioned Congress to preserve their right of suffrage.[14]

The members of the 45th Congress, unfortunately, were not blessed with the gift of prophecy. They could not have foreseen the increasing complexity of governing the District, the heavy burdens which future Congressmen would have to shoulder as aldermen of a great metropolis. The Republican members were for the greater part unaware that the abandonment of popular suffrage in the District would in later years be cited as a precedent for the elimination of the Negro voter in the South, by which the strength of their own party would severely suffer. "The Southern states, which by ingenious constitutional devices practically disenfranchised the Negro," wrote Col. A. K. McClure thirty years later, "have merely followed the teachings of the Republican Congress and President, which disenfranchised him in the capital city."[15] The Republicans in the 45th Congress were not solving the question of the District government; they were merely placing it in cold storage, whence, as from Pandora's box, it would eventually re-emerge to plague their successors.

Neither could the business and property owners who had so eagerly sacrificed their right of suffrage for the financial assistance of the Federal government realize that their advantages would not be permanent. They could not look forward to the time, almost fifty years later, when the 50-50 ratio of Federal contribution to the District budget would be superseded by a formula of payments which would vary from year to year, that the Federal Government, while continuing to own more than half of the land in the District, would contribute less than eight per cent to its maintenance. Nor were they able to anticipate the constant shifts of population within the city of Washington and the enormous expense required to maintain a dual school system for white and colored children, in theory separate but equal. Still hoping for a voice in national representation, members of the Board of Trade could see no inconsistency in opposing at the same time all efforts to regain local suffrage, ignoring the historical fact that national representation had never been granted to territories which had not first proved their ability to govern themselves.

As the passage of time has changed our perspective on the problem of the District, the achievements as well as the failures of the Territorial Government should be carefully reassessed.

Taking a long view of the matter, the benefits which the District enjoyed as a result of the improvements to the city were enormous. The wealth which accrued in Washington during the last decades of the nineteenth century and the first decades of the twentieth more than fulfilled Shepherd's fondest dreams, and the debt which was incurred during his administration was paid off in the course of time without placing undue burdens upon the taxpayers of the District. Yet the question remains whether the price paid by the District for its fifty years of prosperity was not too high. Had Shepherd been a man of different temperament, possessing equal determination but greater patience, the course of the improvements could have been spread out over a longer period, and there would have been fewer costly mistakes, such as the laying down of wooden pavements which had to be replaced within a few years' time.

Shepherd's greatest error was to make the city improvements into a partisan and political issue, thus alienating the Conservatives and Democrats who would have accepted a less hasty and expensive program. Had President Grant shown less partisanship in his appointments to the Territorial Government, and had the Democrats and Conservatives been represented in the Legislative Council which he appointed, that body could have served as an effective brake on the overly-impetuous Board of Public Works. The Territorial Government, as established in 1871, contained fundamental weaknesses, as were brought out in the 1874 Investigation; it was cumbrous, expensive to operate, and the relationship between its Executive and Legislative branches and that of the Board of Public Works was inadequately defined. Yet Congress had provided a system of checks and balances which under other men than Grant and Shepherd might have functioned effectively for many years. In a period less subject to violent political emotions than the Reconstruction it could have been possible to retain the form of the Territorial Government, while abolishing the Board of Public Works and eliminating much superfluous expenditure. At a time, however, when the issue of District suffrage was tied so closely to that of Negro suffrage in the Southern states, such a compromise was unfortunately impossible.

Since so much emphasis has been placed upon the participation of Negroes in the government of the District by local historians such as Walter S. Dodd, Edward Ingle and W. B. Bryan, it is important that this question be re-examined more fully than has been done in the past. In recent years all efforts to revive Home Rule for the District in Congress has been successfully thwarted by a group of Southerners, many of whom have claimed that the participation of the Negro in District politics during the Reconstruction period had been an unmitigated failure.[16] It will be well to conclude this study by recapitulating some of the findings which have been brought out in earlier chapters, and which show that many of the accusations made by these Southern Congressmen rest upon prejudice and folklore rather than upon a careful study of the historical facts.

The most serious accusation brought against Negro suffrage in the District is that of illegal voting. Such charges, which were made by the *National Intelligencer* and *Georgetown Courier* in 1867 and 1868 and by the *Daily Patriot* in 1871 and 1872, have never been fully investigated. Most of the allegations were made by men who were appalled at the size of the Negro vote and the efficiency with which it was organized by the Republican ward commissioners: since the proportion of colored men who voted was greater than that of the white voters they could only conclude that this must have been due to fraud.

The great majority of the white residents of the District had resisted to the utmost the enfranchisement of the colored population, the largest concentration of Negroes to be found in any American metropolitan area at this time.[17] Yet their fears of being dominated by the "refugee freedmen" which Andrew Johnson had voiced in his veto of the District Suffrage Bill in 1867 were never realized. The colored vote of 1867 was phenomenally large, since it was the first occasion in which Negroes had been permitted to vote in the District—or, for that matter, in any place in the South—but not a single Negro in this year was elected to the city Councils. In 1868, despite the fact that the period of residence in city wards prerequisite to registration had been reduced from three months to fifteen days, the colored vote fell 216 beneath that of the previous year. In 1870 the number of Negroes registered declined still further. Only in the year 1869 was the number of colored members in the Washington City Councils equivalent to their proportion of the population, and this was not the case in Georgetown nor in the County, where they had no political power.

It cannot be denied that the overwhelming majority of Negroes voted the Republican ticket—a scarcely surprising situation, since the Democrats were so closely identified with the South and with slavery. Yet it is a fact that in the election of 1870, in which Sayles J. Bowen was defeated by Matthew Emery, a "Reform Republican" who had the support of Democrats and Conservatives, the Negroes did not vote as a bloc. Although Bowen had shown himself to be a warm partisan of the Negro cause, a large proportion of colored voters chose to give their votes to a man who appeared to them a more capable administrator. It is noteworthy that on this occasion the same sources which had raised the cry of illegal voting by Negroes whenever they voted for a regular Republican candidate made no such accusations after the defeat of Bowen at the polls. Emery was given the votes of many Negro laborers who had become dissatisfied with the failure of the Bowen administration to pay them their wages on time. They chose to support another Republican, a businessman, who promised to preserve their civil rights and also to advance their economic interests.

The worst feature of Negro suffrage in the District during the Reconstruction period was unquestionably the rioting which took place in 1868 and 1869 during the Washington municipal elections. It should be remembered, however, that violence at the polls during this period was by no means confined to Washington, and that such outbreaks had been prevalent in many other cities, such as New York and San Francisco, where almost no Negroes had voted. The disturbances were primarily caused by the lack of a secret ballot, which made it possible for voters to be identified while standing in line at the polls by the party tickets which they were carrying. By 1870, however, the situation in Washington was fully under the control of the Metropolitan Police, and there is no mention in the local newspapers of any violence at the polls during the elections which took place under the Territorial Government.

In the 1872 Investigation when the matter of illegal voting came before a House Committee neither the Chief Clerk of the House of Delegates nor the editor of the *Daily Patriot* were able to substantiate charges which they had made that Negroes had voted twice in the same election. The Rev. J. W. Green, a colored minister who opposed the policy of the Board of Public Works, was also unable to prove charges that colored workmen had been imported from Virginia to vote at the special election held in 1871 to ratify the $4,000,000 loan. Some white witnesses, when asked why they had not registered at this same election, complained of having to vote twice in the same year and stated that "property owners did not like crowds." It would seem plain, therefore, that the same circumstances on which the *Evening Star* had commented in 1867—the unwillingness of many white men to vote alongside of Negroes—was the principal factor which deterred them from taking a greater part in municipal elections. Had white Democrats and Conservatives voted in as large a proportion as the colored Republicans, they would undoubtedly have made a far better showing at the polls.

In the Territorial Government the ultimate authority of the electorate had been taken away and given to officers appointed by President Grant, so that the power of all voters, white as well as colored, had been greatly reduced. Some historians, however, such as Walter S. Dodd,[18] have suggested that the Negroes, being for the most part members of the laboring class, were chiefly responsible for the endorsement of the $4,000,000 loan in 1871 which enabled the Board of Public Works to carry out its plans for civic improvements. This statement, however, greatly oversimplifies the facts. Members of other large minority groups among the working classes, such as the traditionally Democratic Irish, were just as enthusiastic as the Negroes in their support of a program which offered them large-scale employment, and the Loan Bill was endorsed by the overwhelming majority of the citizens of the District, who were anxious that the improvements should not be subjected to further delay. Later on, as the Board of Public Works had exhausted the funds of the District Treasury, and as new and stringent methods of taxation were introduced, opposition to the Board developed in every section of the community; some of the colored property-owners, indeed, became as loud-spoken in their condemnation of Shepherd as any of the white "memorialists."

During the Reconstruction period the cooperation between the white and colored groups, especially within the ranks of the Republicans in the District, had developed to a remarkable degree, and voting in many instances actually ran contrary to color lines. In the primary election of 1871 to select the Republican nominee for Delegate to Congress Frederick Douglass received the votes of several white men, and General Chipman was endorsed by many Negroes. In the special election of 1871 Henry Piper, the official candidate of the Republican Central Committee, defeated his wealthy white opponent, Hallett Kilbourn, who was standing as an independent Republican candidate, in a district where the majority of registered voters was white; in this same election in a similarly mixed district the colored lawyer, O. S. B. Wall, defeated a white Republican Independent. Considering that white voters had been so strongly opposed to Negro suffrage only a few years previously, it was remarkable how soon they were able to value colored men of proven political ability. Even such an extreme opponent of the Republicans as James E. Harvey, editor of the *Daily Patriot,* paid tribute in the 1872 Investigation to John Gray, the colored member of the Legislative Council, declaring him to be a better man than some of his white associates.

Nor did the social barriers which still divided the white and colored races during this period extend to members of the

Territorial administration. On New Year's Day, 1872, white and colored members of the District government visited each other's homes; John F. Cook, the Collector of Taxes, entertained at his home on 16th Street "nearly all the officials of the District government and representatives of every interest in the community, in each of which he has warm friends."[19] A few doors away Carter A. Stewart, a former Negro Alderman, James A. Handy, a colored member of the House of Delegates, and William H. Wormley, former Commissioner for the Colored Schools, were receiving their friends of both races. It is more than likely that under a representative government such friendly relationships between the white and colored groups in the District would have become stabilized and that effective cooperation between the most responsible elements in both races could have been established.

Had representative government been permitted to continue in the District, it is also certain that the inflexible party lines which bound Negroes so closely to the Republican Party during Reconstruction would have crumbled. After the death of Charles Sumner, after the Republican Party leaders had become lukewarm to the cause of the Negro and devoted themselves more than ever to the protection and preservation of vested interest, many Negroes in both the North and the South turned to the Democrats. Such men as George T. Downing in the North and Hiram Revels in the South, both ardent Republicans in their youth, realized that Negroes would stand more to gain from an effective two-party system than from being permanently tied to Republican coattails. If the political and economic gains which they had made during Reconstruction could have been consolidated, Negroes in the District would have voted less as a racial bloc and more and more as members of social classes and economic groups. The Congress of the United States, by abolishing local suffrage in the national Capital, injured not only the colored citizens of the District; it also ended a promising experiment in political democracy from which the entire nation could well have benefited.

Notes

NOTES FOR CHAPTER ONE

1. Ellis: *Sights and Secrets of the National Capital,* p. 444.
2. Idem p. 446.
3. Henry Adams: *The Education of Henry Adams* (Modern Library ed.) p. 257.
4. Quoted in *Ellis* op. cit. p. 418. Donn Piatt was a native of Ohio who had settled in Washington after the war.
5. Idem p. 418.
6. Bryan: *History of the National Capital,* Vol. II, p. 505.
7. The actual population percentage of Germans resident in the District of Columbia, as given in The Census of 1870 was 3.73. To this number must be added, however, the German-speaking immigrants from Austria and Switzerland and second-generation German-Americans.
8. George Alfred Townsend (1841-1914) was born in Delaware. During the War he became correspondent to the *New York Tribune* and later the *New York World.* In 1867 he settled in Washington and was a regular correspondent for the *Chicago Tribune,* the *Cincinnati Gazette* and other important papers. Townsend was the author of biographies of Garibaldi and Lincoln, of a play, *The Bohemians,* and of several works of fiction, *Tales of the Chesapeake* and *The Entailed Hat.*
9. Ben Perley Poore (1820-1887) was a native of Newburyport, Massachusetts. He had been attached to the U. S. Legation in Paris, and had edited documents pertaining to American history in the Franch National Archives. In 1854 he had settled in Washington as correspondent to the *Boston Journal* and other newspapers. He edited the first number of the Congressional Directory and also was the author of biographies of such political figures as King Louis-Philippe of France, Napoleon and Zachary Taylor.
10. Allen C. Clark: "Beau Hickman." *Columbia Historical Society Records,* Vol. 40-41, p. 90.

NOTES FOR CHAPTER TWO

1. *Margaret Leech*: Reveille in Washington, p. 1.
2. *New York Times*: March 17th, 1868.
3. *Washington, City and Capital,* p. 74.
4. *Special Report of the U. S. Department of Education on the Condition and Improvement of Public Schools in the District of Columbia,* 1871, p. 195.
5. Ellen O'Connor: *Myrtilla Miner—a Memoir,* p. 65-72.
6. *Congressional Globe*: 34th Congress, 2nd Session, p. 1496.
7. *Records of the Bureau of Freedmen and Refugees* (U. S. Archives).
8. George Alfred Townsend: *Washington Inside and Out,* p. 250.
9. W. W. Moore: "Contraband Suffrage." *Journal of the 64th Council of Washington,* June 6th, 1867.
10. U. S. Department of Education: *Historical Sketch of Education for the Colored Race in the District of Columbia,* 1807-1905, by Winfield S. Montgomery, 1907, p. 111.
11. Wallach interpreted the law as referring to the proportion of colored children aged from six to 17 to the aggregate number of children of both races from birth to the age of 21.
12. According to the Report made by J. O. Wilson and R. T. Morrell, trustees of the Washington Public Schools, only $19,283.72 had been paid to the Colored School Trustees between 1862 and 1866, while the white schools had received during the same period $182,257.25. By November, 1867, the arrears had reached the figure of $55,960.35. It was not until June, 1868, that the trustees of the colored schools received their fair share of the common school fund.
13. Tindall: "Sketch of Mayor Bowen." *Records of the Columbia Historical Society,* Vol. 18, p. 37.
14. McCulloch: *Men and Measures,* p. 234.
15. The bill was passed three times by Congress, but not signed by Andrew Johnson and did not become law until after President Grant had become President on March 19th, 1869.

NOTES FOR CHAPTER THREE

1. Letter to James T. Fields, February 9, 1868.
2. A contrary opinion of Andrew Johnson's alcoholic indulgences is to be found in the *Reminiscences* of Senator William M. Stewart of Nevada, who stated (p. 169) that "Johnson continued to drink at low groggeries after Lincoln's assassination and to associate with toughs and rowdies, both black and white." On the night of the assassination he mentions visiting Johnson at the Kirkwood House recovering from a "bender"; he and his friends

"had the doctor administer a dose," and they cleaned him up and gave him a new pair of clothes (p. 194).

3. Charles K. Tuckerman. *Magazine of American History,* July, 1888.
4. Letter of Andrew Johnson to Col. Benjamin C. Truman, Aug. 6, 1868.
5. Mrs. John A. Logan: *Thirty Years in Washington,* p. 661.
6. Whitelaw Reid: *After the War,* p. 306.
7. *Georgetown Courier*: February 5, 1870.
8. Bryan: *History of the National Capital,* Vol. II, p. 551.
9. *U. S. Senate Records.* 38th Congress. District Committee.
10. *Evening Star*: February 13, 1866.
11. Richardson: *Messages and Papers,* Vol. VIII, pp. 3670-3681.
12. Gideon Welles: *Diary,* Volume II, pp. 3-5.
13. *Baltimore Sun*: January 9, 1867.
14. *Diary of William Owner,* Library of Congress.

NOTES FOR CHAPTER FOUR

1. *Evening Star*: Feb. 5, 1867.
2. *Evening Star*: Feb. 26, 1867.
3. *Georgetown Courier*: Feb. 25, 1867.
4. Idem March 2, 1867.
5. *Evening Star*: March 20, 1867.
6. *National Republican*: June 4, 1867.
7. *Journal,* 65th Council of Washington. June 6, 1867. W. W. Moore: "Contraband Suffrage."
8. *Evening Star*: Dec. 31, 1867.
9. U. S. Statutes 15 and 62. May 28, 1868.
10. *National Republican*: May 13, 1868.
11. Bryan: *History of the National Capital,* Vol. II, p. 563.
12. Crosby S. Noyes: *A Memorial,* p. 66.

In 1867 Mr. Wallach, believing the future of Washington was not promising, decided to sell the paper. Mr. Wallach had promised Noyes some years before that if he ever determined to sell he would give him a first chance to buy. In accordance with this agreement Mr. Wallach one day handed to Mr. Noyes a 48-hour option on the *Star* for the price of $100,000. This was looked on at the time as an extravagant price for the property. Mr. Noyes had invested in the Washington and Georgetown Railroad Company, his stock had increased, and he was able to borrow on the strength of his personality and public confidence . . . He joined with him Samuel H. Kauffmann, then an employee of the Treasury Department and a man of extended acquaintance with the printing art, George W. Adams, one of the best-known correspondents for out-of-town papers, Alexander R. Shepherd and Clarence Baker . . . When Shepherd was made Governor (of the District of Columbia in 1873) he sold his stock to his partners.

13. *New York Herald*: June 4, 1868.

14. Petition of 77 members 12th Infantry Co., Russell Barracks, June 22, 1868, claiming that restrictions on voting should not apply to those men who had previously been registered, and objecting to rights being granted to "refugee blacks from Freedmen's Village." Eleven of the signatories, mostly bearing Irish names, signed with an "X." *U. S. Senate Records.*

15. The Bill striking out the word "white" in the Washington city charter was "pocketed" by Andrew Johnson. It was not signed until March 19, 1869, by President Grant.

16. The Contested Elections Bill became law after passage by both Houses without Andrew Johnson's signature.

17. Washington Corporation Ordinance. Feb. 6, 1869.

18. *National Intelligencer.* May 28, 1869.

19. Idem June 6, 1869.

20. *Evening Star*: June 8, 1869.

21. *Evening Express*: June 3, 1869.

22. Laws of Corporation of Washington: Chap. 42, March 7, 1870.

23. Message of Mayor Bowen. *Journal of 66th Council,* p. 22.

24. Message of Mayor Bowen. *Journal of 67th Council,* pp. 88-90.

25. S. 141. "A Bill to secure equal rights in the Public Schools of Washington and Georgetown."

26. *Evening Star*: November 27, 1869.

27. The Rev. J. Sella Martin was born in Georgia, educated in Michigan and later came to Boston, where he was called to be pastor of the Tremont Temple. At the solicitation of John Bright and others of the Union and Emancipation Society he visited England, where he remained for more than two years. During this period he raised over $100,000 for the American Missionary Association. In 1868 he received a call from the 15th Street Presbyterian Church in Washington.

28. George Vashon was born in Pittsburgh, educated at Oberlin, where he received his M.A. He was called to the Bar in 1847. He taught in Haiti and subsequently at New York Central College. Vashon could read and write Greek, Latin and Hebrew and was the author of many poems. William Wells Brown: *The Rising Son,* p. 476.

29. *Evening Star*: Nov. 30, 1869.

30. 67th Council, pp. 1300-1302.

31. 67th Council, April 25, 1870, pp. 1474-1475.

32. William Chandler had been negotiating to buy the *Intelligencer* on behalf of the Republicans, but had evidently been unsuccessful. Chandler Mss. Library of Congress. Letter to Elihu Washburne, Oct. 19, 1868.

33. This was a particularly false accusation, since Bowen had actively opposed the granting of licenses to grog shops while a member of the Levy Court.

34. Boswell's salary as Register was based upon a percentage of the fees which he collected from taxes.

35. *Evening Star*: June 1, 1870.

36. Anthony Bowen was born of slave parents in Prince George's County, Maryland. After purchasing his freedom he organized with Enoch Ambush the Zion Sunday School in 1856 and later became minister of the African Methodist Church. He also held the position of messenger, later file clerk in the Patent Office.

NOTES FOR CHAPTER FIVE

1. William Tindall: "Alexander Shepherd." *Col. Hist. Soc.*, Vol. XIV, p. 63.
2. Rutherford B. Hayes. Letters. To S. Birchard. March 7, 1869.
3. Henry Adams: *Education of Henry Adams*, p. 262.
4. Papers of Commissioner of Public Grounds and Buildings.
5. Idem.
6. Henry Adams: *Letters.* Vol. I, p. 176.
7. Crook: *Memoirs of the White House*, p. 90.
8. Jesse Grant: *In the Days of my Father*, p. 63.
9. Idem, p. 66.
10. V. Melah remained at the White House until October, 1871. After his resignation Henry Whitelaw, a colored man, was appointed as steward. *Star*, Oct. 31, 1871.
11. *66th Council Journal*, 1870, pp. 10-11.
12. Letters of Sec. Gorham to Sen. Hannibal Hamlin, July 12, 1870. *U. S. Senate Records.*
13. Harvey's appointment as Minister to Portugal seems to have been somewhat of a mystery, according to Gideon Welles, whose opinion of his character was very low. *Diary*, Vol. I, p. 32. Welles also states that Harvey "gave notice to the Rebels of the expedition" to Sumter, thus precipitating the attack which caused the outbreak of the War. Vol. III, p. 514.
14. 41st Congress. 2nd Session. S. 361.
15. Report of William Syphax and William Wormley. U. S. Department of Interior.
16. Report of Charles King. U. S. Department of Interior
17. The Territorial Bill was passed by a vote of 97 to 58; 82 members of the House abstaining.
18. J. J. Coombes in his "Address on District Affairs" of August 19, 1872, charged that Shepherd and his "Ring" were responsible for a paragraph in the 20th clause of the Organic Act of 1871 which provided that special taxes might be levied in particular sections of the District for local improvements, thus evading general tax limitations. These clauses, he claimed, were fraudulently inserted and not discovered by the public until the Bill had been passed.
19. *Evening Star*: Jan. 21, 1871.
20. *Evening Star*: Jan. 13, 1871.
21. *Patriot*: Feb. 22, 1871.
22. *New National Era*: April 6, 1871.
23. *Chronicle*: April 9, 1871.
24. *National Republican*: April 12, 1871.
25. *National Republican*: April 21, 1871.
26. *Patriot*: April 21, 1871.
27. *Evening Star*: May 15, 1871.
28. *Patriot*: June 14, 1871.

NOTES FOR CHAPTER SIX

1. *Patriot*: June 23, 1871.
2. Walter S. Cox was a member of an old and distinguished Georgetown family. He was to become Chief Justice of the District Supreme Court, and was later responsible for the codification of the District laws, approved by Congress in March, 1901.
3. *Evening Star*: August 7, 1871.
4. Signers of the injunction petition included George H. Plant and George W. Riggs.
5. *Patriot*: September 4, 1871.
6. *Patriot*: October 31, 1871.
7. The Third District represented part of Georgetown, the Thirteenth portion of the central Washington city area.
8. *Patriot*: December 4 and 18, 1871.
9. Mr. Corcoran was actually in Europe for his health at the time of the special election.
10. Miller's paper was bought out in 1873 by Werner Koch, editor and publisher of the weekly *Columbia*. A new daily, the *Washingtoner Journal*, appeared under Koch's editorship on March 31, 1873.
11. Idem p. 389.
12. Idem pp. 577-588.
13. Idem p. 739.
14. Idem p. 688.
15. Idem *Report of the Investigating Committee*, pp. IV-XII.
16. Idem *Report of the Investigating Committee*, pp. XV-XX.
17. *Patriot*: May 30, 1872.

NOTES FOR CHAPTER SEVEN

1. Bryan: *History of the National Capital*, Vol. II, p. 610.
2. Barton: *Washington City*, p. 30.
3. *Patriot*: July 12, 1872.
4. *Evening Star*: September 6, 1872.
5. *National Republican*: September 11, 1872.
6. Sumner: *Works*. Vol. XV, pp. 175-195. Letter was addressed to William H. Wormley, Dr. A. T. Augusta, Dr. J. L. N. Bowen, Furman J. Shadd, and others.
7. *Chronicle*: October 23, 1872.
8. Shepherd Papers.
9. Report of the District Board of Public Works, 1872, pp. 16-17.
10. Richardson: *Messages and Papers*, Vol. IX, p. 4158.
11. 42nd Congress, 3rd Session. Executive Documents No. 7.
12. *Evening Star*: January 11, 1873.

13. John H. Crane: The Washington Ring, 1872. More about the District Tammany, 1873.

14. 42nd Congress, 2nd Session. Appendix, pp. 428-437, *Congressional Globe.*

15. 42nd Congress, 3rd Session. Appendix, p. 74, *Congressional Globe.*

16. Including the old Corporation funded debt, the total indebtedness of the District in 1874 was $18,872,565.76.

17. *Evening Star*: February 10, 1873.

18. 1874 Investigation. Vol. I, pp. 480-481.

19. Shepherd Papers.

20. 1874 Investigation. Vol. I, pp. 471-477.

21. Cortissoz: *Life of Whitelaw Reid.* Vol. II, pp. 316-317.

22. *Evening Star*: June 28, 1873.

23. Richard Greener, the first Negro to graduate from Harvard, was named in 1873 to the chair of Philosophy at the reconstructed University of South Carolina. In 1877 he returned to Washington, where he worked in the Treasury Department and subsequently headed the Law School of Howard University. In 1885 he served on the Grant Memorial Association in New York, was appointed shortly afterwards U. S. Consul in Bombay, India, and later became the first American commercial agent to serve in Vladivostock, Russia.

24. H. M. Larson: *Jay Cooke,* p. 405.

25. Ellis P. Oberholtzer: *Jay Cooke,* Vol. II, p. 417.

26. *Evening Star*: September 17, 1873.

27. *Evening Star*: September 19, 1873.

28. *Evening Star*: October 3, 1873.

29. *Washingtoner Journal*: October 10, 1873.

30. *Georgetown Courier*: October 18, 1873.

31. General John Eaton: *Lincoln, Grant and the Freedmen,* p. 289.

32. Richardson: *Messages and Papers,* Vol. IX, p. 4208.

33. *1874 Investigation,* Vol. I, p. 4.

NOTES FOR CHAPTER EIGHT

1. Henry Adams: *Democracy,* p. 295.

2. *Capital*: March 12, 1871.

3. George Alfred Townsend: *Washington Inside and Outside,* p. 176.

4. *Chronicle*: December 1, 1872.

5. James T. Wormley died in Boston on October 18, 1881. When his body was brought back to Washington for interment a few days later the flags of all the leading hotels in the city were at half-mast. The pall-bearers at the funeral included the directors of the Arlington, Willard, Ebbitt House and other principal Washington hotels. *Evening Star*: October 25, 1884.

6. George Alfred Townsend: *Washington Inside and Out,* p. 177.

7. Mark Twain and Charles Dudley Warner: *The Gilded Age,* Vol. II, p. 10.
8. Idem p. 14.
9. *Lippincott's Magazine*: "Life at the National Capital." December, 1873, p. 659.
10. *Evening Star*: January 1, 1874.
11. *Lippincott's Magazine*: op. cit. p. 661.
12. Gail Hamilton: *The Galaxy.* June, 1876.
13. Madeline Vinton Dahlgren: *Etiquette of Social Life in Washington,* pp. 5-12.
14. Mrs. John A. Logan: *Memoirs of a Soldier's Wife,* pp. 269-270.
15. Alexander Hunter: *The New National Theatre,* p. 61.
16. Ben Perley Poore: *Reminiscences of Forty Years,* p. 307.
17. Emily Edson Briggs: *The Olivia Letters,* p. 340.
18. Frank M. Anderson: *The Mystery of a Public Man.*
19. Matthew Josephson: *The Politicos,* p. 105.
20. Mark Twain and Charles Dudley Warner: *The Gilded Age,* Vol. I, p. 277.
21. Idem p. 239.
22. Idem p. 240.
23 Edward Strahan: *The Art Treasures of America.*
24. Jane W. Gemmill: *Notes on Washington,* p. 69.

NOTES FOR CHAPTER NINE

1. *Evening Star*: Jan. 30, 1874.
2. Shepherd's Reply to Investigating Committee. March 1, 1874.
3. *Evening Star*: March 30, 1874.
4. *1874 Investigation.* Vol. II, pp. 345-360.
5. Idem Vol. II, pp. 395-421.
6. Idem Vol. II, pp. 536-542.
7. Idem Vol. II, pp. 614-626.
8. Idem Vol. III, pp. 1184-1229.
9. *Evening Star*: May 1, 1874.
10. *1874 Investigation.* Vol. III, p. 1462.
11. Idem Vol. III, p. 1423.
12. Idem Vol. III, p. 1516.
13. *New York Tribune*: May 6, 1874.
14. *1874 Investigation.* Vol. III, pp. 1809-1956.
15. Idem Vol. III, pp. 2015-2016.
16. Idem Vol. III, pp. 2049-2105.
17. *Evening Star*: May 23, 1874.
18. *Capital*: May 23, 1874.
19. *National Republican*: June 9, 1874.
20. *New York Tribune*: June 9, 1874.

21. *National Republican*: June 10, 1874; *Chronicle*: June 18, 1874.
22. *New York Sun*: June 12, 1874.
23. 1874 Investigation. *Report of Investigation Committee,* Vol. I, p. viii.
24. Idem p. xi.
25. Idem p. xii.
26. *Chronicle*: June 22, 1874.
27. *Capital*: June 21, 1874.
28. *Nation*: June 25, 1874.
29. Shepherd Papers.
30. *New York Sun*: June 19, 1875.
31. *Evening Star*: June 23, 1874.
32. *New York Sun*: June 24, 1874.
33. *Evening Star*: June 27, 1874.
34. *Capital*: June 28, 1874.

NOTES FOR CHAPTER TEN

1. Emily Edson Briggs: *The Olivia Letters,* p. 274.
2. Idem p. 275.
3. *National Republican*: April 16th, 1874.
4. Idem.
5. Idem.
6. *New York Herald*: January 7, 1874.
7. *National Republican*: April 16, 1874.
8. *Philadelphia Press*: March 17, 1870.
9. *James G. Blaine*: *Twenty Years in Congress,* Vol. II, p. 515.
10. *New York World*: February 10, 1872.
11. *Evening Star*: November 25, 1871.
12. *New National Era*: June 18, 1874.
13. *Georgetown Courier*: June 18, 1874.
14. Dr. A. T. Augusta, born in Norfolk, Virginia, worked at first as a barber, learned to read and write, "by stealth," and made his way to Philadelphia, where he worked for a doctor. He earned enough money to reach Canada, where he studied at the University of Toronto Medical College and obtained a medical degree. During the War he became an Army surgeon and rose to the rank of Lieutenant-Colonel, the highest rank attained by any Negro serving in the Union Army. He was placed in charge of a hospital at Savannah, Georgia, and later worked at Freedmen's Hospital in Washington. Dr. Augusta was one of the first members of the medical faculty at Howard University.
15. *Chronicle*: November 4, 1872.
16. Dr. Charles B. Purvis was born in Philadelphia, the son of the famous Negro Abolitionist, Robert Purvis. He graduated in medicine at Western Reserve, was Acting Surgeon in the Army and Assistant Surgeon at Freedmen's

Hospital from 1869 to 1881. From 1872 to 1875 Dr. Purvis was a member of the District Board of Health.

17. *Washington Law Reporter*: Vol. II, p. 2, 1875.

18. See case of Smith v. Bell in District Court, September 1, 1883, which involved the refusal of a Washington restaurant to serve a colored man. The case was nolle prossed, but not until April 4, 1896. *Records of the D. C. Supreme Court,* U. S. Archives.

19. *New York Herald*: October 23, 1869.

20. *Evening Star*: December 20, 1871.

21. *Evening Star, National Republican*: August 20, 1873.

22. Ellis: *Sights and Secrets of the National Capital,* pp. 496-497.

23. John Edward Bruce. Manuscript, Schomburg Collection, New York Public Library.

24. *Congressional Globe.* 42nd Congress, 2nd Session, January 31, 1872, pp. 728-729.

25. Ellis: op. cit. p. 112.

26. *Evening Star*: May 19, 1870.

27. Adams: *The Washers and the Scrubbers,* p. 10.

28. Frederick Douglass: *Life and Times of Frederick Douglass,* p. 487.

29. Harris and Spero: *The Black Worker,* p. 18.

30. Idem p. 19.

31. Miss Abby Simmons, a native of Massachusetts, who came to teach in the District colored schools in 1865, was the last white teacher to remain in service, retiring as late as 1901.

32. Dyson: *History of Howard University,* p. 47.

33. *The Etude*: "The Negro Stephen Foster," July, 1939.

NOTES FOR EPILOGUE

1. *Troy Times,* July 8, 1874.

2. Cortissoz: *Life of Whitelaw Reid,* Vol. I, p. 317. Rollin H. Kirk: *Many Secrets Revealed,* pp. 110-111.

3. *New York Tribune*: July 29, 1874. Many of these claims were subsequently paid in District 3.65 bonds.

4. Henry E. Davis: "The Safe Robbery Case," *Columbia Historical Society,* Vol. 25, p. 151.

The plea for abatement was based upon the argument that the jury had been improperly constituted according to the provisions which had been in force previous to the Territorial Government. In the Organic Act of 1861 the power of appointing officers to select jurymen had been assigned to the District Supreme Court.

5. Idem pp. 175-176.

6. *New York Herald*: September 21, 1878.

7. *National Republican*: November 17, 1874.

8. *Congressional Record*: 43rd Congress, 2nd Session, p. 120.

9. Idem p. 126.
10. Idem p. 127.
11. Idem pp. 128-130.
12. James Keeley: *Democracy and Despotism in the National Capital.*
13. The amount of Thompson's fine as well as Kilbourn's legal expenses were covered by a special congressional appropriation. In 1885 the District courts had previously dismissed Kilbourn's case against House Speaker Michael Kerr and the members of the Investigating Committee.
14. Senate Papers, District of Columbia Committee, 45th Congress. U. S. Archives.
15. *Washington Post*: January 5, 1902.
16. *Congressional Record,* 81st Congress, 2nd Session. Remarks of Senator Olin Johnston of South Carolina, p. 188.
17. According to the U. S. Census of 1870 the percentage of Negroes in the District of Columbia was 32.46. Of other large cities only New Orleans (26.35%) had a colored population of more than one-fifth.
18. Walter S. Dodd: *Government of the District of Columbia,* p. 51.
19. *Chronicle*: January 2, 1872.

Bibliography

Adams, Francis Colburn, *Our Little Monarchy* 1873
The Washers and the Scrubbers 1878
Adams, Henry, *Letters, Education of Henry Adams* 1918
Agar, Herbert, *The People's Choice* 1933
The Price of Union 1950
Ames, Mary Clemmer, *Ten Years in Washington* 1874
Andrews, E. Benjamin, *The Last Quarter Century* 1897
Aptheker, Herbert, *The Negro People in the United States* 1951
Badeau, Adam, *Grant in Peace* 1897
Baker, Lafayette C., *History of the U. S. Secret Service* 1867
Bancroft, Frederick, *Life of William H. Seward* 1900
Barrows, Chester L., *William Evarts* 1941
Barrus, Clara, *Whitman and Burroughs, Comrades* 1931
Barry, David S., *Forty Years in Washington* 1924
Beale, Howard, *The Critical Year* 1930
Beard, Charles and Mary, *The Rise of American Civilization* 1930
Bigelow, John, *Retrospections of an Active Life* 1909
Blaine, James G., *Twenty Years in Congress* 1886
Bouligny, M.E.P., *Tribute to W. W. Corcoran* 1874
Bowers, Claude C., *The Tragic Era* 1929
Boyd's Business Director and Guide to Washington 1865-1878
Briggs, Emily Edson, *The Olivia Letters* 1906
Brown, William Wells, *Rising Son* 1874
Bryan, William Bogardus, *History of the National Capital* 1916
Burgess, John W., *Reconstruction and the Constitution* 1911
Burroughs, John, *Walt Whitman* 1883
Butler, Benjamin F., *Butler's Book* 1892

Centennial History of Washington 1892
Chadsey, Charles E., *The Struggle Between President Johnson and Congress over Reconstruction* 1896
Chester, Giraud, *Embattled Maiden—The Life of Anna Dickinson* 1951
Chidsey, D. B., *The Gentleman from New York* 1935
Clemenceau, Georges, *American Reconstruction, 1865-1870* 1928
Coleman, Edna M., *White House Gossip from Andrew Johnson to Calvin Coolidge* 1933
Conkling, A. R., *Life and Letters of Roscoe Conkling* 1889
Coolidge, Louis A., *Ulysses S. Grant* 1917
Cortissoz, Royal, *The Life of Whitelaw Reid* 1921
Coulter, E. Merton, *The South during Reconstruction* 1947
Cox, Samuel S., *Three Decades of Federal Legislation* 1886
Cranford, J. B., *The Credit Mobilier of America* 1880
Crook, Col. W. H., *Through Five Administrations* 1907
Curry, J. L. M., *Brief Sketch of George Peabody* 1898
Dabney, Lillian G., *The History of Schools for Negroes in the District of Columbia* 1949
Dahlgren, Madeline Vinton, *Etiquette of Social Life in Washington* 1873
De Witt, Daniel M., *Impeachment and Trial of Andrew Johnson* 1903
Dorris, Jonathan Trumbull, *Pardon and Amnesty Under Lincoln and Johnson* 1953
Douglass, Frederick, *Life and Writings of Frederick Douglass,* Edited by Philip Foner 1952-55
Douglass, Frederick, *Calender of the Writings of Frederick Douglass* 1940
Life and Times of Frederick Douglass 1884
Du Bois, Walter B., *Black Reconstruction* 1935
Dunning, William, *Essays on the Civil War and Reconstruction* 1931
Reconstruction, Political and Economic 1907
Eaton, General John, *Lincoln, Grant and the Freedmen* 1907
Edmonds, Franklin S., *Ulysses S. Grant* 1915
Eminent Men of Washington and Virginia 1893
Elliot, Maud Howe, *Uncle Sam Ward and his Circle* 1938

Ellis, John B., *The Sights and Secrets of the National Capital* 1869
Fessenden, Francis, *Life and Public Services of William P. Fessenden* 1907
Flack, Edgar H., *The Adoption of the Fifteenth Amendment* 1909
Fleming, Walter L., *Documentary History of the Reconstruction* 1907
The Freedman's Bank and Saving Company 1927
Flower, Frank A., *Edwin McMasters Stanton* 1905
Forney, John W., *Anecdotes of Public Men* 1875
Foulke, W. D., *Life of Oliver P. Morton* 1899
Fuess, Claude M., *Life of Caleb Cushing* 1932
Carl Schurz 1932
Furnas, J. C., *Good bye to Uncle Tom* 1956
Gemmill, Jane W., Notes on Washington 1883
Gobright, Lawrence A., *Recollections of Men and Things at Washington During the Third of the Century* 1869
Gordon, John M., *Some Letters to the Mayor and City Council of Washington* 1869
Gorham, George C., *Life and Public Services of Edwin M. Stanton* 1899
Gouverneur, Marion, *As I Remember* 1911
Grant, Jesse, *In the Days of my Father* 1925
Grant, Ulysses S., *Personal Memoirs* 1886
Greeley, Horace, *Recollections of a Busy Life* 1868
Gutheim, Frederick, *The Potomac* 1949
Hamilton, Gail, *James G. Blaine* 1895
Harris, Abram, *The Negro as Capitalist* 1936
(with Spero, Sterling) *The Black Worker* 1936
Hayes, Rutherford B., *Diary and Letters* 1925
Hazard, Rowland, *The Credit Mobilier of America* 1881
Hesseltine, William B., *Ulysses S. Grant* 1935
Hilyer, Andrew, *Twentieth Century Union League Directory* 1901
Hollister, O. J., *Life of Schuyler Colfax* 1886
Howard, Gen. Oliver Otis, *Autobigraphy* 1908
Howe, Julia Ward, *Reminiscences* 1900
Howe, M. A. De Wolfe, *Portrait of an Independent, Moorfield Storey* 1932

Hunter, A. and Polkinhorn, J. H., *The New National Theatre* 1885
Hunton, Gen. Eppa, *Autobiography* 1933
Ingle, Edward, *The Negro in the District of Columbia* 1893
Josephson, Matthew, *The Politicos* 1938
Julian, George F., *Political Recollections* 1884
Keeley, James Hugh, *Democracy and Despotism in the National Capital* 1916
Kendrick, Benjamin F., *Journal of the Committee of Fifteen on Reconstruction* 1914
Kerr, W. S., *John Sherman, his Life and Public Services* 1898
King, Gen. Charles, *The True U. S. Grant* 1914
Kirk, Rollin H., *Many Secrets Revealed* 1885
Korngold, Ralph, *Two Friends of Man* 1950
Larson, H. M., *Jay Cooke, Private Banker* 1936
Leech, Margaret, *Reveille in Washington* 1941
Logan, Mrs. John A., *Our National Government* 1908
Reminiscences of a Soldier's Wife 1913
Lomax, Elizabeth Lindsay, *Leaves from an Old Washington Diary* 1943
Lynch, Dennis Tilden, *The Wild 70's* 1941
Martin, Edward W., *Behind the Scenes in Washington* 1875
Mathews, John Mabry, *Legislative and Judicial History of the Fifteenth Amendment* 1909
McCulloch, Hugh, *Men and Measures of Half a Century* 1889
McPherson, Edward, *Political History of the United States during the Period of Reconstruction* 1871
Miller, Charles G., *Donn Piatt* 1893
Milton, George F., *The Age of Hate* 1930
Moore, W. W., *Contraband Suffrage* 1867
Mori, Arinori, *Life and Resources of America* 1871
Morrison's Stranger's Guide to Washington 1866
Nevins, Allan, *Hamilton Fish* 1930
The Emergence of Modern America 1927
Nicolay, Helen, *Our Capital on the Potomac* 1924
Noyes, Crosby S., *A Memorial* 1908
Oberholtzer, Ellis Paxon, *A History of the United States Since the Civil War* 1917
Jay Cooke, Financier of the Civil War 1907

O'Connor, Ellen, *Myrtilla Miner, a Memoir* 1885
Paine, Albert Bigelow, *Thomas Nast, his Period and his Pictures* 1904
Peacock, Virginia T., *Famous American Belles of the 19th Century* 1901
Pendel, Thomas F., *Thirty-Six Years in the White House* 1902
Phelps, Mary Merwin, *Kate Chase, Dominant Daughter* 1935
Piatt, Donn, *Men Who Saved the Union* 1887
Pierce, Edward C., *Memoir and Letters of Charles Sumner* 1893
Pierce, Paul S., *The Freedmen's Bureau* 1904
Poore, Ben Perley, *Reminiscences of Forty Years* 1886
Porter, John Addison, *The City of Washington; Its Origin and Administration* 1885
Quarles, Benjamin, *Frederick Douglass* 1948
Randall, J. G., *The Civil War and Reconstruction* 1937
Rhodes, James Ford, *The History of the United States: 1850-1877* 1906
Richardson, James D., *Messages and Papers of the Presidents* 1917
Richardson, Leon, *William E. Chandler, Republican* 1940
Riddle, A. G., *Life of Benjamin Wade* 1886
Riley, Jerome, *Philosophy of Negro Suffrage* 1895
Roberts, Chalmers, *Washington, Past and Present* 1950
Ross, Earle D., *The Liberal Republican Movement* 1919
Ross, Edmund, *The Impeachment of Andrew Johnson* 1896
Russell, Charles Edward, *Blaine of Maine* 1931
Salter, William, *The Life of James W. Grimes* 1886
Schlesinger, Arthur, *History of American Life, Vol. X The Rise of the City* 1933
Schmeckebier, Lawrence, *Government and Administration of the District of Columbia* 1929
Schouler, James, *History of the United States* 1913
Schurz, Carl, *Correspondence and Political Papers* 1913
Reminiscences 1907
Seitz, Don C., *Horace Greeley* 1926
The Dreadful Decade 1926
Seward, Frederick W., *Seward at Washington* 1895
Sherman, John & Sherman, William, *Recollections of Forty Years* 1895

The Sherman Letters 1894
Singleton, Esther, *The Story of the White House* 1907
Slauson, Allen B., Editor, *A History of the City of Washington* 1903
Smith, Samuel Denny, *The Negro in Congress* 1940
Smith, T. C., *The Life and Letters of James Abram Garfield* 1925
Stevens, William Oliver, *Washington, the Cinderella City* 1943
Stewart, William H., *Reminiscences of William H. Stewart of Nevada* 1908
Storey, Moorfield, *Charles Sumner* 1901
Strahan, Edward, *The Art Treasures of America* 1879
Stryker, Lloyd Paul, *Andrew Johnson, A Study in Courage* 1930
Studies in Southern History and Politics 1913
Sumner, Charles, *Works* 1900
Swanberg, W. A. *Sickles the Incredible* 1956
Todd, Charles Burr, *The Story of Washington* 1889
Towle, G. M., *American Society* 1870
Townsend, George Alfred, *Washington Inside and Outside* 1874
Trout, James Samuel, *Life, Adventures and Anecdotes of Beau Hickman* 1876
Twain, Mark and Warner, Charles Dudley, *The Gilded Age* 1874
"Vera" (Bianca Wright) *Our American Cousins at Home* 1873
Warden, Robert S., *Private Life and Public Services of Salmon P. Chase* 1874
Washington, S. A. M., *George Thomas Downing* 1910
Washington, City and Capital (Federal Writer's Project) 1937
Washington Past and Present, edited by John Claggett Proctor, Edwin M. Williams and Frank P. Black 1930
West, Richard S. J., *Gideon Welles* 1943
White, Horace, *Life of Lyman Trumbull* 1913
Williams, George W., *History of the Negro Race in America* 1873
Wilson, Henry, *History of the Rise and Fall of Slave Power in America* 1874-77
Winston, Robert W., *Andrew Johnson, Plebeian and Patriot* 1928

Wolf, Simon, *Presidents I Have Known* 1922
Woodward, W. E., *Meet General Grant* 1918
Woodward, C. Vann, *Reunion and Reaction* 1951
Young, John Russell, *Around the World with General Grant* 1879

GOVERNMENT DOCUMENTS

U. S. House of Representatives. 42nd Congress, 2nd Session Report No. 72. 1872. Investigation of District of Columbia.
U. S. Senate & House of Representatives. 43rd Congress, 1st Session. Report No. 452. 1874. Investigation of District of Columbia Affairs.
U. S. Department of Education. Special Report of Conditions and Improvement of Colored Schools in the District of Columbia. 1871.
U. S. Department of Education. Historical Sketch of Education for the Colored Race in the District of Columbia. 1907.
U. S. Census 1860 & 1870. District of Columbia.

MAGAZINE ARTICLES

Bernard, Job. "Early Days of the Supreme Court." *Records of the Columbia Historical Society*. Vol. 21.
Borland, William P. "The District and the General Government." *Records of the Columbia Historical Society*. Vol. 18.
Clark, Allen C. "Beau Hickman." *Records of the Columbia Historical Society*. Vol. 40-41.
"Richard Wallach." *Record of the Columbia Historical Society*. Vol. 21.
Cox, William Van Zandt. "Matthew Emery." *Records of the Columbia Historical Society*. Vol. 25.
Davis, Harriet Riddle. "Civil War Recollections of a Little Yankee." *Records of the Columbia Historical Society*. Vol. 44-45.

Davis, Henry E. "The Safe Robery Case." *Records of the Columbia Historical Society*. Vol. 25.

Frank, John P. & Munro, Robert P. "The Original Understanding of the Equal Protection Clause." *Columbia Law Review*. February 1950.

Hamilton, Gail. "The Display of Washington Society." *The Galaxy,* June 1876.

Howe, Franklin H. "The Board of Public Works." *Records of the Columbia Historical Society*. Vol. 3.

"Life at the National Capital." *Lippincott's Magazine*. December, 1873.

Long, Howard H. "The Support and Control of Public Education in the District of Columbia." *Journal of Negro History*. April, 1922.

Noyes, Newbold. "Crosby S. Noyes." *Records of the Columbia Historical Society*. Vol. 40-41.

Preston, E. Delorus. "William Syphax." *Journal of Negro History*. October, 1935.

Taylor, Alrutheus A. "Negro Congressmen a Generation Later." *Journal of Negro History*. April, 1922.

Tindall, William. "Sketch of Mayor Bowen." *Records of the Columbia Historical Society*. Vol. 25.

"Alexander Shepherd." *Records of the Columbia Historical Society*. Vol. 14.

Townsend, George Alfred. "The New Washington." *Harper's Monthly*. February, 1875.

Wormley, G. Smith. "Educators of the First Half Century of the Public Schools in the District of Columbia." *Journal of Negro History*. April, 1932.

Zornow, William Frank. "The Judicial Modifications of the Maryland Black Codes in the District of Columbia." *Maryland Historical Magazine*. March, 1949.

PAMPHLETS, THESES, ETC.

Brown, Bernard B. "Civil Rights in the District of Columbia." Master's Thesis, Howard University. 1940

Bryson, Walter C. "The Founding of Howard University." 1921

Collins, Carolyn B. "Sayles J. Bowen and the Beginnings of Negro Education."
Paper read before Columbia Historical Society, May 26, 1955.
Coombs, Joseph J. Address on District Affairs 1872
Crane, John H. "The District Ring" 1872
"More about the Washington Tammany" 1873
Grant, Major-General Ulysses S. 3rd. "The Territorial Government of Washington, D. C." Address to Women's City Club 1929
Greene, Dorothy. "Negro Suffrage in the District of Columbia." Master's Thesis, Howard University. 1936
Piper, Ada "Negro Members in the Territorial Legislature of the District of Columbia, 1871-1874." Master's Thesis, Howard University. 1930
Lofton, Williston H. "Civil Rights of the Negro in the United States 1865-1887." Master's Thesis, Howard University 1930
Williams, William H. "The Negro in the District of Columbia during Reconstruction." Master's Thesis, Howard University. 1924
Yeldell, Carleton, Jr. "Role of the Negro Question in the Struggle for Home Rule." Master's Thesis, Howard University. 1948

MANUSCRIPTS

Babcock, Orville E. "Correspondence and Letter Books, 1869-1877." U. S. Archives. Office of Superintendent of Public Grounds and buildings.
Bruce, John Edward. "Washington Colored Society." Schomburg Collection. 135th Street Branch, New York Public Library.
Bunche, Ralph. "Political Status of the Negro." 1940. Schomburg Collection. 135th Street Branch, New York Public Library.
Chandler, William E. Papers. Library of Congress.
Bureau of Refugees, Freedmen and Abandoned Lands (known as Freedmen's Bureau) U. S. Archives.

French, Major B. B. Correspondence and Letter Books. Office of Superintendent of Public Grounds and Buildings. U. S. Archives.

Grant, Ulysses S. Papers. Library of Congress.

Johnson, Andrew. Papers. Library of Congress.

Owner, William. Diary. Library of Congress.

Shepherd, Alexander. Papers. Library of Congress.

Stevens, Thaddeus. Papers. Library of Congress.

Sumner, Charles. Papers. Library of Congress. Correspondence. Harvard University Library.

Supreme Court of the District of Columbia. Records. U. S. Archives.

Woodson, Carter. Correspondence and Records. Library of Congress.

NEWSPAPERS AND MAGAZINES

Alexandria, Virginia. *Alexandria Gazette,* 1865-1878.

Baltimore, Maryland. *Baltimore Sun,* 1865-1875.

New York City. *Daily Graphic, Herald, Sun, Times, Tribune, World, The Nation, Harper's Weekly, Leslie's Illustrated Weekly, Harper's Monthly Magazine.* 1865-1875.

Washington, D. C. *Capital, Chronicle, Critic, Sunday Herald, Evening Express, National Intelligencer, National Republican, Daily Patriot, Evening Star, Georgetown Courier, New National Era, Columbia, Anzeiger, Washingtoner Journal,* 1865-1878.

LOCAL GOVERNMENT RECORDS

Washington, D. C. Board of Common Council, Board of Aldermen, Journals, 1865-1871.

Georgetown, D. C. Board of Common Council, Board of Aldermen, Journals, 1865-1871.

District of Columbia Territorial Government. House of Delegates, Legislative Assembly, Journals, 1871-1874.

District of Columbia Board of Public Works. Reports. 1872-1873.

District of Columbia Board of Health. Reports. 1872-1875.

Index